the magazine

The Best and Most of Egypt

There's never enough time to see everything in Egypt...

Best Views
- **Of Cairo:** from the al Azhar Park overlooking Fatimid Cairo (➤ 71).
- **Of Luxor:** from the top of the Theban hills.
- **Of Sinai:** sunrise at Gebel Musa.
- **Of the Red Sea:** naturally from beneath the waves, where you'll also see blue, green and every other colour imaginable.
- **Of the Nile:** from the terrace of Aswan's Old Cataract Hotel (➤ 126).

but don't miss these...

Above: Tutankhamun enamelled jewellery

Pyramids at Giza, the only surviving Wonders of the Ancient World and still wonderful (➤ 62–66).

The Egyptian Museum of Antiquities in Cairo – for Tutankhamun's treasure, of course, but also to bring ancient Egypt to life, right down to the knitted socks (➤ 50–53).

Karnak Temple in Luxor, one of the world's greatest religious centres (➤ 84–87).

Valley of the Kings, for the beauty, awe and complexity of the pharaohs (➤ 91–93).

Sultan Hasan Mosque-Madrasa in Cairo, to appreciate the grandeur and harmony of Islamic architecture (➤ 69).

Above: Relax with a *sheesha*. Previous page: Woman in traditional costume

A bird's-eye view of Thebes

Best Buzzes

• Tea and *sheesha* (water pipe) – the tea comes strong and the tobacco rough – are quintessentially Egyptian.
• Being in an ancient temple or tomb alone – difficult in high season, but there's nothing like it to feel the power of the place.
• Sunrise and sunset – a thrill wherever you are.
• Hot-air ballooning over Luxor's West Bank (➤ 102).

Best for Peace and Quiet

• The courtyards of mosques, but not during prayer times.
• The Nile, anytime, but preferably on a leisurely 7-day *dahabeyya* cruise (➤ 122).
• St Catherine's Monastery, but beware of tour groups (➤ 160–162).
• Downtown Cairo between 4 and 4:20am – it's almost worth staying up late for this (➤ 67).

Best Mosques

• **Al Azhar**, authority on Islam, and one of the world's oldest universities (➤ 70).
• **Abu Haggag**, built in the 13th century on the ruins of Luxor Temple, now hangs spectacularly over the excavated columns (➤ 89–90).
• **New Gurna**, Hassan Fathy's marvel in Luxor, shows just how far you can go with mudbrick (➤ 183).

Rest and watch the world go by over a glass of tea

• Sliding down nearly vertical sand dunes in the Libyan Desert.

Most Quirky

• The **Police Museum** at the Citadel, for a glimpse of crimes and corrective measures (➤ 68–69).
• The chapel **of the Convent of St George** in Coptic Cairo (➤ 54–55), where you can wrap yourself in chains like the martyr .
• The **Cavafy Museum**, Alexandria, where you can sit by the poet's bed and read his more *risqué* works (➤ 137).
• **Fertility charms:** watch what you touch in temples and tombs – some statues and images are reputed to boost fertility.

The Desert

Nothing points out the delicate balance between the fertile and the barren better than a flight over Egypt. Thin strips of agricultural land line the ribbon of the Nile, and fan out into the delta. Beyond are the great deserts that form 90 per cent of the country: the Libyan Desert in the west, the mountainous Eastern Desert and, between the Mediterranean and Red Sea, the Sinai Desert.

Because of this stark contrast and the low rainfall, few countries are as dominated by their geography as Egypt. The welcoming fertility of the Nile valley and the awesome wilderness of the all-encompassing deserts have had a huge influence on Egypt's history and culture. And one of ancient Egypt's most popular and enduring myths – the ongoing clash between desert and sown – is still relevant today.

Most camels in Egypt have come through the desert from Sudan, along the Forty Days Road

Top of the Pyramid

Aware of the need to work together to use the floodwater, early Egyptians created a hierarchy and bureaucracy as the basis for their civilisation. When the hierarchy and government were strong (for instance when the Pyramids were built), the Nile was harnessed and the area used for agriculture was increased. At times of a weaker government, the farmland quickly returned to desert.

Many Egyptian farmers still work the land like their ancestors

& the Sown

Order and Chaos

The ancient god Osiris (► 12–15) brought order and civilisation to the Nile valley, making laws and teaching the Egyptians how to cultivate crops and produce wine. Along this generous if confined strip of land, the Egyptians thrived for thousands of years. It seemed such a wonderful place that ancient Egyptians hoped for its equal in their afterlife. Their idea of the perfect valley is echoed in many religions – in the Garden of Eden, for example, and in the Islamic shaded paradise cut through by running water, with food and drink in abundant supply.

Osiris's brother Seth, on the other hand, was associated with the desert, which was a constant threat to the sown. Perhaps

Intense farming occurs on the thin strip of fertile land along the Nile

not by chance the myth ties in with Egypt's early history, when global warming destroyed the forests on which the people of the Nile depended and the desert closed in on the river. Communities used to hunting and gathering then became reliant on the annual flooding of the Nile to irrigate their crops.

The Desert Was...

The desert wasn't seen in solely negative terms. Despite being the master of chaos, Seth was considered an essential part of the Egyptian world. Ancient Egyptians used the desert as a place to escape; it was where Moses and his people were tested and purified, and where Christianity's first monastic orders were founded in the 4th century. This spiritual place was also a place of wealth, for in spite of the challenging climate and landscape, some of the pharaohs' gold was mined from the Red Sea mountains, while turquoise and lapis lazuli were found in Sinai. The desert also acted as a buffer against the wild Berber tribes of the Libyan Desert and the ambitious Bedouin Arabs to the west. Invasions, when they came, tended to arrive in the north or across the Sinai peninsula.

Disappearing Act

There was, perhaps, a moment when Egyptians blessed the desert. In the 6th century BC, after conquering Egypt and sacking Thebes, the great Persian emperor Cambyses sent an army to destroy the Oracle at Siwa Oasis.

Some 50,000 men marched into the sands.

None of them came out.

Like other temples along the Nile, Kom Ombo suffers from rising water caused by the Aswan Dam

Shifting Sands

Thebes was eulogised as "hundred gated" by the Greek poet Homer and it was the epitome of the ancient city. Alexandria was the model of the classical city and Cairo was extolled as "the Mother of the World" in *The Thousand and One Nights*. But despite this, Egyptian society has always been predominantly rural, until now.

Throughout history most Egyptians were farmers, tending their plots and bartering their produce. At the beginning of the 19th century Cairo was still mostly confined within its medieval walls and Alexandria was smaller than the Greek and Roman city from which it had grown. But since then, and particularly since the 1970s, when the Aswan High dam stopped the annual flooding of the Nile valley, more people are now living in cities than in the countryside. And there have been similarly dramatic changes in the desert.

Above right: Water from the Nile is used to irrigate the fileds via a series of canals

Right: The donkey is a traditional animal of labour for farmers

The Desert Solution

Rather than threatening the stability of life in the Nile valley, the desert now seems to offer solutions. In 1869 the Suez Canal was cut across the desert that separated the Mediterranean and Red seas – it's currently the country's second-largest earner of foreign currency. Elsewhere in the desert, significant reserves of gas, oil, phosphates and fresh water boost Egypt's economy. New satellite cities have been established in the desert to ease the population squeeze in Cairo and are growing larger all the time. In the Libyan Desert mechanical diggers are at work on a project to divert water from the Nile along the new Toshka Canal and into a desert depression. It's hoped that this will create an alternative valley, a mirror image of the Nile. These exciting developments herald the start of a new era in the stormy yet inseparable relationship between the desert and the sown.

It is hard to get away from death in Egypt, as many monuments along the Nile are connected to the cult of death. However the ancient Egyptians were not obsessed with death, they enjoyed life so much they wanted it to go on forever.

Death on the Nile

Osiris, God of the Underworld

Osiris was the archetypal good king and is credited with bringing civilisation to his people, teaching them how to farm and to honour their gods. Although he lived as a man, Osiris was born a god – the son of Geb, god of the earth, and Nut, the sky goddess. In true ancient Egyptian style, he married his sister Isis, while his brother Seth married their other sister Nephthys. But Seth was jealous of Osiris's success and, after inviting him to a feast, Seth presented Osiris with a beautiful box. Suddenly he was bundled into it, thrown into the Nile and drowned.

According to the Greek writer Plutarch (*c*46–120), Isis found Osiris's body in Lebanon, where a tamarisk tree had grown round it. She returned her husband's corpse to Egypt, using magic to revive him for long enough to conceive a child: the falcon-headed god Horus. Later, Seth again found Osiris and this time cut him into 14 parts that were thrown into the Nile. The ever-resourceful Isis collected the parts, finding all of them except his penis, and bandaged them up before burying them. So, in addition to his many other distinctions, Osiris therefore became the first mummy.

Isis's lamentations were said to have been particularly beautiful and the tears she shed over her husband were believed to have caused the Nile to rise. Even today, the night in June when the Nile is seen to rise is known as the Night of the Drop.

Egyptian gods kept things running smoothly and could be petitioned in times of need. Myths developed to explain their origins and powers. Most had human bodies, but were often identified with animals.

Amun the ram
Anubis the jackal
Bastet the cat goddess
Edjo the cobra goddess
Horus the falcon-headed son of Isis and Osiris
Hapi the pot-bellied Nile god
Khepri the scarab beetle
Mut the vulture goddess
Ra the great sun god
Sekhmet the lioness

Top left: Osiris, god of the underworld

Above and right: Corpses were wrapped in natron to dry out for 70 days. Below right: Jackal-headed Anubis, the god associated with funerary rites, attends to the mummy of King Sennutem

Below: Child's sarcophagus

Life After Death

Osiris's myth offered the promise of resurrection, so in the hope of joining him in the next life, Egyptians began to follow his style of burial by having themselves mummified. Isis kept the location of Osiris's tomb a secret, but it was believed that a part of his corpse was buried in each of Egypt's provinces. Temples were dedicated to him in each of these areas, but his main cult centres were at Bubastis in the Nile delta and Abydos on the Nile itself, where his head was believed to be buried and which Egyptians saw as the gateway to the afterlife (▶ 101). He was also held in reverence at Isis's temple on Philae (▶ 116–117).

Going Prepared

Ancient Egyptians believed that happiness in the afterlife depended on making the right preparations in this one.

As well as being well preserved, a dead person also needed help getting to the other side. The essential aids for this were spells and prayers; the Book of the Dead, for instance, was intended as a map to guide the deceased to the afterlife. The final barrier was Osiris's judgement, when the dead person's heart was weighed against the feather of truth. If the scales tipped in your favour, you were through to everlasting happiness. It's a common image on tomb walls and must have been a terrifying prospect, especially to those who had lived less than perfect lives.

Even if you were lucky enough to get through to paradise, your tomb still had to be kept in order, as it contained all the goods, treasures and models of workers that would be needed to provide for you. These, together with prayers and offerings made at your tomb, gave you a good chance of a sweet eternity.

At first corpses were kept intact by being buried in sand, but when tombs developed, bodies had to be mummified

Crossed arms and a false beard symbolise the fact that the god Osiris or the pharaoh in question is dead

Simple Muslim tombstones, facing Mecca, and splendid mausoleums in Cairo's City of the Dead

Islamic Death Rites

Islam, which changed religious rituals, also changed burials. The Prophet Muhammad announced that the best grave was one you could wipe away with your hand – a winding sheet and a hole in the desert were all that you needed. But before long the old ideas began to reassert themselves, especially the ancient cult of the dead and a belief in the ability of spirits to affect the living.

When the Fatimid caliphs (▶ 24) established the city of al Qahira (Cairo), they brought the bones of their ancestors. And when the 15th-century sultan Qaytbay built his tomb, he added a school, monastery and *caravanserai* (lodgings). He wanted the tomb to be maintained after his death, and hoped that prayers would still be said for him long after he had gone. His name has certainly lived on – Qaytbay's tomb complex is one of the glories of Islamic architecture (▶ 179). Although it was built in a desert, outside the city limits, Cairo has since grown so dramatically that this City of the Dead is now well within the city – a city within the city. It's also where many ancient Egyptian funerary traditions are kept alive, from the regular offerings of the family to the spirit of the deceased, to people living in the cemetery alongside the dead.

> "...ppiness in ... afterlife ...ended on ...king the ... prepara-...ns in this ... one"

Death on the Nile

The 1978 film of Agatha Christie's novel was a veritable travelogue, with a host of international stars attempting to baffle Peter Ustinov's detective Hercule Poirot. Pictured from left to right are some of the stars of the film: Angela Lansbury, Maggie Smith, Jack Warden, Bette Davis, Peter Ustinov, George Kennedy and David Niven.

The Land of Believers

The Greek historian Herodotus, who visited Egypt in 450 BC, called the Egyptians "religious to excess, beyond any other nation in the world." Although much has changed over the past 2,000 years, religion still plays a key part in everyday life, and almost all Egyptians will identify themselves as much by their religion as by their city or region of birth. One reason for this is that Egypt has been important to the development of the region's three main religions: Islam, Christianity and Judaism.

Followers of Islam

The Prophet Muhammad never visited Egypt, but several of his companions and close family members are buried there. Today, some 94 per cent of Egyptians are Muslims, or followers of Islam. The holy book of Islam, the Quran, is based on a series of revelations received by Muhammad in about AD 610 to 632. The new religion recognised the validity of Judaism and Christianity, but claimed to have superseded them.

Islam was brought to Egypt along with an army commanded by the great Arab general Amr ibn al As in AD 641, while the country was under the nominal rule of the Christian emperors

Friday noon prayers often block the traff in the streets outside the mosques of Constantinople (Istanbul). Radically, Islam abolished the priesthood that had dominated the older religions. In Egypt, where the ancient priests had often ruled the country, the idea of praying directly to God because all people were regarded as equal in His eyes, must have been especially popular.

After Muhammad's death in around 632, both his friend, Abu Bakr, and his son-in-law, Ali, claimed the title of leader of the faithful. The dispute caused a rift which continues today, with the followers of Ali known as Shi'a (Shi'ite) and the followers of Abu Bakr as Sunni. Most Egyptians are Sunni Muslims.

Five Pillars of Islam

All Muslims should adhere to these principles:

◆ Declare "that there is no God but Allah and that Muhammad is His Prophet"

◆ Pray five times a day

◆ Give alms

◆ Observe the daylight fast during the month of Ramadan

◆ Make the pilgrimage (*hajj*) to Mecca once in a lifetime if health and finances allow it

Most Egyptians may be Muslim, but the celebration of the *moulids* or annual saints' days (➤ 18) has very little to do with Islam – often they refer to the local festivals for ancient deities.

The Egyptian Christian Church

Egypt had links with Christanity from the very beginning, because the young Jesus is said to have been brought to the country by his parents. According to legend the Church in Egypt was founded after the evangelist

St Mark sailed into Alexandria in the 1st century AD. At the time of the Arab invasion most Egyptians belonged to the Coptic (Egyptian Christian) Church. Although Copts now make up some 6 per cent of the population, they still exert a significant influence, particularly in politics and trade, perhaps because they claim to be the true heirs of Egypt's ancient civilisation. However, while Egyptians played an important part in establishing the rituals of the early Church, they were unable to accept an imperial ruling on the dual nature of Jesus as God and man. To the Egyptians, he was inseparably both in one. Refusing to toe the official line, they were condemned as heretics in AD 451 and since then, they have been isolated, their rituals and liturgy essentially uncorrupted by outside influences. Some scholars are now looking to the Egyptian Church to provide them with a glimpse of how the early Christian Church must have been.

Religious tensions have led many young Coptic men to retire to desert monasteries

Many aspects of Coptic rites seem to have preserved the world of the pharaohs. The Coptic language, still in use in churches, would be understood by the last of the ancients, while the liturgy and other prayers contain many phrases and images that seem to come from pagan texts. This idea is supported by the Jewish philosopher Philo of Alexandria (c15 BC–AD 50), who noted that Christians merely changed some of words of the ancient prayers. Many ancient gods seem also to find parallels in the new, from the holy mothers Mary and Isis, to Horus the Elder who is often depicted harpooning a hippo like St George fighting the dragon.

Common Ground

One thing Copts and Muslims share is a love of celebrations, in particular the annual saints' days, called *moulids*. These festivals often last several days and take place all over the country. Some are small gatherings but others, such as the *moulids* of Huseyn in Cairo and Sayyid al Badawy in Tanta, attract millions. Their mixture of religion, social bonding and trade is similar to celebrations held in ancient Egypt. Whether the saint is Christian or Muslim, *moulids* tend to attract a mixed crowd who go for the saint's blessing and the chance to party.

The Jewish Community

The formative years of the early Jews were spent in Egypt, with Moses receiving the Ten Commandments on Gebel Musa in Sinai. In the 3rd century BC, the Jewish holy book was first translated into Greek in Alexandria, making it accessible to a wider audience. Alexander the Great relocated Jews to his new city of Alexandria soon after it was founded in 331 BC and there's been a community in Egypt ever since. Most Jews emigrated or were expelled in the mid-20th century as a result of the creation of the State of Israel and the Arab-Israeli wars, although small and mostly elderly groups do survive in Alexandria and Cairo. Consequently, the Jews are now the smallest religious group in Egypt.

Religious Tension

There has always been tension between the different religions in Egypt. In 2nd- and 3rd-century Alexandria there was fighting between Christians, Jews and pagan sects, while medieval Cairo was a battleground for Copts, Sunni and Shi'a Muslims. In the 1950s and 60s, when Egypt was at war with Israel, the country's remaining Jewish population was discriminated

Always take off your shoes before entering a mosque or a tomb

against. In the decades since then, particularly since the Afghan and Gulf wars (in which Egypt took part) there have been attacks on churches and Christian interests.

This has so embittered some of the Christian community that the Coptic Patriarch, Shenouda III, lifted his ban on Copts emigrating. Recently several young professional Coptic men have retreated to desert monasteries and created a monastic revival.

Often, there are not enough members of the Jewish community in an Egyptian synagogue to perform a service

WHEN IN EGYPT

After thousands of years of invasions, floods, droughts, unreliable harvests, poverty and wars, Egyptians are used to taking what history throws at them. Stoicism has become part of the national character, and the first response to any calamity, whether it is big or small, might well be *maalesh*, *bukra* things will be better, *inshallah*.

Never Mind

Maalesh has a multitude of applications. You'll hear it after some mishap because even calamities are part of the grand scheme of things. If someone's pestering you to buy a plastic wallet or flashing sunglasses, *maalesh* shows you're not interested.

Talk Like an Egyptian

If you speak Egyptian Arabic in another Arab country, chances are you'll get a laugh – and not just for your accent. Egyptians are notorious in the Arab world for their irrepressible sense of humour and love of play and drama. They are the masters of Arab soap opera, which is seen from Morocco on the Atlantic coast to Dubai on the Indian Ocean and beyond.

God Willing

Step into a taxi and tell the driver where you want to go and he'll invariably reply, "*Inshallah*". He means "yes" but is actually saying "God willing". To assume that this is just a hackneyed saying is to underestimate the importance of Allah in everyday life, and to dismiss the fundamental belief in divine intervention.

■ ■ ■

Tomorrow

"*Bukra*" used to be the standard reply for whatever service you were requesting, whether you wanted a train ticket or collect your laundry. "Come back tomorrow", or "not ready till tomorrow" showed that Egyptians had a different sense of time and priorities from many foreigners visiting their country. But it's now a sign of the changing ethos in Egyptian society – particularly in the cities – that people resort less and less to this line of defence.

Exchanging Greetings

Wherever they are and whatever pressing business they have, Egyptians always make time for an elaborate exchange of greetings. A simple version might be a rally of blessings such as *sabah al ishta* ("morning of cream") and *sabah al yasmin* ("morning of jasmine"). Between men there's also likely to be handshaking, kissing, hugging and an insistence that they visit the nearest café there and then. Usually there is an extended series of questions and answers about every member of each other's family and their health.

Family Life

Most Egyptians are passionately patriotic and, if you meet an Egyptian abroad, it doesn't take much to bring on a bout of nostalgia for their homeland and their family. In a country with no social security system, families support out-of-work men and will provide a son with a home for his wife and children until they can afford a place of their own. They will also look after the sick and elderly. Sons are especially important and the birth of a male is greeted with particular joy, while young girls are often treated as dolls. But attitudes to daughters (at least in public) tend to change after puberty, when many of them hide themselves behind veils and voluminous dresses for reasons of modesty, often dictated as much by a desire for social conformity as religious zeal.

EGYPTIAN CHRONICLES

c5000 BC

Neolithic farming communities are already well established in the Nile valley area.

King Menes may have been a composite of several kings

c3000 BC

King Menes (or Narmer) unites the two lands of Upper and Lower Egypt (the Nile delta), establishing its capital at Memphis. Menes is now generally regarded as the first pharaoh of the 1st Dynasty in Egypt.

c2600 BC

Imhotep, architect to the 3rd-Dynasty King Zoser (2667–2648 BC), creates the world's first pyramid, at Saqqara (► 59–61). The ancients were suitably impressed and later deified him. He became the god of medicine, son of the god Ptah and his consort Sekhmet.

1352–1336 BC

The ruling pharaoh Amenhotep IV tries to free his administration from the influence of the priesthood of Thebes by moving the capital to Amarna, some 370km (230 miles) miles north. To promote the worship of a single god, the sun god Aton, he changed his own name from "Amun is pleased" to Akhenaton ("Soul of Aton"). Akhenaton is most famous today for being depicted in art with his beautiful wife Nefertiti and his children (► 51).

1336–1327 BC

After Amenhotep's death, his nine-year-old son-in-law Tutankhaten becomes ruler. Within a short time, he restores the old order, moves the capital back to Thebes and reinstates Amun as the state god, changing his name to Tutankhamun. He dies at the age of 18 with no heirs, the last male of the 18th Dynasty.

The Saqqara step pyramid was the world's first large stone monument

1279–1213 BC

Ramses II rules for more than 60 years – time enough to build grand monuments, marry many wives and father more than 100 children, helping to guarantee his name in posterity. He leaves his mark on almost every significant monument in Egypt, adding huge colossi in his image and decorating temple walls with scenes of his greatest victories. He deifies himself in the

Prolific pharaoh, Ramses II

eighth year of his reign and the two temples that bear his name, at Abu Simbel and in Thebes, are as monumental as his self-esteem. Many of his 50 sons are buried in KV5, the princely gallery tomb that is now being excavated in the Valley of the Kings (▶ 93).

8th–7th century BC

Egypt is ruled for a time by kings from Nubia, the area of southern Egypt and northern Sudan.

332 BC

Alexander the Great (356–23) conquers Egypt, which passes to a general, Ptolemy, and into the Ptolemaic era.

General Alexander the Great

c270 BC

In Alexandria, the Greek architect Sostratos builds one of the seven wonders of the world – the marble lighthouse on the island of Pharos in the harbour.

Cleopatra VII's tomb in Alexandria has disappeared

47–30 BC

At the beginning of her reign, at the age of 21, Cleopatra VII flees Egypt to escape her murderous brother-husband Ptolemy XIII, but is restored to the throne by Julius Caesar. In return she bears his only son, Caesarion. Five years later, with Caesar dead, Cleopatra falls for his successor Mark Antony, by whom she has three more children. But in 30 BC Octavian, the future Emperor Augustus, defeats the lovers' army and captures Alexandria. When Mark Antony commits suicide, Cleopatra causes her own death soon after by the bite of an asp, thus sealing one of the greatest love stories. Cleopatra is the last ruler, until the modern era, of an independent Egypt. The country falls under Roman and Byzantine rule.

The Pharos was said to contain 300 rooms for its mechanics and builders

St Anthony of Egypt lived to the wise old age of 105

AD 251–356

At the age of 18 the future St Anthony, a wealthy young man from the town of Beni Suef, is inspired to become a hermit after hearing the gospel of Matthew. He retreats to an isolated cave on Mount Qalala, where he lives until the age of 105. His followers, settling at the foot of the mountain, found the world's first monastery (► 164).

639–641

When Amr ibn al As visits Alexandria as a young man he is struck by the capital's wealth. He returns in 639 with a 4,000-strong Arab army and meets little opposition from the ruling Byzantines. The Arabs take Heliopolis and then besiege Babylon-in-Egypt. By 641 Egypt is an Arab province. Amr establishes his capital in Fustat (later Cairo), where he builds his mosque and introduces Islam.

973–1171

During the Fatimid Dynasty, al Hakim, who rules from 996 to 1021 is the maddest and most capricious of the caliphs (literally, "Successor to Muhammad"). He persecutes the Jewish and Christian minorities and destroys countless churches. He forbids women to go out, outlawing the manufacture of their shoes. He also hates daylight, decreeing that all work should be done at night. He even declares himself divine as the pharoahs did before him. After mysteriously disappearing while out riding, he is commonly presumed dead, but according to the Druze, a political and religious Islamic sect for whom he becomes a cult figure, he's actually escaped to Lebanon.

Muhammad Ali's mosque now crowns the citadel built by Saladin

1171–1193

Legacies of the reign of the Kurdish general Salah ad Din (Saladin) include Cairo's Citadel and the ending of the Shi'a caliphate rule. He establishes the Ayyubid Dynasty after becoming sultan, and is also notable for uniting Egyptian Muslims in a common cause. For most of his rule he is away fighting a *jihad* ("holy war") to free the Holy Land from the Crusaders. He succeeds in recapturing Syria and Jerusalem, but dies in Damascus, where he is buried. His legendary qualities turn him into a hero throughout Europe and the Arab world.

Below: Cairo was always an important trading post

1250–1517

The Mamelukes – soldiers descended from slaves who made up the Ayyubid army – overthrow the Ayyubids with their highly professional army, led by amirs. Their Muslim dynasty lasts until their conquest by the Ottoman Turks.

The Mamelukes proved their fighting abilities in the Crusades

1517

Egypt comes under the control of the Ottoman Empire, which had been founded in the 13th century by Osman I, but the Mamelukes continue to rule. With increasing trade between the East and Europe, the important route between Alexandria, Cairo and Suez prompts British and French attempts to control it.

1798–1801

Napoleon Bonaparte leads scholars and troops into Egypt to study and to remove antiquities, creating the first systematic record of Egypt's treasures.

1805–1848

Muhammad Ali, an Albanian officer whose army arrived in Egypt with the French, is regarded as the founder of modern Egypt. After the French leave, Ali supports Egypt's rulers against the Mamelukes and becomes viceroy. Influenced by advances in Europe, he modernises the country's infrastructure, building roads and Africa's first railway. He reorganises the army, reforms agriculture with improved irrigation and establishes industry. His dynasty rules Egypt under the title of Khedive and later King, until the revolution in 1952.

1869

After ten years of problematic construction, the Suez Canal is finally opened, linking the Mediterranean at the newly created Port Said with the Red Sea at Suez (► 168–169). The new towns of Port Said and Ismailiya grow as the area becomes wealthy. Port Said is named after Egypt's ruler (although he dies before the project was completed) and Ismailiya receives its name from the subsequent ruler, Khedive Ismail, who opens the canal.

Napoleon defeated the Mamelukes at the Battle of the Pyramids in 1798

1882

Riots begin after an army faction objects to the British and French control of Egypt's finances. As a result, British troops

bombard Alexandria and occupy Egypt under the pretext of restoring peace to the country. They remain as a colonial presence until 1956.

Muhammad Ali laid the foundations for modern Egypt

1952

A military coup by the "Free Officers" over-throws King Farouk and declares a republic. The army officer and politician Gamal Abd al Nasser (1918–70), becomes Egypt's prime minister in 1954 and later president (1956–70). His Arab nationalism and socialism makes him popular in Egypt and the Arab world.

The charismatic Nasser

Above: In 1973 Sinai became a battlefield in the Arab–Israeli war

Scottish troops at the Sphinx in 1882

When he nationalises the Suez Canal in 1956 Britain, France and Israel invade Egypt, but Nasser stands up to them, adding to his cult status.

1970s

Both Egypt and Israel claim victory after several Arab-Israeli wars. Anwar al Sadat (1918–81) becomes president in 1970 and sets about restructuring the political system (founding the National Democratic Party) and diversifying the economy. After some initial aggression, his work towards peace in the Middle East leads to talks with the Israeli Prime Minister Menachem Begin (1913–92). This culminates in the 1978 Camp David Peace Accord, for which the two leaders share the Nobel Peace Prize. Although Egypt becomes somewhat isolated from other Arab countries, the agreement encourages foreign investment and strengthens the economy. However, only a minority become wealthy and the decade ends in social unrest and a general feeling of dissatisfaction.

1981 to present

On 6 October 1981, President Sadat is assassinated by radical Islamists. Hosni Mubarak (born 1928), the vice-president, succeeds him as president, with the support of the armed forces. Mubarak has continued Sadat's policy of liberalisation of trade. In 2005 Mubarak changed the constitution to allow multi-party presidential elections, but the popular fundamentalist Muslim Brotherhood remained banned. He won the elections but Egypt's future is less certain: opposition is growing, the country is in a serious economic crisis and Mubarak seems to have less of a grip on regional politics.

Current president, Mubarak

كُل، كُل...يا اللّٰه كُل!

Kul, kul...yallah kul

The phrase means "eat, eat...come on eat", and you'll hear it often if you dine with Egyptians, who love to eat, to talk about food and to share a meal.

It's always been this way – their forefathers are depicted on the walls of tombs attending lavish banquets. Some dishes are still favourites today, particularly *faseekh*, roast goose and *meloukhia* (see panel).

Modern meals include as many dishes as the host can afford, and the tastiest morsels will be put in your mouth at what can be an alarming rate. In restaurants Egyptians continue the habit of sharing by ordering vast amounts of *mezze*, hot or cold starters, dips and salads.

Sweetness Delight

If you've seen Egyptians piling sugar into their tea, then you'll have noticed their sweet tooth. That's why the country's numerous pâtisseries sell a wide variety of cream-filled Western pastries and finger-licking good Oriental pastries, usually dripping in honey. The "queen" of Egyptian desserts is *Umm Ali*, which some sources suggest was introduced into Egypt by an Irish woman, Miss O'Malley, who was mistress to the 19th-century leader, Khedive Ismail.

Left: Street food is available everywhere

The Egyptian Staple

Fuul (fava beans) is one of the basics of the national diet and, while some poorer Egyptians live on them, even wealthy Cairenes have them for breakfast. The dried beans are simmered for about six hours, and then sold in the morning from carts on street corners. The stew is often eaten with more beans crushed and fried into little patties (*taamiya*).

> **"The tastiest morsels will be put in your mouth at an alarming rate"**

Some Dishes to Sample

Faseekh: salted dried fish
Meloukhia: thick green soup made with a leafy vegetable, Jew's mallow, similar to spinach, served with chicken or rabbit
Kushari: a delicious mixture of macaroni, rice, fried onions, chickpeas and lentils, topped with a spicy tomato sauce
Qawaria: a clear cows' feet soup, said to enhance sexual potency
Lambs' testicles: found in sandwiches or stews, said to have similar properties to *qawaria*
Umm Ali: crisp pitta bread, coconut, cream, nuts, raisins and sugar, soaked in hot milk

Below: Smoking a *sheesha* is the best way to digest a platter of *mezze* (right)

Bakers' boys carry big trays of hot, fresh pitta bread on their heads at all times of the day

Absence Makes the Heart Grow Fonder

During the lunar month of Ramadan Muslims abstain from eating, drinking, smoking and making love between sunrise and sunset. Perversely, although this is a month of fasting, more food is consumed during the nights of Ramadan than at any other time. Ramadan also brings its social obligations, as it's traditionally when people visit friends and relatives for an evening breakfast. They then indulge in meat and more luxurious ingredients than usual to make up for the hardship of the day's fasting.

Café Pleasures

The best thirst-quencher in a hot climate is tea, and there's no shortage of it in Egypt. Tea is drunk black or with milk and lots of sugar at the local *ahwa* (coffee house). The other ubiquitous drink is syrupy Arabic coffee, which soon becomes a compulsion and has the bonus of being the medium for fortune-telling (it's like reading tea leaves). Cafés are also places to relax, chat or ponder while drawing on a *sheesha* (water pipe or hookah), which can usually be ordered with normal tobacco, *ma'assal* (tobacco sweetened with molasses) or *tuffah* (sweetened with apple). Traditional cafés also serve herbal infusions such as *yansoon* (anis), *helba* (fenugreek), *karkadeh* (hibiscus) and *irfa* (cinnamon). Warm yourself in winter with a delicious, custardy *sahlab* – made of arrowroot and cinnamon topped with coconut and other nuts.

Juicy Delights

"Once you drink water from the Nile, you will always return to Egypt" goes the old saying. But ignoring that advice is the best way to ensure you're able to come back. Avoid tap water and river water – look for bottled mineral water or head for the colourful juice bars behind piles of oranges or strawberries and indulge in the delights of the season.

Some cafés serve *shay bin naana* or tea with mint

Above: Freshly brewed herbal infusions are excellent thirst-quenchers

Authentic Restaurants

For a taste of real Egyptian food, try one of these:
- In Alexandria, Muhammad Ahmed, Kadoura
- In Cairo, Felfela (► 75), Andrea's (► 75), Alfi Bey (► 74)
- In Luxor, Restaurant Muhammad (► 105), Nour al Gurna (► 105)
- In Aswan, al Masry (► 126)

Undulations & Gyrations

From Salome's dance of the seven veils in return for the head of John the Baptist, to modern-day sell-out shows at 2am, belly dancing has always pulled the crowds.

Raqs sharqi, or more properly Oriental dance, is a social phenomenon in Egypt. From its origins in the Middle East it stretches back in time, through ancient tomb paintings of women apparently belly dancing, and cuts through social barriers. Everyone, from the haughtiest society princess to the poorest rag-picker, will have a go at some time.

Professional dancers claim it's in the genes and that every Egyptian is born with the ability to dance in this way. But it's not all in the belly. The dance also demands great control of the hips, expression of the hands and (if you can afford it) the backing of a 30-piece band.

As they get older not all Egyptian belly dancers continue to perform in public, except perhaps at weddings and big family parties. There's a growing social stigma about dancing, linked to increasing religious conservatism, which has led to some very public retirements by famous dancers. Strong competition has arrived from foreign dancers, but the biggest stars, Dina, Lucy and Soraya, remain Egyptian.

These days it's not even confined to Egypt, as the energy required and effort involved has made belly dancing a popular way of keeping fit in the West.

In the Egyptian and Arab music world one voice is heard above all others: that of Umm Kalthoum (1898–1975), known as *Sitt al Kull* (The Lady of All) and *Kawkab al Sharq* (The Star of the East).

Star of the East:
Umm Kalthoum

Umm Kalthoum was born in the village of Tumay al Zahayra in the delta's Gharbiya province. Talented from an early age, she starred in six films from 1936. But it was for her extraordinary voice that she stood out, and she gave up films in 1947 to concentrate on singing. She was a social phenomenon. At a time when Egyptians didn't talk about love, emotions or sexual pleasure, she provided them with a vocabulary to do so, using ambiguous lyrics to avoid offending public morals. In the process she liberated both men and women.

On the first Thursday of each month Umm Kalthoum would give concerts that became an institution, attracting dignitaries from around the Arab world. They were also broadcast live to millions on radio.

Like Western celebrities, Umm Kalthoum's life was often controversial. Her success aroused the jealousy of singers and critics, who accused her of being domineering and of stifling younger talent. Her passionate songs also provoked rumours about her love life and she was romantically linked to several people, but she married a doctor and university professor called Dr Hassan Hefnawy in 1953.

Umm Kalthoum was fêted around the world, but attained the status of a guru in Egypt. A firm supporter of the 1952 revolution, she influenced public opinion and had the ear of Presidents Nasser and Sadat.

Millions of fans attended her funeral in 1975, one of the largest and most dramatic ever seen in modern Egy[pt]

The Umm Kalthoum Museum, on the southern tip of Cairo's Rhoda island (Monastirli Palace, tel: 02 362 1467, open daily 10–5), has photographs, memorabilia and archive footage of her performances and funeral.

Among her best live recordings are:
• *Alf Layla wa Layla* (The Thousand and One Nights)
• *Enta Omri* (You Are My Life)
• *Al-Atlal* (The Ruins), was voted one of the top 100 songs of the 20th century by French newspaper *Le Monde*.

Finding Your Feet

First Two Hours

Cairo is traditionally the main point of entry for visitors to Egypt, but there are a growing number of international flights direct to Luxor and Alexandria and also charter flights to Hurghada, Sharm al Sheikh and al Alamein.

Cairo International Airport

- The main airport is **25km (16 miles) from the centre**, or 45 minutes by car.
- There are **two main terminals** connected by a free Egypt Air shuttle-bus that runs through the day and night. **Terminal 1** is used by Egyptian and other Arab airlines and El Al, while **Terminal 2** serves Western carriers.
- Both have **24-hour currency exchange** and automatic cash machines accepting Visa, Cirrus and Mastercard.
- **Taxis** are generally cheaper than in Europe and America, but beyond customs you'll be accosted by taxi drivers, some of whom may overcharge. If you've already booked a hotel they may tell you it has closed down and offer to take you to another hotel where they will earn a commission.
- To avoid the hassle you can book a **limousine** in the arrival hall. These are slightly more expensive, but you fix a price and pay before you ride. However, the driver will expect a tip on arrival. If you do take a taxi, check out limousine prices first and make sure you pay less.
- There are also extremely cheap **buses** (24 hours) and more comfortable **minibuses** into the centre. The best bus is No 356 from Terminals 1 and 2 to Midan Abd al-Moneim Riyad behind the Egyptian Museum in the centre; they run every 20 minutes from 6am until 11pm. On the same route are the No 400 and minibus No 27, which operate 24 hours.
- The **tourist office** at Terminal 1 is open daily from 8am to 9pm (tel: 02-291 4255, ext 2223) and the tourist office at Terminal 2 is open for 24 hours every day (tel: 02-291 4277).

Luxor International Airport

- The airport is about 10km (6 miles) out of town and there's **no public transport** into town, so try to arrange to be met by a travel agent. Otherwise you'll have to deal with Luxor's taxi drivers, who are notorious for overcharging; agree the fare before getting in.
- Beyond the airport run, **taxi fares** in Luxor, as elsewhere in Egypt, are generally relatively cheap.
- The airport **tourist office** is open 24 hours in winter peak season (no phone)

Hurghada Airport

- There's **no public transport** from the airport into the town centre so independent travellers must rely on taxis, which charge reasonable fares into town

Sharm al Sheikh

- Ras Nasrani airport is about 15km (9 miles) north of the tourist centre at Naama Bay, and again there's **no public transport**. Most visitors are met by travel agent, but if you're arriving independently you'll have to take a cab.

Tourist Information Offices

- Most tourist offices in Egypt are **rather limited** in the services and brochures they provide. They can be useful for official prices of *calèches* (horse-drawn carriages), taxis and *feluccas* (boats), or for a city map, but they may not as accurate as maps in this and other guidebooks.
- Tourist offices will rarely help with **accommodation**, except those at airports

Cairo Tourist Office

➕ 196 C4 ✉ 5 Sharia Adly, Downtown

☎ 02-391 3454

🕐 Daily 8:30–8; 9–4 during Ramadan

Good for some dusty brochures, but staff could be more helpful.

Egyptian Tourist Authority, Luxor

➕ 202 B4 ✉ Tourist Bazaar on Corniche, just south of Luxor Temple

☎ 095-237 2215

🕐 Daily 8–8

Provides a useful list of official rates for *calèches*, taxis, *feluccas* and guides.

Hurghada Tourist Information

➕ 201 E1 ✉ Opposite the Grand Hotel in New Hurghada

☎ 065-344 4420

🕐 Sat–Thu 9–8, Fri 2–10

Aswan Tourist Office

➕ 202 C3 ✉ Beside the train station

☎ 097-231 2811

🕐 Sat–Thu 8–3, 6–8, Fri 10–2, 6–8; daily 10–2 during Ramadan

Very helpful staff, who can point you towards the trustworthy *felucca* captains.

Alexandria Tourist Office

➕ 200 A5 ✉ Midan Saad Zaghloul, Downtown

☎ 03-485 1556

🕐 Daily 8:30–6 (also 6–8pm mid-Jul to mid-Aug); 9–4 during Ramadan

Local Issues

In the 1990s anti-Christian and anti-governmental violence coincided with the emergence of the Islamic group, the Gamaiyat al Islamiya, which has carried out attacks not only on governmental institutions but also on tourists in an attempt to force the government to agree to their demands for an Islamic state. Their campaign of attacks against trains, cruise boats and tourist buses culminated in 1997 at Deir al Bahari in Luxor, when 58 foreigners and 10 Egyptians were killed. But the government responded by arresting many suspects and introducing the death penalty for terrorists. Nothing of this sort has happened in recent years, but tourists are protected by police and soldiers at the main sites, and must travel through Upper Egypt in an armed convoy.

However, the subsequent discussion of the role of religion in the state has led to a new wave of religious conservatism. The most obvious sign of this trend is the growing number of middle-class women wearing the veil, the ever-greater numbers who spread prayer mats in the street for Friday's midday prayers and men with "raisins" or bruises on their forehead caused by praying.

Visitors should respect the culture when visiting more traditional areas and mosques by dressing modestly (women should cover their hair, upper arms and legs) and behaving discreetly. Men and women should not show affection in public.

Admission Charges

The cost of admission for museums and other sites of interest mentioned in the text is indicated by price categories:

Inexpensive = under 25LE **Moderate** = 25–50LE **Expensive** = over 50LE

Getting Around

On the whole the public transport system in Egypt works well, with regular buses and trains to most major destinations, and service taxis (*beejous*) covering the rest.

Urban Transport
Cairo

- Cairo has a whole fleet of **buses**, but they're usually packed, and women may get hassled. You might be happier sticking to the smaller **mini-** and **microbuses**, which are slightly more expensive but take only as many passengers as there are seats. Minibuses are orange and white, and follow the usual bus routes. Microbuses are more like a shared taxi.
- **Taxis** are cheap and more comfortable than buses.
- The **metro** is clean and easy to use, especially from Downtown Cairo to Coptic Cairo. Tickets are inexpensive (£) and there are special carriages for women only (at the back or front). Women getting in a mixed carriage will be stared at.
- **River buses** are becoming scarce, but are still a good way to avoid the traffic jams and dangerous driving.
- Private **motorboats** (launches) and *feluccas* make excursions on the river.

Elsewhere

- Outside Cairo it's a different story. In most other cities, except perhaps Alexandria, you may prefer taxis to the **scant public transport** service.

Buses

- **Intercity buses** are inexpensive, faster and usually more reliable than trains and often serve areas not covered by the rail network, such as Sinai and the oases. Almost all intercity buses now leave from one bus station, the **Turgoman Garage** (Mo'af Turgoman) on Sharia al-Gisr in Bulaq, 600m (650 yards) southwest of Ramses train station. Buses 983 and 984 or minibus 32 go there from the Abd al-Moneim Riyad Terminal in downtown Cairo. Buses, particularly the long-haul air-conditioned services, fill up quickly, so it is advisable to book seats one day in advance.
- The four bus companies listed below all have offices at Turgoman, and all run both **air-conditioned** and **non air-conditioned services**.
- The **West Delta Bus Company** (tel: 02-576 5582) runs services to Alexandria, Marsa Matruh and the Nile delta.
- The **East Delta Bus Company** (tel: 02-574 2814) operates to Sinai and the Canal zone. Some buses also stop at the old Sinai Terminal on Sharia Ramses in Abbaseya.
- The **Upper Egypt Bus Company** (tel: 02-575 0261) serves all cities south of Cairo along the Nile, the Fayoum, the Western Desert oases and the Red Sea coast up to Marsa Alam. There are no direct buses to Siwa from Cairo; you have to take a bus to Mersa Matruh or Alexandria and change there.
- **Superjet** (tel: 02-579 8181) runs more luxurious air-conditioned buses (with video, snacks and toilet) from Cairo to Alexandria, Luxor, Aswan and Hurghada. There are also five fast buses daily to Sharm al Sheikh.

Taxis

- Taxis in Cairo are **black and white** and tend to be four-seater cars.
- Taxis are **cheaper** than in Europe, but rarely use their old meters.

Even if they do, the amount shown will probably bear little resemblance to the fare charged by the driver.

▪ Cairenes usually **hail a taxi** by shouting out their destination as it drives past. They don't discuss the fare as they know roughly what to pay, but as a visitor it may be best to agree a fare and ask someone in your hotel for the going rate before you travel. Be prepared to haggle for a reasonable price.

▪ **Estate-car cabs**, known as **service taxis**, usually charge limousine rates if they're working as normal taxis. These serve everywhere in Egypt and can be the fastest way of getting around. As they're usually Peugeots, they're known as *beejous*. The drivers announce their destination and leave as soon as there are six or seven passengers. The fares charged are similar to buses (again, check that you are not charged tourist rates).

▪ Due to **travel restrictions** for foreigners, it can be difficult to take a service taxi. Often you have to pay for all seven seats and use the car as a private taxi in an armed convoy.

▪ **Beware:** *beejous* have been nicknamed **"flying coffins"** as they tend to be driven fast and recklessly. Accidents are common, especially at night.

Trains

▪ The government-owned **Egyptian State Railway** operates services through the Nile Valley to Aswan, Alexandria, Suez, Port Said and Marsa Matruh. The line from Safaga on the Red Sea coast to Qena, Kharga and Baris is expected to be connected to the Toshka region in the Western Desert in the coming years.

Egyptian State Railway tickets are inexpensive and must be **bought in advance** from the railway station.

The privately owned **Abela Sleeping Trains** operates a rather worn, but good, sleeper train from Cairo to Luxor and Aswan, and several fast and comfortable turbo trains a day to Alexandria (2 hours). In summer there are three sleeper trains a week to Marsa Matruh.

▪ Abela Sleeping Trains tickets must be booked in advance from **Ramses Station** in Cairo (tel: 02-574 9474; www.sleepingtrains.com).

Domestic Flights

▪ As **Egypt Air** almost has a monopoly on domestic flights, fares are uncompetitive and have become quite expensive. If you are flying into Egypt with Egypt Air, book your internal flights at the same time to save up to 50 per cent on published fares. Egypt Air flies **daily** from Cairo to most of Egypt's main cities (tel: 02-392 7649/7680; www.egyptair.com.eg).

Book well in advance, especially during the busy winter season, and be aware that overbooking is unfortunately quite common. To minimise the risk of being "bumped", always reconfirm bookings well in advance, and turn up earlier than the recommended check-in time at the airport,

All domestic flights leave from **Terminal 1** of Cairo airport, also known as the Old Airport (*al matar al qadim*).

You can also book **Air Sinai** flights to Hurghada, Sinai, and Tel Aviv in Israel. Same contact information as Egypt Air.

Orascom Aviation (tel: 02-305 2401), a private airline, operates regular flights from Cairo and Luxor to Gouna.

Driving

Driving in Cairo can be nerve-wracking, and in rural areas it's often dangerous, so consider **renting a car with a driver** if you are nervous.

Since the terrorist attack in Luxor in 1997 **security** is tight along Egypt's roads and it's almost impossible for foreigners to pass the many roadblocks along the Nile without the protection of an armed convoy.

Driving Essentials

- Speed limits on **highways:** 100kph (62mph)
- On other **roads:** 90kph (56mph)
- In **urban centres:** 50kph (31mph)
- **Seat belts** are compulsory.
- Driving is on the **right**-hand side of the road.
- Avoid driving in the **dark** outside cities as most people drive without headlights, saving them for the moment before collision, when they use full beam. In the countryside, remember that villagers walk their animals home just after dusk and that people often sit on the side of the road.
- Many roads have **checkpoints**, where the police may ask for your papers, so be prepared for delays.
- Always carry your **passport and driving licence**. Failing to do so makes you liable to an instant fine, and onward travelling may be prevented.
- If your car hits someone in a rural area, **report it** immediately at the nearest police station, and be aware that you may be attacked by angry villagers.

Car Rental

- **Car-rental agencies** operate in most major hotels.
- **Credit cards** are accepted.
- Drivers must be at least **25 years old** and hold an International Driving Licence.
- Car-rental contracts must be sold with a **third-party liability insurance**, but check if **accident and damage insurance** is included. If you're involved in an accident, you'll need to provide the insurance company with a written report from the police and from the doctor who first treats the injuries.

Upkeep

- Main towns and cities will have many petrol (*benzene*) **filling stations**, but there are fewer in the countryside. To be safe, always fill the tank to the limit, and clean the oil filter regularly because dust and impurities in the fuel tend to clog up the engine.
- Larger **filling stations** are often open until late at night.
- Fuel is much **less expensive** than in Europe.
- The cheapest petrol is **normal** (*tamaneen*), but **super** (*tisaeen*) is better quality. Lead-free fuel is available only from a few filling stations in more affluent areas of Cairo and Alexandria.
- Egyptian car **mechanics** are often masters of invention and can usually fix breakdown.
- Most large garages stock a good range of **spare parts**.
- If you run into trouble, **people will often gladly help** you push your car to the next garage or to the side of the road.

Motoring Club

Automobile and Touring Club of Egypt
10 Sharia Qasr al Nil, Downtown Cairo
✚ 196 C4 ☎ 02-574 3355 (Sat–Thu 9am–1:30pm)

Travel Restrictions

- Incidences of terrorist violence against tourists have led to **tight security** and travel restrictions for visitors on certain overland routes, notably between cities along the Nile, with travel possible only in armed convoys.
- Officially, tourists are also allowed only on two guarded air-conditioned **trains** between Cairo, Luxor and Aswan.
- The **situation changes frequently** so check with the tourist office before travelling, or use river transport where possible.

Accommodation

There's a large choice of accommodation in Egypt's main tourist centres, but elsewhere it's often down to the very basic. This guide includes a cross-section of places to stay, from luxury hotels in palaces to good inexpensive pensions.

Hotels

- Hotels are rated from **deluxe to budget**, with a few unclassified hotels geared mainly towards backpackers and Egyptian families.
- **Deluxe** hotels, almost always part of international chains, usually have international facilities, but although service is getting better it may not always be up to international standards.
- **Mid-range hotels** include some of the more characterful old hotels, such as the Cecil in Alexandria, and also more modern concrete resort hotels on the Red Sea.
- **Budget hotels** are rarely air-conditioned, but some will have cooling fans. A few are real gems, old art-deco buildings with high ceilings, old-fashioned furniture and unreliable plumbing. The less said about others, the better.

Pensions

Pensions are similar to budget hotels but, as they're often run by one family, the atmosphere tends to be much friendlier and relaxed, and the rooms better maintained.

Hostels

- Egypt has **15 cheap hostels** in the main towns, recognised by Hostelling International. Rooms are cheaper if you have a HI membership, but it is not strictly necessary.
- Information is available from **Egyptian Youth Hostel Association**, 1 Sharia Ibrahimy, Garden City, Cairo (tel: 02-794 0527; fax: 02-795 0329).

Camping

- Camping is **not popular** in Egypt and the country's few campsites are mostly along the coast and in the oases, where they're generally a long way from the sights and poorly equipped. Campsites attached to hotels are usually slightly better.
- Camping outside designated sites along the coast is not advisable as some empty beaches are still **mined**. This is less of a problem in the desert.

Booking Accommodation

Rooms at more expensive hotels are often cheaper when booked either through the chain's international reservation system or when bought as part of a package. Other places recommended here should preferably be **booked in advance**, particularly in high season when hotels fill up fast.

Check the website **www.egyptreservation.com** for hotels, reservation services, travel agents and other related services.

Accommodation Prices

- many hotels, it is possible to bargain over the advertised room rate, particularly in off-peak periods and if you are staying for a few days. The set price of accommodation featured in the guide is indicated below. The prices are for a double room per night.

£ = under 450LE   **££** = 450–1000LE **£££** = over 1000LE

Food and Drink

You can eat well in Egypt, but don't expect to find a variety of gourmet food
Egyptian cuisine is peasant food, a lot less sophisticated, for instance, than
its Lebanese neighbour (➤ 28–30).

The Egyptian Way of Eating

- **Lunch** is usually served from 12:30 to 3pm and dinner from 8 to 10:30pm
  but many places in tourist areas stay open all day.
- At a **restaurant**, Egyptians tend to start a meal with a good selection of cold
  and/or hot *mezze* (small dishes) with drinks. If the spread is big enough,
  this can sometimes make a whole meal.
- **Flat pitta bread** is often used in place of a fork to scoop up food.
- An important point of etiquette to remember: only use the **right hand** while
  eating this way, because the left hand is traditionally used for ablutions.

On the Street

Everywhere in Egypt you will come across street vendors selling everything
from cheese sandwiches and delicious *shawarma* to cow's-feet soup and lamb
testicle sandwiches. However tempting these may look and smell, street food
is only recommended for the adventurous or those with a strong stomach, as
hygiene conditions on these stalls can be quite poor and very few have
running water.

International Cuisine

- You can now find most styles of cooking in **Cairo** and, unlike in Europe,
  ethnic restaurants are usually more expensive.
- **Outside Cairo** the choice is more limited. Most international restaurants are
  in the luxury hotels, with prices to match. Hotel food can often be bland,
  especially set menus or open buffets, but some restaurants are excellent.
- International **fast-food** chains are a relatively recent arrival in Egypt, but
  have proved to be immensely popular and just about every tourist resort
  now boasts McDonald's, PizzaExpress and so on.
- In spite of this success, Egyptians have not entirely abandoned their own
  interesting varieties of fast food. Examples include *kushari* (a spicy mix of
  pulses, pasta and rice) and *falafel/taamiya* (deep-fried, spiced, mashed
  chickpeas/ground beans) or *fuul* sandwiches.

Vegetarians

Although most Egyptians can't afford to eat meat more than once a week,
there is little understanding of why a foreigner should choose to live off
vegetables alone. Having said that, there are usually plenty of vegetable stew
or other vegetarian dishes on restaurant menus and fish, usually from the Nile
or the Red Sea, is available for those who eat it. **Ana nabaati/iya** is Arabic for
I'm a vegetarian.

Eating Out

- If you have a **sensitive stomach**, try to avoid raw vegetables, unpeeled fruit,
  ice-cream, open buffets and food that has been cooking for a while, such
  as *shawarma*.
- Drink plenty of **water and fresh juices** to replace fluids, but avoid heavily
  chilled drinks in the midday sun, particularly alcohol.
- Egyptians love to **dress up** to go to a fancy restaurant, but other places are
  fairly casual about clothes.

Useful Reading

■ The *Egypt Today Restaurant Guide*, available from local bookshops, has reviews of a wide selection of restaurants and watering holes.
■ The monthly magazine *Egypt Today*, which also has a restaurant selection, reviews new places in Cairo.

Best for Fresh Fish

The Fish next to the Hilton Fayrouz, Sharm al Sheikh (➤ 172)
Americana Fish Market, Cairo (➤ 74)
Fish Market, Alexandria (➤ 147)
Qadoura, Alexandria (➤ 148)

Drinks

■ **Tap-water** and ice made from it is heavily chlorinated but can still cause problems.
■ **Bottled mineral water** (*maaya maadaniya*) is widely available.
■ Most Egyptians drink a lot of tea, coffee, herbal drinks, cold drinks and juice (➤ 30). Everywhere you'll find stalls making inexpensive, **fresh juices** from whatever is in season: orange, pomegranate, strawberry, carrot and mango, as well as bananas in milk. Fresh lime juice is a perfect thirst-quencher, but it's often served with lots of sugar. If you want drinks without sugar, be sure to mention it when ordering.

Alcohol

■ Egypt is officially a Muslim country and, although alcohol is widely available in tourist centres, it's **prohibited** in some parts of the country, particularly away from the main towns. Even where it is available, show your respect for the culture by drinking it only in moderation.
■ Hotels and some restaurants usually sell **local beer and wine**, but imported alcoholic drinks are often only available in the luxury hotels and at hugely inflated prices.
■ **Locally made liquors**, with names such as Johnny Talker and Good Gin, are best avoided; there have been several cases of serious illness resulting from bootleg liquor. Zbib, quite similar to Greek ouzo, is the exception.
■ Several good **beers**, including Stella and Sakkara, are brewed in Egypt.
■ The long-established and recently privatised **Gianaclis Vineyards** in the delta region produce drinkable red, white and rosé wines, although you may not want to take any home.
The other local wine, red, white, rosé and sparkling **Obelisk**, is made in Gouna from good-quality grape concentrates from Sicily.

Best Watering Holes

After Eight, Cairo (➤ 74)
Greek Club, Cairo (➤ 76)
Sequoia, Cairo (➤ 75–76)
Cap d'Or, Alexandria (➤ 147)
Little Buddha Bar, Sharm al Sheik (➤ 172–173)

Restaurant Prices

Below is the price of establishments featured in this guide, based on the amount you should expect to pay per person for a three-course meal, excluding alcoholic drinks and tips.

£ = up to 100LE   **££** = 100–200LE   **£££** = over 200LE

Note that some hotels charge an extra service tax of 22 per cent.

Shopping

Wherever you go in Egypt, there will be no shortage of shopping opportunities. Egyptians are traders at heart and they also love to shop, so it often seems as if most of the country is one big bazaar. Shopping can be a lengthy process involving exchanging greetings, drinking tea, choosing the items you want to buy and then, eventually, bargaining and agreeing on the price.

Shopping Hours

- **Department stores**, often state run, are usually open Monday to Saturday from 9am to 1pm and again from 5 to 8pm, while smaller shops tend to be open all day, and often until 8pm or later in tourist areas.
- Most **bazaars** are closed on Sundays, but some tourist shops might still be open.
- Some Muslim shopkeepers close during the **Friday noon prayers**, but will reopen as soon as they come back from the mosque. At the regular prayer times you may find the shopkeeper performing his prayers behind the counter. Just hang around, as these will not take very long.
- Major **credit cards and travellers' cheques** are now widely accepted in tourist areas, but many smaller shops still accept only cash or will add a surcharge for using credit cards.

Bargaining

Western visitors are often too embarrassed or impatient to haggle over a price, but for Egyptians this is the normal state of affairs: when Egyptians go shopping they expect to bargain for everything. You may prefer the few shops with fixed prices, but they are often more expensive and tourists who cannot read Arabic numerals are still likely to be overcharged. Just remember that bargaining can be fun once you understand the rules. Window-shop at the fixed-price stores to get an idea of prices before venturing into the bazaars, where haggling is the norm. As a general rule, try halving the asking price and watching the trader's reaction. If he's quick to accept, you're still offering too much. If he's not interested, you could offer a little more, or try walking away: if your price was fair he will call you back.

Handicrafts

- The **variety** of Egyptian handicrafts is endless and prices are very good, but the quality of the work has deteriorated as Egyptian tastes have changed; most crafts are now produced for the tourist trade. Typical souvenirs are mostly cheap reproductions of pharaonic art. Papyrus, for example, is often made of banana leaves, painted with scenes copied from original papyri and tomb paintings. Also look out for poorly executed reproductions of ancient statues.
- Several **aid organisations** are trying hard to revive old crafts, such as embroidery, pottery and weaving, particularly as a way of making the women in rural areas who produce them more financially independent. A sign of their success is the appearance of a few new shops selling better-quality products, such as **Fair Trade Egypt** (➤ 77), a fair-trade shop selling quality products from projects all over Egypt, **Khan Misr Touloun** (➤ 77), or **Oum el Dounia** (➤ 77).
- The cheapest place to buy crafts is in **Khan al Khalili** in Cairo (➤ 70), or in the bazaars at Luxor and Aswan. The best buys are painted papyrus, hand-blown recycled glass, mother-of-pearl inlay work, brass and copper work, woven tablecloths and alabaster.

Antiques and Antiquities

Genuine pharaonic, Islamic and Coptic antiques can be exported only with a licence from the Department of Antiquities, best obtained by the dealer. Be aware that most antiquities on offer are fakes, although there is still an important and damaging trade in stolen antiquities.

Cotton and Other Fabrics

Good-quality **Egyptian cotton** is hard to come by in Egypt as most of it is exported, but it's still possible to find inexpensive cotton casual clothes almost everywhere.

■ For traditional **Egyptian clothes** it's best to try looking in the markets in the main towns.

■ The small towns of **Akhmim** and **Nagada** in Upper Egypt are famous for their superb woven textiles, available from better fabric shops in Cairo and Luxor. Bedouin women produce beautifully **embroidered shawls** and clothes.

■ Cairo is probably the best and the cheapest place to buy **belly dance outfits**. You can either buy ready made clothes or have them tailored to your whims with as much beading, glitter, bells and sequins as your heart desires. The best place is the Haberdashery emporium in Khan al Khalili (➤ 70).

Jewellery

■ Many Egyptian women still prefer to put their money in **jewellery**, preferably gold, rather than in a bank, so jewellery is readily available.

■ Bedouin and rural women prefer 21-carat gold, but most Western-style jewellery is 18 carat. **Gold and silver jewellery** is sold by the gram, with an additional fee for the workmanship. Bullion prices are printed daily in the *Egyptian Gazette*.

Jewellery is **relatively inexpensive** in Egypt, as wages are still very low.

■ Gold or silver **cartouches** with names written in hieroglyphics are probably the most popular jewellery buy for tourists. These usually take the form of pendants on chains.

Perfumes and Spices

Cairo has long been the **largest perfume and spice market** in the Middle East. Try the spice market in Khan al Khalili (➤ 70) for the best selection. Essences are sold by the **ounce** (28g), to be diluted in alcohol for perfume. Take care when buying **scents**. Egypt produces many pure essences that are used in Western perfumes, and several shops offer close copies of famous brands. Some shops offer the real thing, but overcharging and diluting pure essences is a common scam.

Spices such as black pepper (*filfil*), cumin (*kammum*), red pepper (*shatta*) and cinnamon (*irfa*) make inexpensive and welcome souvenirs, useful for recreating Egyptian cuisine back home.

Stick to the spices used locally as more exotic spices such as saffron (*zaafaran*) or green pepper (*filfil akhdar*) may be considerably cheaper than back home, but since they are often artificially dyed and have no taste whatsoever, are of inferior quality.

In Aswan look out for the red **hibiscus** flower (*karkadeh*), which makes a delicious hot or cold drink.

Best Markets...

…souvenirs: Khan al Khalili, Cairo (➤ 70–71; 77)
…antiques and junk: Attarin Market, Alexandria (➤ 149)
…camels: Daraw (➤ 122)
…spices: *souk*, Luxor Town (➤ 105), Aswan (➤ 127)
…Nubian baskets, silk shawls: *souk*, Aswan (➤ 127)

Entertainment

Most visitors to Egypt have such a full schedule that they have very little energy left for sports or nightlife. But if you have the time and the inclination, you can find information about what's on in the *Egyptian Mail* (Saturday), the daily *Egyptian Gazette*, *Al Ahram Weekly*, and the monthly magazines *Egypt Today* and *Insight*. If you have access to a computer or Internet café, also try th websites www.egypttoday.com, www.cairocafe.com and www.cairotimes.com

Bars and Clubs

- Cairo has a wide variety of bars and clubs, but elsewhere in the country most of the nightlife happens in the hotels. The **music** on offer is partly Western and partly Egyptian, with the occasional Sudanese or Greek song thrown in.
- Some places will refuse you entry if you are dressed too **casually** or in jeans, and others have a couples-only policy to avoid trouble, although single foreign women will invariably be let in.
- **Outdoor cafés** are a great place to watch the world, but this is usually done over tea, coffee or cold drinks and a *sheeshas* (water pipe), as alcohol is rarely served.

Belly Dancing

Belly dancing has become less popular in recent years as many younger Egyptians and Arabs opt for Western-style entertainment. When religious leaders condemned belly dancing as sinful, many Egyptian dancers took early retirement, and their places were filled by foreign dancers. You'll find the bes shows in the nightclubs of the luxury hotels, which charge a flat fee for the show and a four-course meal. The dancers to look out for are Lucy, Dina and the British-born Yasmina. Less salubrious clubs can be rather sleazy but fasc nating, where beer flows at a price and where men shower dancers with pape money. (See also Undulations and Gyrations, ➤ 31)

Nile-side Entertainment

On hot summer nights many Egyptians like to go down to the Nile to catch the cooler breeze. Many towns have casinos, or café terraces on the banks of the Nile where families come for cold drinks and a snack, and where lovers meet to discuss their future. At almost any time of the year it's possible to rent a *felucca* (sailing boat) or a motorboat to watch the sunset or to spend a pleasant evening with drinks and a picnic.

Spectator Sports

Egyptians are crazy about soccer and the adventurous can attend matches during the season (September–May). Cairo has two premier league teams. Ahli's stadium is in Zamalek and, rather confusingly, Zamalek Club plays at Muhandiseen. The national stadium is in Madinet Nasr. Another popular spe tator sport is horse-racing, which is held at Cairo's Gezira or Heliopolis hippodromes, between October and May.

Festivals

October: Pharaoh's Rally, a desert 4WD race attracting an international field.
November: Arab Music Festival at Cairo Opera House, featuring classical and traditional Arabic music.
December: Cairo International Film Festival held in several Downtown cinema

Cairo

Getting Your Bearings

In a tale from *The Thousand and One Nights*, a man who is talking of wondrous cities claims:
"He who has not seen Cairo has not seen the World. Its dust is gold; its Nile is a wonder; its women are like the black-eyed virgins of paradise: and how could it not be otherwise, when she is the Mother of the World?"

The Nile still runs like a mirage through the city and some of the women are indeed beauties, but the dust is more concrete than gold, and the Mother of the World now nurses a population close to 20 million.

Cairo is full of extremes: poverty and wealth, widespread illiteracy and Internet cafés, mudbrick buildings beneath skyscrapers. There's always a surprise around the corner, but somehow the city continues to function, and even to flourish.

★ **Don't Miss**

At Your Leisure

At first sight you may think of
hell rather than paradise, for the
traffic is usually solid, pollution
leaves a brownish haze on the
horizon and the cacophony of
noises produces instant headaches.
Less than 200 years of urban and
industrial sprawl is now threatening
to engulf monuments that have stood
for 5,000 years. Yet in the face of turmoil,
Cairenes merely go about their business. You may lose patience
– some people hate the city, but most are exhilarated by the
chaotic overdose of humanity, and its unpredictability.

The secret of enjoying Cairo is perhaps to do as the Cairenes
and take it as it comes, with humour and heaps of patience.
The reward is instant and you'll soon discover one of the most
fascinating cities in the world, where history is just another
part of everyday life.

Previous page:
Cairo glitters
by night. Far
left: View from
Gezira Island.
Left: Herbalists
in Khan al
Khalili bazaar

It would take months to explore all of Cairo's treasures, but in three days you can get a sense of the many facets of this fascinating city.

Cairo in Three Days

Day One

Morning
Start with a long morning visit to the **① Egyptian Museum of Antiquities** (left, ➤ 50–53), then stroll over to **② Downtown Cairo** (➤ 67) for lunch in one of the numerous restaurants. Try either the stylish Sabaya (➤ 76) or the less expensive Felfela (➤ 75).

Afternoon
Walk back to Midan Tahrir (Liberation Square), cross the Nile over Qasr al Nil Bridge, passing the modern Opera House and walk to the **③ Mr and Mrs Mahmoud Khalil Museum** (➤ 67). Walk back towards the Nile and take a *felucca* to watch the sun setting over Cairo.

Day Two

Morning
Start early and take a taxi or the metro to **④ Coptic Cairo** (➤ 54–55) to visit the Coptic Museum and old churches. Take a taxi to the **⑧ Sultan Hasan Mosque-Madrasa** (➤ 69) and from there another cab to the **Al Azhar Park** (➤ panel 71) for a stroll and lunch at one of the restaurants (➤ 74–76).

Afternoon
After lunch, it's a short cab ride to **11 Khan al Khalili** (➤ 70). Stroll through the *souks* towards the Barquq Mausoleum and on to the merchant's house, **Beit al Suhaymi** (➤ 57). Afterwards, return along **12 Sharia al Muizz li Din Allah** (➤ 56–58) up to the Tentmakers Bazaar. Return to Khan al Khalili for a cup of mint tea and water pipe at the al Fishawi café (right, ➤ 75).

Evening
Finish the evening watching a belly dance show at one of the top-quality hotels (➤ 78).

Day Three

Morning
Take a taxi to Memphis, and continue from there to the Step Pyramid and tombs at **13 Saqqara** (➤ 59–61). Have a late lunch at Andrea's (➤ 75) or in the garden of the Mena House Oberoi (➤ 73).

Afternoon
Take another cab or walk over to the **14 Giza Pyramids, the Sphinx** and the **Solar Boat Museum** (➤ 62–66) for a leisurely visit. Head for the stables and rent a horse or camel to go for a sunset trip in the desert.

Evening
Head back into town and join the in-crowd at the bar-restaurant Sequoia (➤ 76) with wonderful views over the Nile.

🚻

The Egyptian Museum of Antiquities

The Egyptian Museum in Cairo houses the world's most exquisite and extensive collection of ancient Egyptian artefacts, covering more than 3,000 years, from the Old Kingdom to the Roman period. It's said that if you allowed one minute for each exhibit, it would take nine months to see everything here. But if that's a little too long, take at least a morning (or better still two) to see the museum's many highlights, even though the exhibits are often badly lit and displayed. The ground floor is arranged chronologically, moving clockwise from the entrance hall (pictured below), while exhibits on the first floor are grouped thematically.

Ground Floor Highlights

The beginnings of Egyptian art are marked by the **Narmer Palette** in Room 43, which records the unification of Egypt by King Menes (► 22), and by the museum's oldest **statues** (Room 48) – that of the seated King Zoser was found near his step pyramid at Saqqara. The smooth black statue of the pyramid

---

➕ 196 B4
✉ Midan Tahrir, Downtown ☎ 02-575 4319;
www.egyptianmuseum.gov.eg
🕐 Daily 9–6:45
🍴 Museum cafeteria (£);

Italian restaurant (££) ;Abu Ali café terrace
(£) at the Nile Hilton
🚇 Sadat station
💲 Moderate; extra charge for the Mummy
Room from its first-floor entrance (expensive

Grand Egyptian Museum

When the present Egyptian Museum first opened it saw about 500 visitors daily, but the ever-growing collection now attracts some 7,000 visitors a day. A running joke has it that the museum's basement is the last important dig in Egypt. The new 38,000sq m (410,000sq feet) Great Egyptian Museum is expected to open on a site near the Giza Pyramids in 2009. More than 100,000 objects will be on show, and it will include a museum shop, an Egyptology library, an auditorium and a media centre. The current museum will still be used to exhibit 5,000 masterpieces.

builder Khafre is a masterpiece, as is the striking wooden man known as the Sheikh al Balad or Village Chief (both Room 42).

Room 32 is dominated by the striking double statue of the harmonious couple Rahotep and Nofret, which has exceptionally well-preserved colours. Rather more bizarre is the statue of the dwarf Seneb and his wife, with his children placed to hide his short legs. The remarkably colourful chapel of Hathor, with a life-size statue of the cow goddess (Room 12), was found at Hatshepsut's Temple, Deir al Bahari, in Luxor (▶ 94–95).

One of the museum's most fascinating collections, in Room 3, shows the ground-breaking realistic art from the time of the rebellious pharaoh Akhenaton (▶ 22). In four large statues here Akhneton is shown with a long face, a gorgeous mouth, and oversized hips and belly. He's seen with his famously beautiful wife Nefertiti, and playing with their children.

Now walk along the eastern wing to the southeast staircase leading to the first floor.

Above: The statue of Khafre radiates a sense of his power

Below: Taking time to look at the smaller details can be rewarding

Left: Tutankhamun probably died before the age of 20 from brain tumour and a lung disease. Below: This gold jewel from his tomb is inlaid with semi-precious stones

The First Floor

Tutankhamun's splendid mask is made of solid gold with decorations in lapis lazuli, turquoise, carnelian and glass paste

The biggest crowd-puller among the museum's many world-class treasures is undoubtedly **Tutankhamun's treasure**. Akhenaton's son-in-law only ruled for nine years, but he became famous when the English archaeologist Howard Carter (1874–1939) discovered his intact tomb in 1922 in the Valley of the Kings, packed to the roof with the dazzling objects that were intended to see him through the afterlife.

By walking up the southeast stairs you encounter the items more or less as they were placed in the tomb. Room 45 starts with two life-size statues of the pharaoh that guarded his burial chamber, and the next galleries show the vast amount of refined furniture, often gold-plated, that was placed in this modest tomb. Rooms 7 and 8 are filled with the gilded wooden shrines that fitted into each other and contained the pharaoh's sarcophagus. You may have to queue in Room 3 to see the biggest treasure of all, Tutankhamun's solid-gold death mask, encrusted with semi-precious stones, his golden sarcophagus and his jewellery.

In Room 4 you'll find more ancient jewellery from all over the country, and Room 2 has the spectacular jewellery found in Tanis tombs. The newly arranged Rooms 53 and 54 have a wonderful collection of animal mummies.

The Royal Mummy Room

Room 56 houses the **mummies** of 11 of Egypt's most illustrious pharaohs, including Seti I, his son Ramses II (➤ 23) and Tuthmosis II. Former President Sadat had the room closed in 1981, considering it disrespectful to the dead. But since it partly reopened in 1995, visitors are asked to keep respectfully quiet and tour groups are not allowed.

TAKING A BREAK

The museum cafeteria is rather dull, but the **Nile Hilton** (➤ 73) is just a few steps away. Their Abu Ali's terrace café offers snacks and *sheeshas* (water pipes), the Italian **Da Mario** does good pastas and pizzas, or you can stop for coffee and cakes at the coffee shop. The **Semiramis** hotel near by has several excellent restaurants.

The Aten sun-disc shines on the intimacy of the royal couple

THE EGYPTIAN MUSEUM OF ANTIQUITIES: INSIDE INFO

Top tips Most tour buses get to the museum around 10am, so avoid the crowds by going earlier for an hour of peace and quiet, or in the afternoon.
• The amount of things to see is staggering so try to spread your visit over at least two half days, maybe exploring one floor at a time.

Ones to miss The eastern wing of the ground floor, mostly devoted to the Late Period, is badly labelled and less interesting than the rest, except for the Graeco-Roman art in Room 34.
• You could also skip the western outer galleries of sarcophagi on the first floor and the eastern inner galleries (except Room 14) for the same reasons.

Hidden gems Room 14 on the first floor is rather poorly presented but has a superb collection of Graeco-Roman mummies with beautifully painted face masks, known as the Fayoum portraits.
• Also on the first floor (in Rooms 32 and 27) are some amazingly detailed, lifelike models of fishing boats, butchers, cattle with herdsmen and a villa with garden that give a fascinating insight into life in the Middle Kingdom.

In more depth A digital guide (moderate) is available inside the museum. For more details of the antiquities visit the museum's bookshop. *The Illustrated Guide to the Egyptian Museum in Cairo*, by Zahi Hawass, the secretary-general of Egypt's Supreme Council of Antiquities, is a descriptive guide with pictures of the main exhibits and some useful itineraries (AUC Press). A wonderful illustrated book by Francesco Tiradritti is *The Treasures of the Egyptian Museum in Cairo* (AUC Press).

❹

Coptic Cairo

One of the oldest-inhabited parts of the city is Masr al Qadima (Old Cairo), the Coptic neighbourhood that provides a fascinating link between Egypt's pharaonic and Islamic civilisations. In the 6th century BC a garrison known as Babylon-in-Egypt guarded a river crossing here. There are some Roman fortifications, but the area's real attraction is its narrow lanes lined with early churches, and Egypt's oldest synagogue. Cairo's first mosque, built by Amr Ibn al As in AD 642, is near by.

The first thing you'll see when you get here are two Roman towers, which were part of the fortifications built by Emperor Trajan in AD 130, and some fragments of the walls of Babylon-in-Egypt. Behind these lies the fascinating **Coptic Museum**, which gives an overview of Coptic art from the Graeco-Roman

Enthusiastic Coptic volunteer may show you around al Muallaqa Churc

Coptic Museum
✚ 196 B1
✉ Masr al Qadima (Old Cairo)
☎ 02-363 9742;
www.copticmuseum.gov.eg
🕐 Daily 9–5
🍴 Cafeteria in garden (£)
🚇 Mar Girgis (from Midan Tahrir)
💰 Moderate

Coptic Churches
✉ Masr al Qadima (Old Cairo)
🕐 Churches and synagogue daily 9–4 and during services
🚇 Mari Girgis (from Midan Tahrir)
💰 Free; donations welcome

period to the early Islamic era (from about AD 300 to 1000). It is clear that some Christian symbols may have evolved from pharaonic ones, including the cross and the image of the Virgin and Child.

The Copts were excellent weavers and the upper floor contains a beautiful collection of early textile fragments.

A passage near the cafeteria leads to the **al Muallaqa Church** (Hanging Church), built over one of the Roman bastions, visible at the back of the church. The building is reached via a steep staircase and a vestibule where Coptic souvenirs are on sale. The church probably dates from the 7th century, although some Copts claim it's older. Its dark interior is magnificent, with cedar panelling, a wooden Ark-like ceiling, a fine carved marble pulpit supported by 12 pillars representing the Apostles, and superb 13th-century panels inlaid with bone and ivory hiding the three *haikals* (altars).

Probably the oldest church here is the 5th-century **Abu Sarga (St Sergius)**, with an even older crypt where the Holy Family is said to have rested during their exile in Egypt. In the chapel of the Convent of St George visitors wishing to be blessed can be wrapped in chains by the nuns.

The Jewish community has long gone but the **Ben Ezra Synagogue**, at the other end of the street, has been restored to its former glory. Originally a Coptic church, the building was transformed in the 11th century and the decoration remained very similar to that of the nearby churches. According to Jewish tradition, this is where the prophet Jeremiah preached in the 6th century BC, while the Copts believe that it marks the site where baby Moses was found in a basket.

The Holy Family in Egypt

"The angel of the Lord appeared to Joseph in a dream, saying, 'Arise, and take the young child and his mother, and flee into Egypt...for Herod will seek the young child to destroy him'...He took the young child and his mother by night, and departed into Egypt." Matthew 2:13–14.

It's believed that the Holy Family – Mary, the infant Jesus and Mary's husband Joseph – spent four years on the move, crossing Sinai and then travelling along the Nile to Asyut. Coptic churches and monasteries were built in many of the places where they are believed to have rested.

TAKING A BREAK

The **cafeteria** in the museum garden is a peaceful place.

COPTIC CAIRO: INSIDE INFO

Top tip Attend a **Coptic Mass** at the Hanging Church (Friday 8–11am and Sunday 9–11am) and hear the sound of the pharaohs, as the Copts claim to be their direct descendants. The instruments, music and language you hear are similar to those in ancient Egypt. On 1 June, a festival commemorates the Holy Family's stay in the area.

Hidden gems To the right of the entrance of the Hanging Church is a beautiful 10th-century **icon of the Virgin and Child** with obvious Egyptian facial features.
• Walk along the alleys behind the 11th-century St Barbara's church to discover a hidden Christian cemetery.

🔢

Sharia al Muizz li Din Allah

This is the main thoroughfare of the original Fatimid city of al Qahira (Cairo), and is lined with some of the city's most glorious mosques and palaces. As it was customary to build shops outside mosques, it's also home to some of Cairo's less touristy bazaars.

➕ 197 E4

🕐 Most monuments daily 9–5; mosques may close for Fri noon prayers; less-visited monuments such as the ramparts and Qasr Bashtak may appear closed, but a custodian is usually on duty near by

💰 Moderate; the mosques are free but remember to tip the custodian

The 11th-century **Fatimid walls** and the gate called **Bab al Futuh** mark the northern end of Sharia al Muizz. Built before the Crusades by Armenians (using stones from pharaonic structures), they were reinforced by Saladin (➤ 25) a century later. To appreciate the architectural and military genius, take a torch and walk the ramparts to **Bab al Nasr**, and back for marvellous views over the Northern Cemetery and Cairo.

Adjacent is the **mosque of al Hakim** (➤ 24), with a marble courtyard and huge minarets that are among the oldest in the city. You may guess from the smell that this part of the street is also home to the onion and garlic market.

Farther to the right, the **mosque and *sabil-kuttab* of Sulayman Agha al Silahdar** is built in a mixture of Turkish and Cairene styles, and has a slim pencil minaret. Opposite is **Darb al Asfar**, a narrow side street with several renovated merchant houses, a sign of the government's plans for the entire old city. The finest mansion is **Beit al Suhaymi**, two 17th- and 18th-century houses knocked together. Its rooms are decorated with inlaid marble and *mashrabia* woodwork, and a fabulous shaded courtyard is filled with birdsong.

Back along Sharia al Muizz to the left is the elegant mosque of **al Aqmar** ("the moon-lit"), a rare surviving Fatimid monument. On the next left corner is the prominent ***sabil-kuttab* of Abd al Rahman Katkhuda**, which has a fountain downstairs and Quranic school upstairs, with a beautiful carved ceiling. Here, Sharia Muizz opens out to **Bayn al Qasrayn** ("Between the Two Palaces"), after the long-gone Fatimid palaces at the core of the original city. Only two of the original five storeys of the 14th-century palace of Qasr Amir Bashtak have survived (on the left of the street), but this is one of Cairo's most impressive secular medieval buildings.

Opposite is the 185m (610-foot) facade of the epitome of Mameluke architecture. This complex includes the cruciform ***madrasa-khanqah* of Sultan Barquq** (1384), the ***madrasa*-mausoleum of al Nasir** (1304) with a marble Gothic doorway, and the ***madrasa*-mausoleum and *maristan* of Sultan Qalawun**, al Nasir's father. The *maristan* functioned as a medical centre until the 19th century.

Top: Courtyard of al Hakim Mosque.
Above: The Bab al Futuh gate

Enjoy the peacefulness of the delightful shady courtyard of Beit al Suhaymi

Opposite Qalawun's complex, **Sultan Ayyub's *madrasa-mausoleum*** was built in 1242 as Cairo's first Quranic school. Lined with coppersmith shops, the street turns into the Gold Bazaar, where a small alley to the left leads into **Khan al Khalili** (➤ 70–71). Past the busy shopping street of al Muski is the imposing ***madrasa* of Sultan Barsbay** (1425), and at its southern end an alley leads into the **Perfume and Spice Market**. Across Sharia al Azhar is the impressive **Ghuriya complex** of the Mameluke Sultan al Ghuri, with its mausoleum on the left and *madrasa* on the right.

Beyond the city's last two *tarboush* (fez) shops, the street ends at **Bab Zuwayla**, the beautifully restored southern city gate, former place of execution. Beside the gate is the **mosque of Sultan al Muayyad** (1415) with a splendid raised facade and twin minarets on top of the gate.

TAKING A BREAK

For a sumptuous street café with drinks, snacks and water pipes head for the **Naguib Mahfouz café** (➤ 76) or the more authentic **al Fishawi** (➤ 75), both in Khan al Khalili bazaar.

SHARIA AL MUIZZ LI DIN ALLAH: INSIDE INFO

Top tips Explore the street in the **morning or late afternoon** when it's cooler.
• **Dress modestly**, covering arms and legs, as this is a socially traditional part of town. Women should take a scarf to cover their heads and everyone should remove their shoes before entering a mosque.
• Climb up one of the **minarets** for a view over the historic centre and then stop for a rest in one of the mosque courtyards, which are often oases of calm.

Hidden gems Stroll around in the area between al Azhar Mosque and Sharia al Muizz to discover several workshops and fine mansions.

13

Saqqara and Memphis

Saqqara was one of the largest burial grounds in Egypt and in use for more than 3,000 years. Most of it remains unexcavated, but among the wonders on show is the impressive Step Pyramid of Zoser. The tomb was built by the innovative architect Imhotep for King Zoser in the 27th century BC. But instead of the king's traditional mudbrick *mastaba* grave, Imhotep built in stone and stacked several *mastabas* on top of each other to create the first pyramid and the first large stone building.

Originally the Step Pyramid complex was enclosed in a limestone wall, which had fake doors to confuse intruders

A narrow portal leads through a Hypostyle Hall into the impressive complex at Saqqara

Some tomb decorations at Saqqara are among the finest of the Old Kingdom period

With its original shiny limestone casing, Zoser's pyramid stood 62m (203 feet) high and 118m (387 feet) by 140m (460 feet) around its base. A 28m (92-foot) deep shaft leads into the burial chamber. Part of the original limestone enclosure wall has been rebuilt near the entrance in the south-eastern corner. Enter the complex via a pillared corridor, and on the right is the Heb Sed Court, where the king's vitality was symbolically renewed at a festival held every seven years. The Houses of the South and the North are thought to represent older shrines of Upper and Lower Egypt, and the Serdab has a copy of Zoser's statue (the original is in the Egyptian Museum of Antiquities in Cairo, ➤ 50–53). Across the Great Court is the deep shaft of the South Tomb that probably contained the king's internal organs.

Other Tombs

To the south rises the less impressive **pyramid of Unas**, built 350 years after Zoser's with its interior walls

---

Saqqara
✚ 200 C4
✉ 21km (13 miles) south of Giza pyramids; 32km (20 miles) from Cairo
🕐 May–Sep daily 8–5, Oct–Apr 8–4
🚌 Bus from Downtown to Pyramids Road (Sharia al Haram); from the Marioutiya Canal (1km/ 0.5 mile before the pyramids) get a microbus to Saqqara
🎟 Step Pyramid moderate; separate charge for other tombs

Memphis
✚ 200 C4
✉ Mit Rahina, 3km (2 miles) from Saqqara
🕐 May–Sep daily 8–5, Oct–Apr 8–4
🍴 Cafeteria across the road (£)
🚌 No public transport
🎟 Inexpensive

covered with the Pyramid Texts, the earliest-known examples of decorative writing in a tomb. To the southeast of Unas's pyramid are the recently opened **B Tombs** (separate charge, moderate) and the Persian Tombs.

Northeast of Zoser's complex you can see the magnificent 6th-Dynasty *mastabas* of the viziers Mereruka, Ankh-Ma-Hor and Kagemni, containing the finest reliefs of the Old Kingdom. The double *mastaba* of Akhti-Hotep and Ptah-Hotep shows the different stages of tomb decoration and also has some superb reliefs. The walls of the *mastaba* of the royal hairdresser Ti are covered with wonderful scenes of daily life in ancient Egypt. But the strangest place in Saqqara is the **Serapeum**, where mummified sacred bulls were buried like pharaohs in underground, rock-hewn galleries.

Memphis

Just a short way from Saqqara lie the remains of Memphis, the world's first imperial city, founded in about 3100 BC by King Menes (➤ 22). Old Kingdom pharaohs and nobility were buried in its necropolis at Saqqara.

As the first capital of a united Egypt, Memphis was symbolically built at the place where

the delta met the southern valley. Even after the 5th century BC, when Thebes had long taken over as the capital of Egypt, it was a splendid city, a thriving commercial centre and an important cult centre dedicated to the God Ptah. It's hard to imagine such splendour today, as the mudbrick palaces have dissolved and the stones of its temples, including the grand temple of Ptah, were plundered centuries ago for other buildings.

The sleepy village of Mit Rahina has a few minor statues. Its tiny museum has a fine limestone colossus of Ramses II as a young man, and a beautiful alabaster sphinx in the garden.

The lush green area around Saqqara and Memphis ends abruptly at the necropolis

TAKING A BREAK

Saqqara has a small **café** selling cold drinks and tea, but Egyptian families like to picnic in the shade of the ruined 6th-century Monastery of Jeremiah, near the car-park. If the weather's not too hot you could also **picnic in North Saqqara**, with Imhotep's masterpiece as a backdrop.

SAQQARA AND MEMPHIS: INSIDE INFO

Top tips The most spectacular approach to the Step Pyramid is on horseback across the desert. You can rent a horse from the stables in Giza (➤ 78).
• It gets hot in Saqqara, so make sure you take enough liquids.

Ones to miss The *mastabas* beyond the pyramid of Unas have some fine reliefs, but can be skipped if time is short.

[14]

Giza Pyramids and Sphinx

The Pyramids of Giza (al Haram in Arabic), sole survivors of the seven wonders of the ancient world, embody the mystery and magic of antiquity. Along with the Sphinx, they have attracted more speculation and explanation than any other monument. Despite their enduring fascination, countless questions remain that may never be answered.

Many people dream of seeing these pyramids once in their lives but, strangely enough, the first sight can be disappointing. Perhaps because they are so familiar, the pyramids seem smaller than you might expect and the mystique often disappears in the face of relentless hassle from touts and camel drivers. But if you take time to walk around them, preferably

Above: The pyramids and the Sphinx remain mysterious

✚ 200 B4
✉ Giza, 18km (11 miles) southwest of Cairo
☎ 02-383 8823 (tourist office); www.guardians.net/hawass
🕐 Daily 7am–7:30pm, Great Pyramid 8:30–4:30
🍴 Cafeteria (£)
🚌 CTA buses 355 and 357 from beside the Egyptian Museum to Oberoi hotel at the foot of the pyramids. Microbus to al Haram from Abd al Moneim Riyad bus station
🎟 Pyramid plateau and Sphinx moderate; extra charges for Khufu's pyramid (expensive), and two other pyramids (inexpensive); Solar Boat Museum moderate

Right: The Muslim cemetery of Nazlet al Semaan overlooks the pyramids' plateau

Right:
Exploring the
inside of the
pyramids is
not for the
claustrophobic

early in the morning, it's still possible to sense their over-whelming grandeur and to evoke the 45 centuries of history they represent.

The **Great Pyramid of Khufu** (second king of the 4th Dynasty, 2589–2566 BC) is the oldest and largest of the three main pyramids. Built out of 2.3 million blocks weighing an average of 2.5 tonnes each (but sometimes up to 15 tonnes), with its original casing it reached a height of 146.6m (481 feet) but is now 10m (33 feet) lower than that.

Since it was first reopened in the 9th century, three chambers have been found inside the pyramid, all empty except for Khufu's sarcophagus. But some archaeologists believe there's a fourth chamber, containing the king's treasure. From the entrance a claustrophobic corridor descends steeply into an unfinished chamber. Alternatively, an ascending corridor leads left into the Queen's Chamber or right into the spectacular

Above: The pyramids at Giza are the most instantly recognisable monuments in the world
Right: The area can get crowded during the day

47m (154-foot) long Great Gallery and, beyond it, the King's Chamber with the sarcophagus. East of the pyramid are the remains of the king's funerary temple and causeway, and the three smaller Queens' Pyramids.

The King's Guardian

Khufu's son **Khafre** (fourth king of the 4th Dynasty, 2558–2532 BC) built the second pyramid, which is 136.4m (448 feet) high – but the higher ground makes it appear taller than his father's. This pyramid has two chambers, one of which houses the king's sarcophagus. To the east are the remains of Khafre's Funerary Temple and of the causeway leading to his Valley Temple, guarded by the legendary **Sphinx**, which was carved out of the hillside.

Known as *Abu al Hol* ("the Father of Terror") in Arabic, this massive statue remains a mystery: the face is clearly Khafre's,

Camel and horse drivers around the pyramids can be annoying. Try to ignore them and concentrate on the grandeur of the monuments

but the lionesque body has been suggested to be as much as 2,600 years older. The Sphinx is in a poor condition – the old story goes that its nose fell off after apparently being used as a target by Mameluke and Napoleonic soldiers, while its beard is in the British Museum in London. The soft limestone has not stood the test of time but recent restorations have added thousands of hand-cut limestone blocks to support the legs and haunches.

Khafre's son **Menkaure** (2532–2504 BC) built the third pyramid, which is only 70m (230 feet) high but surrounded by the smaller pyramids of the royal family.

TAKING A BREAK

There are a few fast-food restaurants in Nazlat al Samaan, but for a more sumptuous lunch with a view of the pyramids, head for the poolside restaurant of the **Mena House Oberoi** hotel (➤ 73), or relax in the garden of **Andrea's** (➤ 75).

GIZA PYRAMIDS AND SPHINX: INSIDE INFO

Top tips Visit the pyramids in the **early morning or late afternoon** to avoid the crowds. Follow the road past the pyramids to reach a plateau for a panoramic view of all three, but souvenir stalls and touts may disturb your enjoyment.
• A great way to view the pyramids is on **horseback** from the desert beyond. Before hiring a horse, camel or horse-drawn cart agree the price (per animal or cart) and specify the time you wish to ride. To avoid problems, use the stables near the Sphinx (➤ 78), or check the official price on the board next to the ticket office. If you have any trouble at all contact the on-site tourist police immediately.
• A *son et lumière* show is held several times daily at a theatre beside the Sphinx. For infomation tel: 02-386 3469 or check online at www.sound-light.egypt.com

Hidden gem The **Solar Boat Museum** (Jun–Sep daily 9–5, Oct–May 9–4) behind the Great Pyramid contains a superb 43m (140-foot) boat that was intended to carry the king through the underworld. The vessel was found in 1,200 pieces which restorers spent a total of 10 years putting back together. Another well-preserved boat was found nearby, but it remains unexcavated.

At Your Leisure

2 Downtown (Wust al Balad)

Midan Tahrir (Liberation Square) is the centre of modern Cairo. Landmarks to look out for include the Egyptian Museum of Antiquities (➤ 50–53); the Nile Hilton (➤ 73; built over the British barracks after the 1952 revolution); the Mugamma, a Soviet-inspired "temple" of

bureaucracy; Umar Makram Mosque and the American University.

Khedive Ismail developed the downtown area in the 1860s as part of a modernisation drive connected to the opening of the Suez Canal. The scheme was heavily influenced by Hausmann's plans for Paris boulevards. The main streets of Talaat Harb and Kasr al Nil are lined with elegant buildings that now house offices, shops and banks. The famous but dilapidated Groppi Café graces Midan Talaat Harb, while the picturesque food market of Tawfiqiya sits at the north end of Sharia Talaat Harb, a road lined with shoe shops. With its seedy nightclubs and backstreet bars, 26th-of-July Street leads to the once-grand Ezbekiya Gardens.

➕ 196 C4

Men's reception room at the Beit al Kritliya

3 Mr and Mrs Mahmoud Khalil Museum

This splendid museum houses Egypt's finest collection of Western art. The works of French Impressionist and Post-Impressionist artists, including Rodin, Monet, Gauguin, Renoir, Van Gogh and Delacroix, belonged to the prewar minister Mahmoud Khalil and his French wife, who bequeathed them to the State on condition that they were exhibited in their elegant former residence.

➕ 196 A3 ✉ 1 Sharia Kafour, near the Cairo Sheraton, Giza ☎ 02-338 9720; www.mkm.gov.eg ⏰ Tue–Sun 10–5:30 (holidays 10–3) Ⓜ Doqqi ♿ Moderate (passport required)

5 Gayer-Anderson House (Beit al Kritliya)

The Beit al Kritliya gives a fascinating insight into the life of stylish and wealthy medieval Cairenes. Englishman Major Gayer-Anderson, a doctor to the royal family from 1935 to 1942, joined two houses together and lovingly restored and furnished them with Oriental *objets d'art* and paintings picked up on his travels. The ornate reception room on the ground floor featured in the James Bond movie *The Spy Who Loved Me* (1977). The museum is vast paved courtyard has a peaceful quality and is surrounded by elegant arcades. A 2km (1-mile) long sycamore frieze below the ceiling is inscribed with about one-fifth of the Quran.

➕ 197 D3 ✉ Sharia Saliba, Midan Ahmed Ibn Tulun 🕐 Summer daily 8–6 🚌 Bus 174 and minibus 54 from Midan Tahrir 💰 Free

🏯 Citadel (al Qalaa)

The largest fortification in the Middle East and still dominating Cairo's skyline, al Qalaa stands on a spur of the al Muqattam hills. It was the royal residence for more than 700 years. The citadel was built in 1176 by Salah ad Din (Saladin, ▶ 25) as part of his programme of fortifications against the Crusaders. The impressive walls still remain, but the original buildings were torn down first by Sultan al Nasir, whose striped mosque with faïence minaret is the only reminder of that period. In the 19th century Muhammad Ali (▶ 26) tore down more to build his mosque and palaces. The Muhammad Ali Mosque, built between 1824 and

Above: Fine plasterwork at the Mosque of Ibn Tulun

even more splendid after its recent restoration. The entrance is via the Ibn Tulun Mosque.

➕ 197 D3 ✉ Midan Ahmed Ibn Tulun ☎ 02-364 7822 🕐 Sat–Thu 8–4, Fri 8–noon, 1–4 🚌 Bus 174 and minibus 54 from Midan Tahrir 💰 Moderate

🏯 Ibn Tulun Mosque

A masterpiece of classical Islamic architecture, and the largest and oldest intact mosque in Cairo, Ibn Tulun's mosque impresses with its vast scale and elegant simplicity, despite the controversial restoration. It was built in AD 879 by the Abbasid sultan Ahmed Ibn Tulun, who was clearly influenced by the mosques in his native Iraq. The spiral minaret was probably based on the mosque in Samarra (Iraq), although legend has it that Ibn Tulun was in fact inspired by a rolled-up piece of paper. The

1848 and modelled on Istanbul's Sultanahmet Mosque, is more striking from a distance than close up. The interior is disappointing, but the views from the terrace are impressive. The clock in the court-yard was a gift from King Louis Philippe of France (1773–1850), given in return for the obelisk that now stands in Paris.

The Gawhara Palace houses a small museum of Muhammad Ali's family belongings. Of the other museums, only the Carriage Museum and the bizarre National Police Museum are interesting.

🚹 197 E3 ⊠ Midan al Qalaa (entrance in Sharia Salah Salem)
☎ 02-512 1735 🕔 Summer daily 8–6; winter 8–5; museums 8:30–4:30
🍴 Cafeteria (£) 🚌 Bus 174 from Midan Ramses and minibus 54 from Midan Tahrir 🎫 Moderate

❽ Sultan Hasan Mosque-Madrasa

One of the finest Islamic monuments in Egypt, this was built between 1356 and 1363 on an unprecedented grand scale, as it included shops, schools and apartments. The first mosque to have a cruciform plan, it has four *iwans* (vaulted spaces around a courtyard), and within each corner is a *madrasa* (Quranic school)

Left: Muhammad Ali's mosque is a Cairo landmark
Right: Spectacular view from the citadel over the mosque of Sultan Hasan

Five Best Viewpoints
• **Top of Cairo Tower on Gezira Island:** terrace, cafeteria and revolving restaurant
• **Citadel terrace** before sunset
• **The Pyramid Bar** on the roof of the Nile Hilton hotel (➤ 73), glorious bar and terrace with views of the pyramids on a clear day
• Top of the minaret of **al Muayyad Mosque** (➤ 58), Bab Zuwayla
• **Al Azhar Park** (➤ 71), magnificent views over Fatimid Cairo and beyond

dedicated to the four main legal rites of Sunni Islam.

The entrance to this splendid building is through a dark corridor leading into the dazzling courtyard, with its sense of overwhelming peacefulness and monumental simplicity. The light is most beautiful in the morning. Huge portals on either side of the *mihrab* (niche indicating the direction of Mecca) lead into a sombre mausoleum. There's some confusion as to whether anyone is buried here – some sources say the Sultan's sons are interred inside, while others say that the grave is empty.

🚹 197 D3 ⊠ Midan Salah ad Din
🕔 Summer daily 8–6; winter 8–5
🚌 Bus 174 and minibus 54 from Midan Tahrir
🎫 Free

❾ Islamic Art Museum

A visit to this rich collection is essential for a clearer understanding of the Islamic monuments in Cairo, as most of the objects were salvaged from local mosques, *madrasas* and palaces. Recently renovated and arranged, the collection contains some exquisite masterpieces. Highlights include an elegant Mameluke fountain and mosque lights, gorgeous *mashrabeya* wood-work, some unusual woodwork decorated with birds and animals from the Tulunid period, superb

illuminated manuscripts and some
fine Egyptian glass.

➕ 197 D3 ✉ Sharia Bur Said, Bab al
Khalq ☎ 02-390 1520 ⏱ Daily 9–4.
Closed Fri 11–1 💲 Moderate

🔟 Al Azhar Mosque

Al Azhar ("the most blooming" or
"the radiant"), was built in AD 971 as
the first mosque in Fatimid Cairo. It
is often claimed to be the oldest
university in the world, and is also
Egypt's supreme theological authority, presided over by the influential
Sheikh of al Azhar. The entrance to
this splendid mosque is the ornate
15th-century Barber's Gate, where
students traditionally had their heads
shaved. The *sahn* (courtyard), part
of the original Fatimid
design, is

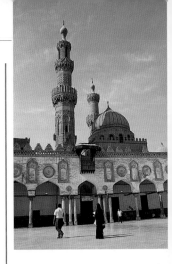

**Al Azhar has been a great conservator of
Islamic traditions for the past 1,000 years**

over the Muslim world, is now
housed in modern buildings behind
the mosque.

➕ 197 E4 ✉ Sharia al Azhar
⏱ Daily 8–5. Closed during prayer
times, particularly Fri noon
💲 Free, but tips are requested

🔟 Khan al Khalili

The Khan, a confusing maze of
alleys and bazaars that are mostly
organised by trade, has been the
bustling commercial soul of Cairo's
old city since the Middle Ages. The
main street, al Badestan, is now
mostly devoted to souvenirs, but for
more interesting buys stroll into the
smaller alleys to find out where the
locals shop. A good place for lunch

**The cafés around al Husayn Mosque serve
endless *sheeshas*, tea and juices**

overlooked by three minarets and
flanked on the right by a Mameluke
madrasa with rooms for the students.
The university itself, which offers
religious studies to students from all

Five Places for Children

- **Cairo Zoo**, Midan al-Gamia, Giza (daily 9–4, tel: 02-570 8895, inexpensive)
- **Dream Park**, Oasis Road, 6th of October City, 20km/12.5 miles south of Cairo (tel: 02-840 0087, www.dreamparkegypt.com, Sat–Thu 4pm–midnight, Fri noon–9pm, expensive) more than 30 rides for kids.
- **Dr Ragab's Pharaonic Village** St Jacob's Island, 2km/1 mile south of Giza Bridge on the Corniche, Giza (tel: 02-571 8675; www.touregypt.net/village; summer daily 9–9; winter 9–6). A kitsch but fun two-hour boat tour taking in scenes of ancient Egypt, all performed by costumed Egyptians.
- **Horse- or camel-riding** at the pyramids (➤ 78).
- **Fagnoon Art School**, Saqqara Road, Sabil Om Hashim (tel: 02-815 1014; daily 10–5). Children can let their creativity loose in Mohammed Allam's wonderful art centre.

or a snack is the Naguib Mahfouz Café-Restaurant (➤ 76) on al Badestan. The gold market around Sharia al Muizz li Din Allah (➤ 56–58) is big and busy, as the amount of gold given by a groom to his bride is still an important part of the marriage contract. The spice and perfume bazaar in an alley to the side of the Barsbay mosque, on Sharia al Muizz li Din Allah (just follow your nose), still has an authentic medieval

atmosphere. Near the mosque of al Husayn is al Fishawi (➤ 75), a café that claims to have been serving continuously since it opened in 1773 – perhaps something of an exaggeration but still worth a visit.

✚ 197 E4 ✉ Between Midan al Husayn and Sharia al Muski ⏰ Mon–Sat 9–6 🍴 Al Fishawi and Naguib Mahfouz café and restaurant (£–££) 🎫 Free

Fountains are a feature of the Royal Palm Promenade in Cairo's al Azhar Park

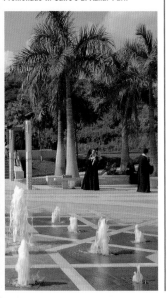

Al Azhar Park

The Aga Khan Trust for Culture created **al Azhar Park** (Sharia Salah Salem, daily 10–10, inexpensive), a much-needed green zone, **behind al Azhar Mosque**, from an ancient rubbish tip. The result is stunning – over 1.5km (1 mile) of 12th-century Ayyubid city walls were uncovered and restored, the neighbourhood of Darb al Ahmar is being restored and revitalised, and 30ha (74 acres) of **beautifully landscaped gardens**, in Islamic tradition with over 50 different water features, have been created. Just how needed this green space was in one of the world's most densely populated areas is clear from the numbers of families who come for **a stroll or a picnic**. The grounds include a theatre, a children's playground, fruit orchards, a lake, a gallery and a wonderful tearoom-restaurant, Citadel View (➤ 75), all with 360 degree views over the city.

Where to... Stay

Prices
The prices are for a double room per night.
£ under 400LE ££ 400–900LE £££ over 900LE

As Egypt's main city, Cairo has a huge range of accommodation, from the sleazy fleapits near Ataba market to sumptuous palaces with spectacular views of the Nile or the pyramids.
Whatever your priorities might be, in summer try to get a room with air-conditioning, as it can get incredibly hot and sticky even at night. Try to book ahead during high season or you'll be lucky to find a bed anywhere.

Cairo Marriott £££

The 19th-century ruler Khedive Ismail built this superb palace on the Nile to house the French empress, Eugenie, and other foreign guests attending the opening of the Suez Canal in 1869. The palace and garden now form the central part of the hotel, and the bedrooms are in two modern towers. Many of the well-equipped rooms have splendid views over the Nile and the city, but they lack the pomp and grandeur of the palace. The *khedival* garden with its swimming pool is an oasis of calm in busy Cairo, while you can drink cocktails in Empress Eugenie's impressive bedroom. There's also a casino for those seeking extra excitement.

🚹 196 B5 ⊠ Sharia Saray al Gezira, Zamalek ☎ 02-735 8888; www.marriott.com

Cosmopolitan ££

Downtown Cairo is one of the noisiest places on earth, but the Cosmopolitan is tucked away in a surprisingly quiet back street in the heart of the area, its magnificent art-nouveau building a reminder of Cairo's *belle époque*. The hotel has been carefully renovated and has spacious and comfortable rooms, full of character. The service is slow but perhaps that's all part of the charm.

🚹 196 C4 ⊠ 1 Sharia Ibn Taalab, Downtown ☎ 02-392 3845; fax: 02-393 3531

Horus House ££

Small, friendly hotels are in short supply in Cairo, which is why the Horus House is such a well-kept secret by regular visitors. Located in the quiet heart of the residential area of Zamalek, it's close to many shops, restaurants and bars. Book well in advance because enthusiasts tend to stay for a while. The restaurant offers a good-value lunch and counts among its regulars some older couples who have lived on the island for years.

🚹 196 A5 ⊠ 21 Sharia Ismail Mohamed, Zamalek ☎ 02-736 0694

Luna £

One of the more recent arrivals on the downtown budget hotel scene, but by far the best. The rooms are spacious and clean, with fresh crisp bedlinen provided on a daily basis, and air-conditioning. Some rooms have a private bathroom, other share an immaculate communal bathroom, and guests can use the kitchen or salon to hang out. Friendly and helpful staff

🚹 196 C4 ⊠ 5th floor, 27 Sharia Talaat Harb, Downtown ☎ 02 396 1020; www.lunacairo.com

Mena House Oberoi £££

Here, you can be one of the lucky few with a view of the pyramids from their room. The beautifully decorated, Oriental-Moorish rooms in the 19th-century wing of this former *khedival* hunting lodge sit right beside the Great Pyramid. Standard rooms in the modern garden annexe are spacious and comfortable and, although they lack the grandeur and immediacy of the palace rooms, you might still get a glimpse of the ancient wonders. Even the swimming pool has a view. Eat breakfast on the garden terrace, and the garden restaurant is perfect for lunch or afternoon tea, while the Moghul Room is the best Indian restaurant in town.

✚ 196, off A2 ☒ Sharia al Ahram, near the pyramids ☎ 02-383 3222; fax: 02-383 7777; www.oberoihotels.com

Nile Hilton £££

Cairo's oldest and most central five-star hotel has had a facelift, and it is still a good place to stay. Right in the middle of Cairo, opposite the Egyptian Museum and downtown, and facing the Nile on the other side, its location is hard to beat. Apart from the spacious well-equipped rooms with balconies, it also boasts some of Cairo's most popular restaurants and now also its trendiest bars. The pool in the garden offers a welcome retreat from the city's hustle and bustle.

✚ 196 B4 ☒ 1113 Corniche al-Nil ☎ 02-578 0444; www.hilton.com

Nile Plaza Four Seasons £££

One of two Four Seasons establishments in town, this is the newest and most impressive of Cairo's luxury hotels. The stylish rooms are spacious, with large marble bathrooms and sweeping views over the Nile or the old city and citadel. The level of service here is unmatched and the hotel boasts two swimming pools, a spa and wellness centre, and five excellent restaurants. This is a real treat!

✚ 196 B3 ☒ 1089 Corniche al Nil, Garden City ☎ 02-791 7000; www.fourseasons.com

Pension Roma £

Madame Cressaty's diligence has maintained this 1940s hotel as one of the best inexpensive options downtown. Behind the Moorish facade, the clean rooms have polished wooden floors, high ceilings and comfortable old furniture. Book ahead as the hotel is extremely popular with backpackers, students and other visitors travelling on a budget.

✚ 196 C4 ☒ 4th Floor, 169 Sharia Muhammad Farid ☎ 02-391 1088; fax: 02-579 6243

President ££

Modern and unassuming from the outside, but cosy, quiet and friendly on the inside, the President offers good value and comfortable rooms in the middle of the leafy residential area of Zamalek, with its many shops and restaurants. The hotel boasts a business centre, an excellent bakery, a rooftop restaurant, and a basement bar which can get quite lively.

✚ 196, off A5 ☒ 22 Sharia Taha Hussein, Zamalek ☎ 02-735 0718; email: preshotl@thewayout.net

Talisman ££

Cairo's one and only boutique hotel is full of atmosphere, and wonderfully located in a quiet alley off a busy shopping street. The hotel, in a large downtown flat, has colourful and luxuriously decorated rooms with Egyptian and Syrian furniture, great bathrooms with Egyptian toiletries. Communal spaces are equally pleasant with a lovely breakfast room, a sumptuous salon and a library full of books about Egypt. The staff is friendly, and refreshments are included in the price.

✚ 196 C4 ☒ 5th floor, 39 Sharia Talaat Harb ☎ 02-393 9431

Where to...
Eat and Drink

Prices
Expect to pay per person for a meal, excluding drinks and tips.
£ up to 100LE ££ 100–150LE £££ over 150LE

Cairo's wide variety of restaurants reflects the city's cosmopolitan character. National dishes such as *fuul*, *koshari* and kebabs are inexpensive and widely available from food vendors and eateries on many street corners, but most of these places don't serve alcohol. Restaurants serving ethnic or international cuisine, often part of a hotel, are more upmarket. Note that wealthy Cairenes like to dress up for dinner in the trendier restaurants.

Abu al Sid ££–£££
This very popular and trendy Egyptian restaurant serves well-prepared classics such as stuffed pigeon and *meloukhiya* (a soup of a spinach-like vegetable with chicken, served with bread, onion and condiments), as well as *mezze* and *sheeshas* (water pipes). The atmosphere is great, and the place is decorated with wonderfully kitsch Louis Farouk-style furniture with work by local artists on the wall. Reservations are essential.

➕ 196 C4 ☒ 6 Sharia Qasr al Nil (beside Nadi el-Sayarat) ☎ 02-574 0855; www.after8egypt.com ☻ Daily noon–3, 8pm–2am

After Eight ££
This old night haunt is now a popular restaurant serving Middle Eastern and Mediterranean specialities, quiet for lunch, but pretty wild at night, particularly at weekends. There is live music nightly with international and Oriental jazz and the hip Cairene band Wust al Balad (Arabic for "Downtown"). The food is pretty average. Book ahead and check the programme.

➕ 196 B5 ☒ 157 Sharia 26 July, Zamalek ☎ 02-735 9640 ☻ Daily noon–2am

with a plate of *mezze*, followed by one of the house specialities: pigeons stuffed with *firkh* (crushed wheat) or *mozza* (roast lamb). Traditional desserts are made without thought to calories or waistlines – the ice pudding and *mahalabeya* (dessert made of rice flour) are particularly good. No alcohol.

➕ 196 C4 ☒ 3 Sharia al Alfy, Downtown ☎ 02-577 4999 ☻ Daily 1pm–1am

Americana Fish Market ££
An excellent fish restaurant, situated on the upper deck of a permanently moored boat on the Nile. You choose from the large catch of the day with a wide selection of Mediterranean fish and seafood. Your choice is weighed, cooked to order, and served with hot freshly made bread and Middle Eastern salads. Reservations are essential.

➕ 196 A1/2 ☒ Americana boat, 26 Sharia al Nil, Giza ☎ 02-570 9693 ☻ Daily noon–2am

Alfi Bey ££
Alfi Bey is an unashamedly old-fashioned Cairo institution, where the cooking is simple Egyptian, the decoration and paper table-coverings are without complications and service comes with a smile. Start

Andrea's £–££

The real pleasure here is to be had outdoors, sitting at tables covered in red-and-white checked cloths, in a garden of bougainvillea and shady trees. Start with a selection of *mezze* and fresh salads that are presented on a large tray, and scooped up with delicious pitta bread (made by women working at the entrance). Main courses are limited to grilled meat and poultry, with the roast chicken coming particularly recommended. Andrea's is perfect after a visit to the pyramids, though it does sometimes suffer from an influx of four groups.

🚼 **200 B4** 🖂 **59–60 Marioutiya Canal, near the Giza pyramids** ☎ **02-381 0938** 🕐 **Daily 10am–10pm**

Aqua £££

This is an expensive but excellent fusion restaurant with some of the best sushi in town, Pacific Rim cuisine and wonderful views over the Nile. Book ahead and dress for the occasion.

🚼 **196 B3** 🖂 **Four Seasons Nile Plaza, 1089 Corniche an Nil, Garden City** ☎ **02-791 6876** 🕐 **Daily 7pm–1am**

La Bodega ££–£££

This very hip lounge bar serves great Asian fusion food in a stylish contemporary Asian décor, while the more down-to-earth bistro on the same floor has an inventive selection of Mediterranean dishes, ranging from a good couscous to fresh pasta and delicious paella.

🚼 **196 B5** 🖂 **157 Sharia 26 July, Zamalek** ☎ **02-735 6761** 🕐 **Daily noon–2, 7pm–4am**

Citadel View ££

Overlooking the beautiful al Azhar Park (▶ 71) and the city of Cairo, this is a perfect place to lunch on the terrace, take tea in one of the upstairs traditional salons, with cushions and low tables, or have a more intimate dinner. At lunch time there is a good-value buffet with a wide choice of Egyptian *mezzeh* and main courses. Recommended, but book ahead on Fridays.

🚼 **197 E4** 🖂 **Al-Azhar Park, Sharia Saleh Salem** ☎ **02 510 9150/51** 🕐 **Daily lunch and dinner**

Egyptian Pancake House £

Places to eat in and around Khan al Khalili bazaar are limited, but this one has long been reliable. Egyptian pancakes (*fiteer* in Arabic) are a cross between a pizza and a crêpe. *Fiteer* can come sweet with nuts and honey, or savoury with cheese, tomatoes and chilli. Inside the restaurant is calmer, but outside you get to sit still and see the endless fascination provided by Islamic Cairo.

🚼 **197 E4** 🖂 **Between Sharia al Azhar and Midan al Husayn, Khan al Khalili** 🕐 **Daily from morning until the last customer leaves late evening**

Felfela £–££

If you know nothing about Egyptian food but are keen to find out, then this is as good a place to start as any. The clientele is predominantly foreign, but locals come here as well for the traditional dishes, if not the wacky décor of stuffed animals and Egyptian artefacts. Try a selection of salads and *mezze* to start, followed by a kebab or grilled pigeon. However, the desserts are less exciting (you won't often see Egyptians eating them here) and the tea is better at the café around the corner. Felfela has now become a chain, but this is the original and best.

🚼 **196 C4** 🖂 **15 Sharia Hoda Sharawi, Downtown** ☎ **02-392 2833** 🕐 **Daily 8am–midnight**

Al Fishawi £

The claim that they have never closed al Fishawi since 1773 may be a slight exaggeration, but this is the oldest teahouse in Cairo. It's also one of the few cafés where you'll find Egyptian women and families sitting with their men. It's a great place to relax, sip mint tea or smoke a sweet water pipe and watch the world go by. During the day it's a good place to stop for a break while visiting the old city, and at night it gets very lively with locals. As it's close to the mosque of al Husayn no alcohol is served.

197 E4 ⊠ Khan al Khalili, just off Midan al Husayn
Daily 24 hours

Greek Club £

For nostalgic souls this is the perfect place to be. This old fashioned club, with its faded neo-classical interior and noisy outdoor terrace, is the perfect place to stop and enjoy a cold and cheap Stella beer with some *mezzeh*. A Cairo institution!

196 C4 ⊠ 3 Sharia Mahmoud Bassioni, above Groppi, Downtown
02-575 0822
Daily 8am–midnight

Marriott Garden ££

Cairo doesn't have many secluded outdoor spaces where you can have a drink or a meal in relative peace. However, the Marriott Garden, all that remains of the original 1869 design, is a perfect place to restore your spirits and energy after sightseeing. Beyond the tourists, it's also a great place to watch wealthy Cairenes or young Gulf Arabs relaxing. It serves drinks and ice-creams as well as a range of tasty sandwiches, some good pizzas and several excellent grilled Egyptian specialities.

196 B5
⊠ Cairo Marriott Hotel, Sharia Saray al Gezira, Zamalek
02-735 8888
Daily 9am–1am

Naguib Mahfouz Coffee Shop £ & Khan al Khalili Restaurant ££

This popular combination of coffee shop and restaurant is the only "quality" place to eat in the bazaar area and, just as important, has the only decent lavatories. The coffee shop serves traditional Egyptian hot drinks (including delicious mint tea), fresh juices, *sheeshas* (water pipes) and sweets in an attractive Oriental decor. The more expensive restaurant serves *mezze* and a wide selection of authentic Egyptian or Middle Eastern main courses. Although the clientele is comprised almost exclusively of tourists, it's still a cosy and quiet place – a haven of tranquillity situated off a very busy street.

197 E4
⊠ 5 Sikket al Badestan, an alley in Khan al Khalili 02-590 3788
Daily 10am–2am

Sabaya ££-£££

In this delightful Lebanese restaurant the best of authentic Lebanese cuisine is served, with an amazing selection of *mezze* and salads. The friendly waiters often recommend the delicious specialities of the house, like *kibbeh nayyeh* (raw pounded lamb) or *hummus* (chickpea paste) served with fried lamb and pine nuts.

196 B3/4
⊠ Semiramis InterContinental, Corniche al Nil, Garden City
02-795 717 Daily 7:30pm–1am

Sequoia ££

Sequoia, a recent addition to Cairo's restaurant scene has everything going for it, and it has proved to be hugely popular with wealthy Cairenes. Situated on the tip of the Gezira Island, this outdoor restaurant (there are heaters during the winter months) has all-round views of the Nile. The excellent Egyptian food is reasonably priced for such a hip venue and they have the largest selection of flavours for the *sheesha* and an extensive cocktail list to choose from. *The* place to see and be seen.

Off 196 A5
⊠ End of Sharia Abou al Feda, Zamalek 02-735 0014
Daily lunch and dinner

Where to... Shop

Cairo often seems like one big bazaar, so there should be no shortage of shopping opportunities, from exotic spices to cotton clothing and silver Bedouin jewellery.

Books and Music

The most extensive range of books on Egypt and the Middle East, many published by the American University in Cairo (AUC Press), is available at the **AUC Bookshop** (Hill House on the AUC campus, Sharia Mohammed Mahmoud, Downtown). **Lehnert and Landrock** (44 Sharia Sherif, Downtown) also has a good book selection as well as old photographs and postcards of Egypt. In Zamalek there is **Diwan** (159 Sharia 26 July)

with a great selection of books, Arabic videos/DVDs and music. The best places to buy music are **Mirage Megastore** (71 Sharia Gami'at al Duwal al Arabiya, Mohandiseen) or **Vibe** (1A Sharia Sayed al Bakry), behind the Diwan bookshop.

For valuable antiquarian Oriental books, maps and prints check out **l'Orientale** (Shop 757 in the basement of the Nile Hilton Shopping Mall, Midan Tahrir, Downtown).

Craft Shops

Khan al Khalili (▶ 70) sells a selection of souvenirs, but the better crafts are in more specialised shops. Dr Ragab, who reinstated the making of papyrus, sells top-quality papyri with matching prices at **Dr Ragab's Papyrus Institute** (Corniche al Nil, near Cairo Sheraton, Giza). Ring the doorbell at **Senouhi** (54 Sharia Abdel Khalek Sarwat, 5th floor, apt 51, Downtown; tel: 02-391 0955) to find a treasure trove filled with carpets, jewellery and paintings.

Khan Misr Touloun (opposite Ibn Tulun Mosque; tel: 02-365 2227) and **Fair Trade Egypt** (27 Sharia Yahia Ibrahim, 1st floor, apt 8, Zamalek; tel: 02-736 5123) both promote high-quality Egyptian crafts, including pottery, tablecloths, embroidery and carpets at fixed prices. **Oum el Dounia** (1st floor, Sharia Talaat Harb, Downtown; tel: 02-393 8273) is a colourful shop filled with the best crafts in Egypt, at fixed and reasonable prices. **Makan** (4 Sharia Ismail Mohamed, Zamalek; tel: 02 738 2632) is another great shop where old furniture blends in with contemporary designs by local artists. **Nagada** (8 Sharia Dar al Shefa, 3rd floor, Garden City, by appointment; tel: 02-792 3249) sells superb hand-woven cotton and pottery made in Fayoum Oasis. Crafts from Siwa oasis are on sale in the elegant **Nomad Gallery** (14 Saray al Gezira, 1st floor, Zamalek; tel: 02-736 1917), or at the Cairo Marriott shopping arcade. Shops in

al Khiyamiya (Tentmakers' Bazaar), outside Bab Zuwayla, sell traditional appliqué work for tents, cushion covers or wallhangings.

The **al Khatoun Gallery** (3 Sharia Mohammed Abduh), behind the al-Azhar Mosque, sells contemporary Egyptian crafts, often with a great sense of humour. On the same street is Abd al Zaher, a traditional bookbinder who makes beautiful leather bound notebooks and albums, and engraves them with your name in gold leaf.

Clothes

Arcadia (Corniche al Nil, Bulaq) is Cairo's top-quality shopping mall, where chains sell casual cotton clothing. However, the mall at the **First Residence** (35 Sharia al Giza, Giza) provides some competition. For belly dance outfits go to **Haberdashery**, reached via a dark stairway signposted "Everything a Belly Dancer Needs", on Sharia Gawhar al Qayed near al Fishawi Cafe in Khan al Khalili.

Where to...
Be Entertained

Cairo is as alive at night as it is during the day. Check the daily *Egyptian Gazette*, the *al Ahram Weekly* and the monthly *Egypt Today*.

Ahwas (Coffee Houses)

Egyptian men like to spend the evening in their local *ahwa* or café, chatting over a water pipe and coffee – no alcohol is served (▶ 28–30). **Al Fishawi** (▶ 75) and the area near the mosque of al Husayn in the old city are particularly lively at night.

Music

Most classical concerts are performed at the **Cairo Opera House** on Gezira Island (tel: 02-739 8144; www.opera house.gov.eg), where men must wear a jacket and tie. Various performances of Arabic music and theatre take place, particularly during Ramadan nights, at **Beit al Harrawi** (behind al Azhar Mosque, Islamic Cairo; tel: 02-510 4174). On the first Thursday of every month there is a free classical Arab music concert. The **Al Sawy Cultural Centre** (Sharia 26 July, Zamalek, under the bridge to Aguza; tel: 02-736 6178) is an active cultural centre with nightly performances of experimental theatre, Arabic music or jazz, lectures and film. The **Cairo Jazz Club** (197 Sharia 26th July, Aguza; tel: 02-345 9939; www.cairo jazzclub.com) has daily live music.

Belly Dancing

The best dancers perform at clubs in expensive hotels, at 8pm for tourists and 1am for Egyptians. Shows at **Cairo Sheraton** (tel: 02-336 9700) and **Semiramis InterContinental** (tel: 02-795 7171) are popular.

Downtown nightclubs such as **Palmyra**, in the alley beside the Chemla store on Sharia 26 July, are sleazier – better dancers arrive only when enough money has been thrown on to the stage. Ask the price of things before you order.

Sufi Performances

The Mawlawiyya is an Egyptian Sufi sect known as **Whirling Dervishes**. The **Tannoura Egyptian Heritage Dance Troupe** gives whirling performances at the Mamluk Al-Ghoury palace (at the pedestrian bridge over Sharia al-Azhar, Islamic Cairo) every Saturday and Wednesday at 9pm when in town (tel: 02-510 0823).

Discos

The big night out in Cairo is Thursday. Discos in hotels will admit non-members or non-residents on quieter nights, or impose a hefty minimum charge. The hippest places are **Latex** (Nile Hilton Hotel, Corniche al Nil, Downtown; tel: 02-578 0444) and **Absolute** (Casino al Shaggara, opposite the World Trade Centre, Corniche an-Nil, Bulaq; tel: 02-579 6512). **Al Morocco** (Blue Nile boat, 9 Saray al Gezira, Zamalek; tel: 02-735 3114) is a bar-restaurant that turns into a lively disco later at night. **Exit** (Atlas Hotel, 2 Sharia Mohamed Rushdi, Downtown; tel: 02 391 8127) is more down to earth, while **Rive Gauche** (Zamalek Hotel, Sharia Maahad al Swissry, Zamalek; tel: 012 735 1846) has the best DJs.

Horse-riding

Only rent horses from renowned stables. In the village near the Sphinx, Nazlet al Semaan, the best stables are **AA** (tel: 02-385 0531) and **MG** (tel: 02-385 3832). The best of all is the **International Equestrian Club** (on Saqqara Road at the end of the al Moneeb ring road; tel: 02-742 7654/385 5016). The **Saqqara Country Club Hotel** (Saqqara road to Abu al Nomros; tel: 02-384 6115) offers temporary membership.

Getting Your Bearings

It was the capital of the New Kingdom for more than 500 years, and Luxor boasts some of the world's most extraordinary monuments, many of which have defied the passing of time. As a provincial Egyptian town it also offers relative peace and quiet, especially on the West Bank.

Luxor is a bustling town, with the Temple of Luxor at its centre surrounded by a crowded *souk* and hotels. By day the Corniche is busy with locals coming off the ferry, tourists getting off their boats, and buses touring the sights. But at night, when people come to catch the breeze along the Nile after a hot day, it's calm.

There were settlements here from an early age, but the town (then known as Waset and later as Thebes) only became important when the princes of Thebes established the New Kingdom (1550–1069 BC). Successive pharaohs vied to build ever-greater additions to the state temple of Amun in Karnak and its sister temple in Luxor. As secular buildings were made of mudbrick, little else remains of the fabled city that Homer described as "hundred-gated".

Luxor Temple and its god Amun were popular even after the Romans camped in the sacred precinct. Previous page: The Court of Ramses II at Luxor Temple

★ Don't Miss

At Your Leisure

9 Valley of the Kings

10 Deir al Bahari   DRA ABU AL NAGA

Valley of the Queens

Deir al Madina   **11** Tombs of the Nobles

7 **6** **8**   AL GURNA

12 Ramesseum

Colossi of Memnon   NEW GURNA

Tomb of Nefertari   Ticket Office

5 Madinat Habu

GEZIRAT SAAD   Nile   **1** Karnak

al Fadliya Canal

GEZIRAT

2 km
1 mile

2 Luxor Museum

3 Mummification Museum

4 Luxor Temple

LUXOR

The dead were buried on the west bank of the Nile, and the kings hid extraordinary treasures in a secluded valley in the Theban mountains, although their security measures failed to foil the tomb robbers. The queens and nobles had less secretive burial grounds, facing the pharaohs' mortuary temples. Ferries sail between the two banks, leaving just opposite Luxor temple, or a bridge crosses the river, 6km (3.75 miles) further south.

In 1997 Luxor suffered Egypt's worst act of terrorism, when 58 tourists were shot at Deir al Bahari. Since then it has been peaceful, but security remains tight and visitors leaving town by road do so as part of an armed convoy.

The mosque of Luxor's patron saint Abu al Haggag sits atop Luxor Temple

This is where the ancient Egyptians were most prolific, where great temples stand as testimony to their creators' wealth and imagination, and where monuments slowly crumble into dust.

Luxor in Three Days

Day One

Morning
Start early, before it gets hot, by taking a *calèche* (horse-drawn carriage) to **❶ Karnak Temple** (left, ➤ 84–87), where you can easily spend a morning. Have lunch in the pleasant outdoor restaurant Dawar al Umda (➤ 104).

Afternoon
After lunch stroll over to **❹ Luxor Temple** (➤ 88–90) for a leisurely walk around the ruins. It's then a short walk to the **Old Winter Palace** (➤ 103) for a touch of grandeur and tea on the terrace. That will take you to early evening, and time for shopping in the *souk*.

Day Two

Morning
Make another early start, especially in the summer. Take a taxi to the ticket booth on the West Bank, where you must buy tickets for all West Bank sites you want to visit. Back in the cab, head first for the exposed **❾ Valley of the Kings** (right, ➤ 91–93), which gets very hot by noon. Ask the driver to wait for you, as there's little other transport back. The Nour al Gurna (➤ 105) is good for a simple lunch.

Afternoon
Walk next door for a visit to the
12 Ramesseum (➤ 100). There's no
problem getting a cab here, but for
some local flavour flag down a passing pick-up truck (*kabut*), most of
which go to the ferry terminal (*al
mina*). Once across the river, walk to
the small, but beautifully arranged
2 Luxor Museum (Coptic relief carving
pictured left, ➤ 98) for a short visit.
Afterwards, rent a *felucca* and, wind
permitting, sail into the sunset. After
dinner, visit the **4 Luxor Temple**
(➤ 88–90), which is perhaps even
more striking when floodlit.

Day Three

Morning
Rent a bicycle (➤ 182–183) or take a taxi (first agree a price that includes all
your chosen sights) and then take the ferry to the West Bank, stopping again at
the ticket booth as tickets are valid only for the day they're purchased. Carry on
to the temple of **10 Deir al Bahari** (below; ➤ 94–95), passing the two **Memnon
Colossi** (➤ 183). From Deir al Bahari retrace your steps to the **11 Tombs of the
Nobles** (➤ 96–97), with their realistic depictions of daily life. Have a late lunch
in the garden of Restaurant Muhammad (➤ 105), near the ticket office.

Afternoon
After lunch, walk or cycle to the
5 Temple of Madinat Habu (➤ 98–99),
which is at its best in the softer afternoon light. Take time to walk around
the temple precinct and watch the
sunset from one of the cafés opposite, or head back to the stables near
the ferry (➤ 106) for a ride through
the countryside.

Evening
Take a taxi to al Moudira Hotel
(➤ 103; and arrange to be picked up
again later) for a wonderful dinner at
one of its restaurants.
Book ahead.

Karnak

The ancient Egyptians called Karnak "Ipet-Isut" ("The Most Perfect of Places"), and for 1,500 years this was the most important place of worship in the country, dedicated to their great god Amun. Much more than just a temple, it was also an important intellectual centre, a spectacular complex of temples, chapels, pylons, obelisks and sanctuaries, covering more than 400ha (990 acres) – enough space for 10 cathedrals. Every pharaoh of note built, destroyed, enlarged, embellished or restored part of the complex to express his devotion to Amun. In the process, Karnak became one of the largest and most magnificent temple complexes in the ancient world.

Take a *calèche* or taxi along the Corniche to get to Karnak which, with all its splendour and history, can be a confusing place to visit. The complex consists of several temple compounds and many additions by different kings. But, as Egyptologist T G H James put it, "Karnak is an archaeological department store containing something for everyone". One rule to remember is that the monuments mostly get older the deeper inside you go.

The temple, and particularly the Great Hypostyle Hall in Karnak never fail to impress the visitor with their overwhelming grandeur

 202 B4
✉ 2.5km (1.5 miles) north of Luxor
🕐 Daily 6–5:30 (6am–6pm in summer)
🍴 Café by the Sacred Lake (£)
🎟 Complex moderate; museum inexpensive

The Triad of Thebes

The temples of Luxor and Karnak are both dedicated to the Theban triad of the gods Amun, Mut and Khonsu. Amun, the most important of these, later became a state deity as the Supreme Creator Amun-Ra, the fusion of Amun with the sun-god Ra. Mut, the Mistress of Heaven, was his wife or consort and Khonsu, also known as "the traveller" or the moon-god, was their son.

The most accessible part of Karnak is the **Precinct of Amun**, which seems like an endless succession of massive pylons (temple gateways), monumental statues and grand hypostyle halls. The precinct is approached from the **Processional Way** of ram-headed sphinxes (Amun was often represented as a human wearing ram horns), which connected with the temple of Luxor (➤ 88–90). This leads to the **First Pylon** which, at 43m (141 feet) high and 130m (426 feet) wide is the largest in Egypt, even though it was never finished. In the forecourt you'll find **Seti II's shrine**, which

Every day, water birds were led through a ston tunnel from the fowl yard to th Sacred Lake

housed the sacred boats of the triad and, in the south corner, the superb **Temple of Ramses III** (20th Dynasty), also thought to be a way station for the sacred boats. The walls of this small temple, which follows the perfect plan of the classical temple, are decorated with scenes of the annual Opet festival. In front of the **Second Pylon** rises the granite colossus of the ubiquitous Ramses II with one of his many daughters beside him.

Behind the Second Pylon lies the most spectacular sight of all, the 13th-century BC **Great Hypostyle Hall** – an amazing "forest" of more than 140 tall papyrus pillars covering 5,500sq m (59,200sq feet), built by Seti I and his son Ramses II. Beyond the Hypostyle Hall lies a rather larger and more confusing section of the temple, built during the 18th Dynasty (1550–1295 BC). In the courtyards beyond the Third and Fourth Pylons are the finely carved **obelisks** of Tuthmosis II and, farther on, of the female pharaoh, Queen Hatshepsut (1473–58 BC, ➤ 94). The tip of her second fallen obelisk lies on the way to the Sacred Lake.

Past the Sixth Pylon stand two elegant pillars carved with lotus and papyrus flowers, symbolic of Upper and Lower Egypt, and the granite **Sanctuary of Amun**, built by Philip Arrhidaeus,

An avenue of ram-headed sphinxes connected Karnak Temple to Luxor Templ

the half-brother of Alexander the Great. This is where Amun's effigy was kept and where, as the images on the walls show, daily offerings were made in his honour. Beyond lies a large **Central Court** and the **Jubilee Temple of Tuthmosis**, where the king's vitality and authority was symbolically renewed during his Jubilee. It's interesting that this huge temple complex was only entered by the powerful priesthood; lay Egyptians were excluded and used intermediary deities, whose shrines they built against the temple's enclosure wall. One such series of chapels, known as the **Chapels of the Hearing Ear**, lies at the back of the Jubilee Temple.

Between the Third and Fourth Pylons the temple spreads southwards along the side of the **Sacred Lake**. In 1903, in the Cachette Court in front of the lake, some 17,000 bronze and 800 stone statues were uncovered. The finest of them are now in the Egyptian Museum of Antiquities in Cairo (➤ 50–53).

The **Open Air Museum** houses a few reconstructions of earlier buildings, two fine *barque* shrines and an elegant 12th-Dynasty white chapel with fine carvings.

Two monumental colossi of Ramses II guard the Second Pylon

TAKING A BREAK

The **café** near the Sacred Lake is a relaxing place to have a drink under the trees. For a later lunch leave the site and head for **Dawar al Umda** on the Corniche (➤ 104), or the coffee shop of the quiet **Luxor Hilton Hotel** near by.

KARNAK: INSIDE INFO

Top tips The temple **can get very crowded** with tour groups from 10am to 3pm, but earlier or later, when the light is at its best, you could have the place more or less to yourself.
• A splendid 90-minute **son et lumière show** is held three or four times, in different languages, each evening. The first part of the show is a walk through the floodlit temple, the other part is viewed from a theatre beyond the Sacred Lake. Buy your ticket at the site. For information check the ticket booth (tel: 02-385 2880) or website: www.sound-light.egypt.com.

Hidden gems The **bas-reliefs** on the northern side of the Hypostyle Hall, representing Seti I's victories and battles, are exquisite – much better than the crudely executed sunk reliefs from the reign of his son Ramses II on the other side.

Ones to miss The badly ruined **Precincts of Mut** to the south and of Mont to the north are rarely visited, as are the courts beyond the 7th Pylon.

4

Luxor Temple

This magnificent structure, known in ancient times as the "Harem of the South", is connected to the Temple of Karnak (► 84–87) by a 3km (2-mile) processional Avenue of Sphinxes. Like Karnak, Luxor's temple was dedicated to the Theban triad of Amun, Mut and Khonsu, whose statues stood here during the Opet festival.

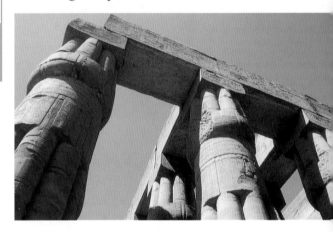

Even though Luxor Temple was expanded several times throughout the ages, it's much more compact and coherent than Karnak, perhaps because its core was built by just one pharaoh, Amenhotep III (1390–1352 BC). The walls are decorated with some of the finest (and often best-preserved) carvings in Egypt, protected because much of the temple was buried until 1885. Before excavations, only the heads of the Ramses II (1279–1213 BC, ► 23) colossi and the tips of the obelisks stuck out above the pile of debris on which Luxor village was built. The village was removed bit by bit as the excavations started, but when it came to destroying the tomb and mosque of Luxor's patron saint, Abu al Haggag, the people refused. As a result, the pretty mosque now perches awkwardly on top of the excavated temple.

Abu al Haggag

The patron *sheikh* of Luxor, Abu al Haggag, was born in Baghdad in around AD 1150, moved to Mecca and later made his way to Luxor where he founded a Sufi school. Every year during the saint's *moulid* (festival), huge floats move slowly through the streets and a few *feluccas* are dragged around his mosque by local people. These represent the boats that were pulled around the temple during the ancient Opet festival.

✚ 202 B4
✉ Corniche, East Bank
🕐 Summer daily 6am–10pm; winter 6am–9pm
🎟 Moderate

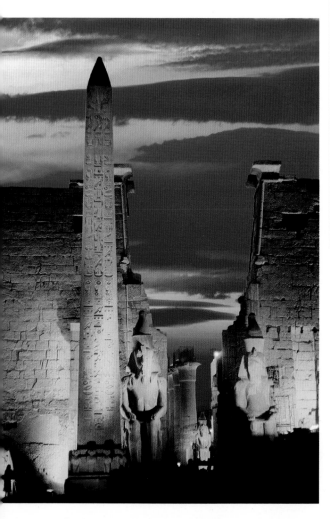

The **Avenue of Sphinxes** leads to the monumental **First Pylon** built by Ramses II, which was once fronted by two obelisks and six colossi of the man himself. One obelisk and two of the statues were taken to France in the 19th century, but the remaining ones are still very impressive. The pylon is decorated, as so many other Egyptian temples, with Ramses II's favourite story, the Battle of Qadesh. Beyond the pylon, the large Court of **Ramses II** is surrounded by two rows of papyrus-bud columns, interspersed with more statues of the king.

To the left of the court, the **Mosque of Abu al Haggag** hangs over the temple, while to the right is the *barque* shrine that was used for the three statues that came from Karnak during the annual Opet festival (see panel, ➤ 90). Also of interest on this

Top left: Luxor Temple is dramatically illuminated at night

Above left: The mighty columns of the temple of Amun at Luxor

side are reliefs of the temple itself and of a funerary procession led by Ramses II's sons. Beyond the Second Pylon the impressive **Processional Colonnade** of Amenhotep III, with huge papyrus columns, was the model for the Great Hypostyle Hall at Karnak. The carvings on the walls were added by Tutankhamun and give a picture of the Opet celebrations: one wall shows the outward journey, the other the return of the procession.

At the end of the colonnade is perhaps the temple's most impressive part, the **Great Sun Court**, also built by Amenhotep III, its fine decorations developed over the millennium between the reigns of Amenhotep and Alexander the Great. Unfortunately this court has suffered badly from the rising water level and a major restoration project is underway. A large cache of statues unearthed here in 1989 can now be seen in Luxor Museum (➤ 98).

Behind a columned portico, used as a chapel by Roman soldiers, lies the temple's **inner sanctuary**, with Alexander the Great's Sanctuary of Amun's Barge and Amenhotep III's Birth Room, which has images of the king's divine conception and birth, and his nurturing by goddesses. The bedrock on which this part of the temple was built was believed to be the site where Amun was born.

The late afternoon sun gives the monuments a warm pinkish glow

TAKING A BREAK

Enjoy Nile views down by the water and a cool beer at the pleasant **Metropolitan Café** (➤ 104).

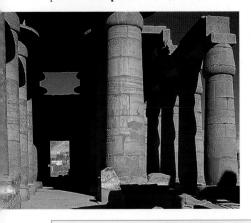

The Opet Festival

During the splendid annual Opet (fertility festival) priests would bring the statues of the gods Amun, Mut and Khonsu in a procession of holy barges up the Nile from Karnak to Luxor, where they would spend a symbolic honeymoon. This festival, held during the second month of the Nile flood, was intended to ensure a good harvest for the coming season.

LUXOR TEMPLE: INSIDE INFO

Top tips It's best to explore Luxor Temple during the day, and return at night when **floodlights** add to the mysterious atmosphere and accentuate the fine carvings.
• Ask the tourist office when the *moulid* happens, as it's quite spectacular.

Hidden gem Study the reliefs on the walls carefully to understand the **rituals of the Opet festival**.

⑨

Valley of the Kings

Ever since Howard Carter discovered Tutankhamun's tomb in 1922, filled to the brim with untold wonders (► 52), the Valley of the Kings (Wadi al Muluk) has excited, intrigued and fuelled the imagination of the world. For more than 500 years this barren and secluded valley, also known as "The Place of Truth", was the last abode of the mighty New Kingdom pharaohs. Their elaborate tombs were carved into the mountain, their mummies covered with gold and jewels, and surrounded with treasure and everything else they would need in their afterlife.

Top: The barren hills hide richly decorated tomb interiors

🗺 202 B4
✉ West Bank, beyond al Gurna
🕐 Summer daily 7–6; winter 7–5
🍴 Cafeteria (£). Closed at present
💷 Expensive; Tomb of Tutankhamun: expensive

These tombs were intended to be secure places where the mummies could rest eternally, ensuring the deceased pharaohs a happy afterlife. But the prize was too great – treasure hunters and tomb raiders were not easily deterred and most tombs had been raided before much time had passed. But even without the mummies and their treasure, the massive scale of some of these tombs and the magnificence of their wall paintings allows you to imagine the original splendour, particularly if you can get away from the crowds.

Into the Underworld
As the pyramids had proved relatively easy to break into, pharaohs of the New Kingdom chose to be buried with less ostentation. The architecture of the tomb in some way reflected the journey the dead pharaoh was making, so rock-hewn tombs with long corridors leading down into antechambers and finally

The Royal Mummies

In 1876 the greatest cache of mummies was discovered near the Temple of Hatshepsut. The mummies of 40 pharaohs, queens and nobles including Amenhotep I, Tuthmosis III, Seti I and Ramses II, were found in a huge burial pit (tomb No 320). It's believed that New Kingdom priests, realising the mummies' allure to robbers, moved them to this secret communal tomb. Some are now on display in the Mummy Room of the Egyptian Museum of Antiquities in Cairo (▶ 50–53).

into the burial chamber represented the underworld. Artists and workers from Deir al Madina (▶ 99–100) decorated the tomb walls with mysterious and complicated inscriptions and images from the Book of the Dead, to help guide the pharaoh to the underworld.

It's All Relative

Tutankhamun's tomb may be famous for the treasure it contained, but as the king died young and insignificant, his tomb is small and the decorations hastily executed. Just try to imagine the amount of gold and wealth that would have been buried with more powerful pharaohs such as Ramses II or Tuthmosis III. Tuthmosis (1479–1425 BC) was one of the first to be buried in the valley; his is a very secretive space, high up in the cliffs past a ravine. That the Tomb of Ramses IV was already a tourist attraction in antiquity is obvious from the centuries of graffiti near the entrance.

The Tomb of Ramses III is one of the longest and grandest in the valley, his sarcophagus is in the Louvre in Paris. Horemheb's tomb is interesting as it was left in different stages of decoration. As to be expected the Tomb of Ramses II was the largest, but it suffered serious damage from floods. The most beautiful tomb belongs to his

The Theban Mapping Project

The Theban Mapping Project (TMP) has been working since 1978 at a comprehensive map of Thebes, one of the world's most important archaeological sites, in order to protect and preserve the area. During the last decade TMP has focused its attention on the Valley of the Kings. In 1995 they rediscovered and started excavating KV5, so far the largest tomb in the valley, with more than 128 rooms. This tomb probably belonged to the 50 sons of Ramses II. In 2006 another tomb was discovered, KV63, with several intact coffins (www.thebanmappingproject.com).

father Seti I (1294–1279 BC), with carvings even finer than those in the pharaoh's temple at Abydos (▶ 101), but it will not be open to the public for the foreseeable future.

TAKING A BREAK

At the time of writing the café at the entrance to the Valley of the Kings was closed. Stalls sell cold drinks and ice-creams.

The Greeks visited the tomb of Ramses VI in ancient times, as they believed that it belonged to Memnon. Right: The red granite sarcophagus of Tuthmosis III remains in his tomb, but his mummy is in Cairo's Egyptian Museum of Antiquities

VALLEY OF THE KINGS: INSIDE INFO

Top tips Tomb openings are **rotated to protect paintings** from damage caused by human sweat and touch. **Check which tombs are open** with the ticket office near Deir al Madina before you go.
- Tickets are sold per **three tombs**, with a **separate ticket for Tutankhamun's tomb**.
- To **avoid the crowds** head for the tombs farther away from the entrance.
- Early **Tuesday morning** is **market day** on the West Bank. The market is held at the start of the **road to the Valley of the Kings**, in an open space behind the modern cemetery and across from the temple of Seti I. The tombs in the market are often similar to the paintings in some of the tombs.

Ones to miss Tutankhamun's tomb is **small and often disappointing** because the treasure is in the Egyptian Museum of Antiquities in Cairo, and the poor decorations have been blackened by a fungus caused by the humidity created by the crowds.

10

Deir al Bahari

The magnificent Mortuary Temple of Hatshepsut is set dramatically against the cliff face of the Theban hills. The imposing terraces look surprisingly stark and modern, but you have to imagine them in Hatshepsut's days, when they were filled with exotic perfumed trees, and fountains to cool the air. Hatshepsut called her temple Djeser Djeseru ("the Sacred of Sacreds"). It was a ruin when excavated in 1891, but it's been carefully restored over many years.

In ancient times the temple was connected to the Nile by a wide avenue of sphinxes. The Lower Terrace (closed for restoration at the time of writing) would have been lined with sweet-smelling myrrh trees and refreshing fountains. The pylons have disappeared and the colonnades were defaced by Tuthmosis III, but you can still see the stumps of a few 3,500-year-old trees. A massive ramp connects the terraces and the fabulous reliefs on the portico of the Second Terrace. On the north side is the Birth Colonnade, with scenes confirming the queen's divine parentage and her right to rule. To the south is the Punt Colonnade, depicting the expedition to Punt (probably in present-day Somalia) sent by Queen Hatshepsut to bring back myrrh trees, ebony, ivory and spices.

Beyond lies the Chapel of Hathor, with a hidden representation of the queen's favourite, and architect of the temple, Senenmut. The Third Terrace, architecturally the finest part of the temple, has a pink granite portico leading into the rock-cut Sanctuary of Amun.

TAKING A BREAK

Several vendors sell cold drinks, but for a rest head for one of the **cafés at al Gurna**.

✚ 202 B4
✉ Al Gurna, West Bank
🕐 Summer daily 6–5; winter 6–4:30 💲 Moderate

The Female Pharaoh

Tuthmosis I's daughter, Queen Hatshepsut, was one of Egypt's rare female rulers and her life was full of intrigue. Her husband Tuthmosis II died before she produced a son, so she usurped Tuthmosis III, son of another wife, and became the absolute ruler of Egypt from 1473 to 1458 BC. She is often represented as a man. After her death Tuthmosis III tried to obliterate her name from history, defacing her images and cartouches.

The setting of Hatshepsut's mortuary temple against the pink Theban hills is spectacular

DEIR AL BAHARI: INSIDE INFO

Top tips Tickets for this temple, as for every monument on the West Bank, are available only from the ticket office near the crossroads before Deir al Madina.
• Visit early in the day to avoid the worst of the heat and bring lots of water.
• Two paths lead up the mountain near Deir al Bahari. Climb to the top for some fabulous views, or walk across the hill to the Valley of the Kings (▶ 91–93).

🔢

Tombs of the Nobles

The nobles – local rulers, ministers and governors under the pharaohs – enjoyed a good life and were keen for pleasures to continue after their death. As a result, their tombs are not decorated with cryptic texts from the Book of the Dead, but with realistic and vividly coloured depictions of their lives. The work is inferior to that of the royal tombs, but it provides a wonderful insight into ancient Egyptian society and the daily life of wealthy Egyptians and their servants.

Whereas the pharaohs' tombs were hidden in the Theban hills, the nobles built theirs ostentatiously on the frontline, facing the mortuary temples of their masters. There are many tombs in this necropolis, but only seven are open to the public. The farthest two are the tombs of **Rekhmire** and **Sennofer**. The first

has scenes of the vizier Rekhmire receiving tributes from foreign lands and overseeing the agricultural revenue, while the second is known as the "tomb of the vines" for its ceiling of beautifully painted vines. The decorative style of the nearby tomb of **Ramose** reflects that he was a vizier immediately before and after the Amarna revolution (➤ 22). The superb carvings along the entrance wall are all in the classical style, showing Ramose making offerings, but on the opposite side they also reveal the more naturalistic Amarna style. Immediately south, the tomb of **Khaemhat**, a royal scribe, contains a variety of fishing, family and funerary scenes and has exceptionally well-preserved colours.

Farther north lies another beautiful group of tombs. The Tomb of **Nakht** has fascinating scenes of a banquet with dancers and a blind harpist, with a cat

**Above: Entrance to the tomb of the supervisor Menna.
Right: Sennofer's tomb, decorated with vines, is one of the most pleasing tombs in this valley**

eating fish under his chair, while that of **Menna**, an inspector of estates, depicts scenes of rural life and of Menna and his wife performing ceremonies for the gods.

TAKING A BREAK

Two cafés in **al Gurna** sell cold drinks or tea. The **Nour al Gurna** hotel restaurant (➤ 103), near by, is good for lunch.

➕ 202 B4
✉ Old Gurna
🕐 Daily 7–5, but smaller tombs often close around 3pm
🍴 Cafés (£)
🎟 Tickets per group of tombs inexpensive (from the kiosk near the crossroads)

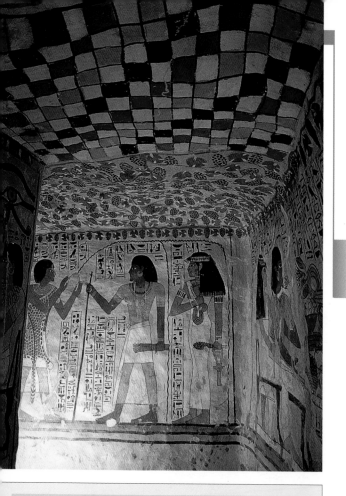

TOMBS OF THE NOBLES: INSIDE INFO

Top tips A visit involves walking and climbing stairs, so avoid the midday heat.
• Tombs are divided into four groups, each requiring a separate ticket. It takes an hour to visit all the tombs, but most visitors limit themselves to the best of each group, or just one group. Signposting is poor but the tombs are close together and local children or villagers are always eager to show you the way.
• Guards will light up tombs the traditional ancient way, using a mirror to reflect sunlight, in return for *baksheesh*. Be sure to refuse their services on arrival if you don't want them.

Ones to miss The tombs of Khonsu, Userhet and Benia are the least impressive.

Hidden gem Many visitors skip Sennofer's tomb as it requires a good climb, but it's delightful and colourful, reflecting Sennofer's eternal love for his beautiful wife.

At Your Leisure

2 Luxor Museum

This small museum of antiquities is an absolute gem. The choice selection of statues and objects found in local tombs and temples is well labelled in English and perfectly displayed against a dark background to bring out the best features. Among the many highlights are a strikingly beautiful statue of an eternally young King Tuthmosis III, an extraordinary statue of Amenophis III held by the crocodile god Sobek, and furniture from Tutankhamun's tomb. There are

Fine relief of King Tuthmosis III wearing the long royal beard and the "atef" crown

also two fine heads of the rebellious Pharaoh Akhenaton and some lovely carvings taken from his temple, illustrating the bizarre physiognomy of that period. The important cache of statues, among them Ramses II and Tutankhamun, found a few years ago under Luxor Temple, is also on display here in the New Hall.

➕ 202 B4 ✉ Corniche al Nil, Luxor ☎ 095-238 0269
🕐 Summer daily 9–1, 5–10; winter 9–1, 4–9 💰 Moderate, camera permit extra

3 Mummification Museum

This interesting little museum highlights the beliefs and the historical development of mummification, and also explains the different stages of the lengthy process. Exhibits include mummification instruments and even some fine animal mummies.

➕ 202 B4 ✉ Corniche al Nil, East Bank, near the ferry terminal
☎ 095-238 1501 🕐 Summer daily 9–1, 5–10; winter 9–1, 5–9
💰 Moderate

5 Madinat Habu

The grand mortuary temple of Ramses III (1184–1153 BC), modelled on the Ramesseum (► 100) of his ancestor Ramses II, was the last great classical pharaonic temple to be built in Egypt. Ramses III, however, was more fortunate than his namesake because this temple has survived the millennia remarkably well, but the Hypostyle Hall and Sanctuaries were severely damaged during an earthquake in the 1st century BC. The entrance to the temple complex is a lofty Syrian-style gatehouse with an upper room decorated with musicians and dancers, where Ramses III apparently entertained guests. To the right are several older chapels and what remains of the Sacred Lake, where local women still come in search of a cure for infertility. The towering First Pylon, like the Second Pylon, is decorated with scenes of battles fought by Ramses II and leads to the First Court,

All around Madinat Habu are reminders of the Coptic settlement of Djeme

which features well-preserved carvings of Ramses himself making offerings to the gods.

Mudbrick remains of the Coptic town of Djeme, which covered the entire enclosure until the 19th century, can be seen above the perimeter wall.

🚹 202 B4
✉ Kom Lola, near the ticket office
🕐 Daily 7–5
🍽 Café-restaurants opposite the entrance (£) 🎟 Moderate

Tomb of Nefertari

The New Kingdom pharaoh Ramses II created one of the most beautiful tombs in Egypt as a shrine to the beauty of Nefertari, his wife of some 34 years. The corridors and walls in its three chambers are decorated with brightly coloured images, most famously of the stunning queen in a transparent white dress with a two-feathered golden head-dress. The ceiling is painted with bright golden stars. The tomb was reopened in 1995 after extensive restoration, but closed again in 2003 until further notice.

🚹 202 B4
✉ Valley of the Queens, West Bank (see above right)
🕐 Closed until further notice
🎟 Expensive; only 150 tickets are on sale from 6am each morning, when the tomb reopens

☷ Valley of the Queens

This is a slight misnomer as the 80 tombs belong not only to queens, but also to princes and princesses. But only four, including the tomb of Nefertari, are open to the public. The tomb of Amun-Her-Khopshef, son of Ramses III, shows beautiful scenes of the father introducing his son to the gods. Also in the tomb is the mummy of a five-month-old foetus, believed to be lost when the mother heard of the death of her nine-year-old son Amunwas. Another son of Ramses III, Prince Khaemweset, is also buried here, surrounded by similar scenes of Ramses leading him through the underworld.

🚹 202 B4 ✉ West Bank 🕐 Daily 7–5
�　No public transport 🎟 Inexpensive; separate charge for Tomb of Nefertari

☷ Deir al Madina

This village sheds a rare light on the lives of less exalted Egyptians. The artists, masons and labourers who worked on the tombs in the Valley of the Kings (➤ 91–93) lived here with their families, segregated from the rest of the population to keep the location of the royal tombs secret. Many inhabitants were literate and a large amount of papyri records the strict organisation of their lives, as well as their complaints about hardship and working conditions. Despite this, they

Entrance to the temple of Deir al Madina

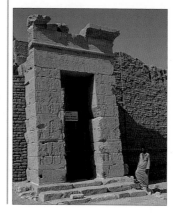

worked 8-hour days, staying in the Valley of the Kings for 10-day shifts, so there was plenty of spare time to work on their own tombs.

Near the entrance to the village are the tombs of artists Sennedjem and Ankherkha, with colourful interpretations (often parodies) of designs they worked on in the royal tombs. The tomb of Peshedu has a painting of the dead artist praying under the tree of regeneration, while Iphy's

> "I met a traveller from an antique land
> Who said: Two vast and trunkless legs of stone
> Stand in the desert…Near them on the sand,
> Half sunk, a shattered visage lies…
>
> … Nothing beside remains. Round the decay
> Of that colossal wreck, boundless and bare
> The lone and level sands stretch far away."
> *From "Ozymandias", Shelley*

tomb is decorated with scenes of everyday life.

A temple dedicated to the goddesses Maat and Hathor stands at the northern end of the village.

🚩 202 B4 ⊠ West Bank, opposite the ticket office
🕐 Daily 7–5
💰 Inexpensive; separate ticket for Peshedu's tomb (Inexpensive)

Parts of Ramses II's colossus are scattered all over the Ramesseum

12 Ramesseum

Ever since the English poet Percy Bysshe Shelley (1792–1822) eternalised the broken statue of Ramses II in his poem "Ozymandias", left, as a symbol of the vanity of transient human glory, visitors have come to the Ramesseum looking for its colossal fragments. Ramses II, who built some awe-inspiring monuments elsewhere in Egypt, intended this mortuary temple to be his eternal monument, but unfortunately chose a site that was annually flooded. It would almost certainly have been as grand as his fabulous temple at Abu Simbel (▶ 118–120), but it's ironic that only this one, intended to be the most important, fell to pieces.

The colossal statue, once the largest in the world at 18m (60 feet) high and weighing more than 900 tonnes, destroyed the Second Pylon and the Second Court as it fell. You can still see its remains and marvel at the proportions. In addition to the statue itself, at the far end of the court is a smaller colossus with a more intact face. The walls of the

First and Second Pylons are decorated with scenes of Ramses' famous victories, as are the walls of the Great Hypostyle Hall, where 29 of its original 48 columns still stand. Beyond lie two smaller hypostyle halls, one with an astronomical ceiling which boasts the oldest-known 12-month calendar. The vaulted mudbrick rooms surrounding the temple were used as workshops, servants' quarters and storage houses.

➕ 202 B4 ✉ al Gurna, West Bank, Luxor 🕐 Daily 7–5 🚌 No public transport, so cycle or take a taxi 🖐 Inexpensive

⑬ Abydos

Abydos is situated about 130km (80 miles) north of Luxor. For nearly 2,000 years Abydos was Egypt's prime

Best for Kids

• *Felucca* ride on the Nile (➤ 106)
• Horse-riding (➤ 106)
• Mummification Museum (➤ 98)
• Tombs of the Nobles (➤ 96–97)
• Al Aboudi bookshop (➤ 105–106): a huge selection of children's books on Egypt

The wall carvings at Seti I's temple in Abydos are among the finest from the New Kingdom

burial ground, as it marked the entrance to the underworld and is where Osiris's head was buried (➤ 12–13). Ancient Egyptians aspired to make a pilgrimage once in their lives and, if they weren't buried here, endeavoured to have their mummies brought here before burial elsewhere in Egypt.

The 14th-century BC Temple of Seti I is one of Egypt's finest monuments, with exquisite decoration, but the facade was finished less carefully by Seti's son, Ramses II, who also built a smaller temple here.

➕ 202 B5 ✉ Al Araba al Madfuna, 10km (6 miles) southwest of al Balyana 🕐 Summer daily 8–5; winter 8–4 🍴 Café opposite 🚌 Train or bus from Luxor to al Balyana, then in convoy to the site 🖐 Inexpensive

Hypostyle Hall at the Temple of Hathor

style by the Ptolemies and the Romans, between 125 BC and AD 60. Hathor, wife of Horus, was the goddess of pleasure, beauty and love, often associated with the Greek Aphrodite. During the annual New Year festival, Hathor's statue was taken to the roof to be exposed to the sun-god, before being reunited with Horus at his temple in Edfu (► 121). Scenes of this festival decorate the walls of the temple.

🚩 Dendera

The well-preserved Temple of Hathor was built here in the classic Egyptian

🔢 202 B5 ✉ 4km (2.5 miles) across the Nile from Qena, 64km (40 miles) north of Luxor 🕐 Summer daily 7–6, winter 7–5 🍴 Café (£) 🚌 Train or bus to Qena, horse-carriage to the site (check first for travel restrictions) 🎟 Inexpensive

Luxor From the Air

You'll get the most spectacular view of Luxor's monuments and villages from a hot-air balloon. Each flight of about one hour is slightly different depending on the wind, but the experience is unforgettable. Two companies offer flights in the early morning, ending with a champagne breakfast. Trips are arranged through the hotels or directly: **Hod Hod Soleiman** (tel: 095-237 0116) and **Magic Horizon** (tel: 095-236 5060; www.magic-horizon.com).

Where to... Stay

Prices

The prices are for a double room per night.
£ under 400LE **££** 400–900LE **£££** over 900LE

EAST BANK

Mövenpick Jolie Ville Luxor £££

This excellent family hotel is on its own island on the Nile, 6km (4 miles) south of Luxor. Recently renovated rooms are spartan but comfortable, all with a little terrace giving onto lush gardens. The wonderful breakfast buffet is served outside on the Nile-side terraces, weather permitting, and the restaurants serve some of the best food in town. Kids will love the great pool, small zoo and playground.

✚ 202 B4 **⊠ Crocodile Island, 6km (4 miles) south of Luxor**
☎ 095-237 4855;
www.moevenpick-hotels.com

New Emilio Hotel ££

All the rooms in this excellent hotel are equipped with private bathroom, air-conditioning, minibar, TV and a hotel video channel. There's also a small rooftop pool with relaxing chairs for sunbathing. The staff are particularly helpful and friendly. Book in advance in high season, as it can fill up with tour groups.

✚ 202 B4 **⊠ Sharia Yussef Hassan**
☎ 095-237 3570; fax: 095-237 0000

Old Winter Palace £££

The Old Winter Palace is a colonial building overlooking the Nile and the Theban Hills beyond, while the interior mixes colonial paraphernalia with new fabrics and *objets d'art* inspired by the old glory days. The large and comfortable rooms have high ceilings and are elegantly decorated, and there's a large swimming pool in well-tended gardens filled with songbirds. Service can be shambolic.

✚ 202 B4 **⊠ Sharia Corniche an Nil**
☎ 095-238 0422; email:
h1661@accor-hotels.com

WEST BANK

Al-Moudira £££

This palatial desert retreat is like no other hotel in Egypt. The wonderful Egyptian architect Olivier Sednaoui excelled himself in this formidable building, with its vast luxurious rooms, beautifully decorated with locally made furniture and finds from antique markets. Set on the edge of the desert and the farmed land, the beautiful pool is surrounded by the perfumed garden that overlooks the Thebes mountains. This hotel is a real delight!

✚ 202 B4 **⊠ Daba'iyya, 15km (9 miles) south of ticket office on the**

Nour al Balad ££

Beautiful sister hotel to the Nour al Gourna (below) with spacious rooms overlooking the Theban hills and fields. It is slightly further from the sights, but peaceful. Breakfast is served in a well-kept garden and dinner is available if ordered in advance. A good place to stay if you have a bit more time to visit the sites on this side of the Nile.

✚ 202 B4 **⊠ Ezbet Bisily, follow the track behind the Medinat Habu temple**
☎ 095 242 6111

Nour al Gourna £

In this delightful small hotel, the simple, stylish rooms overlook sugarcane fields or a pretty palm grove. All rooms have fans and mosquito nets, local furniture and a stereo.

✚ 202 B4 **⊠ Opposite the ticket office, Gurna, West Bank** **☎ 095-231 1430/010-129 5812**

West Bank **☎ 012-325 1307/392 8332; email: moudirahotel@yahoo.com**

Where to...
Eat and Drink

Prices
Expect to pay per person for a meal, excluding drinks and tips.
£ up to 100LE **££** 100–150LE **£££** over 150LE

Most hotels on the East Bank have adequate restaurants serving international cuisine, while a few restaurants along the Corniche specialise in Egyptian food. Most restaurants on the West Bank are basic, offering simple but fresh Egyptian stews, grilled chicken and kebabs. To sample more elaborate dishes, such as duck or stuffed pigeon, order them earlier in the day, before sightseeing.

EAST BANK

Dawar al Umda ££
A good Egyptian restaurant set in the pleasant hotel gardens, offering an excellent selection of *mezze* and classical Egyptian fare such as kebabs, *kofta* and vegetable stews. On winter evenings there is often a belly dancer or folkloric show.

➕ 202 B4 ⊠ Mercure Inn, Sharia al Karnak 📞 095-237 3321 ⏰ Daily lunch and dinner

Kings Head Pub £–££
This popular British pub has all the necessary trimmings from darts, billiards, and soccer on TV to cold beers, lagers and pub food.

➕ 202 B4 ⊠ Near the passport office, on Sharia Khaled Ibn Walid 📞 095-237 1249 ⏰ Daily 10am–2am

La Mamma ££
In the middle of the hotel garden and beside a pond with ducks and pelicans, La Mamma is one of the most reliable restaurants in town, and is especially popular with kids. Fresh pastas, thin-crust pizzas and Italian meat dishes make a change from Egyptian fare.

➕ 202 B4 ⊠ Sheraton Hotel, Sharia Khalid Ibn Walid 📞 095-237 4544 ⏰ Daily lunch and dinner

Metropolitan Café £–££
Pleasant café down by the water, overlooking the Nile and the *felucca* captains going about their business. Food, Egyptian and international cuisine, is served but this is a perfect place for a cold beer while watching the sunset over the East Bank.

Miyako ££
As if the culture shock of being in Luxor wasn't enough, you can now sample excellent Japanese food by the banks of the Nile at the Sonesta St George Hotel. The décor is simple Asian, while the food is excellent and fresh. The sushi and grills are particularly recommended.

➕ 202 B4 ⊠ Sonesta St George Hotel, Sharia Khaled Ibn Walid 📞 095-238 2575

Mövenpick Garden Terrace ££
This beautiful garden terrace overlooking the Nile is perfect for a lunchtime treat. The menu offers good sandwiches, including a copious grilled *kofta* sandwich, excellent salads and fresh pastas. But for many the greatest attractions are the desserts, including huge scoops of the best ice-cream in town.

➕ 202 B4 ⊠ Lower level, Corniche an-Nil, opposite the Old Winter Palace, East Bank 📞 No phone ⏰ Daily 10am–11pm

⊞ 202 B4 ⊠ Crocodile Island, 6km (4 miles) south of Luxor, near the new bridge ☎ 095-237 4855 ⓖ Daily breakfast (in fine weather), lunch, dinner inside

Oasis Café £

A great café-restaurant in a 1920s building in the heart of Luxor, with simple but cosy décor. The food ranges from snacks and pastas to pastries and grilled meats.

⊞ 202 B4 ⊠ Sharia Dr Labib Habashi ☎ 012-336 7121 ⓖ Daily 10–10

WEST BANK

Al Moudira £££

Be it at the poolside restaurant or at the Oriental fantasy indoor restaurant, al Moudira offers the most romantic dining in town. The food, a mixture of the best of Western and Middle Lebanese cuisine, is delicious and superb, and the whole experience is definitely worth travelling the few miles from Luxor. Book ahead.

⊞ 202 B4 ⊠ Daba'iyya, 15km (9 miles) south of the ticket office on the West Bank ☎ 012-325 1307/392 8332

Nur al Gurna £–££

This simple restaurant, in a shady garden, serves local dishes like *meloukhiya* (a soup of a spinach-like vegetable), served with chicken, served with bread, onion and condiments), roast duck and stuffed pigeon are often on the menu. No alcohol is served.

⊞ 202 B4 ⊠ Opposite the ticket office, Gurna ☎ 095-231 1430 ⓖ Daily 10–10

Restaurant Muhammad £

Simple, Egyptian dishes in a cool house with a shaded terrace. The menu is small, but if you pass by in the morning, he may be able to serve a delicious *meloukhiya*, stuffed pigeon or grilled duck for lunch.

⊞ 202 B4 ⊠ Next to the Pharaoh's Hotel, near the ticket office, West Bank ☎ 095-231 1014 ⓖ Daily noon–10 or later

Where to... Shop

Luxor Town, particularly around the temple, is one big tourist bazaar with hundreds of vendors selling cheap souvenirs, from small statues and colourful skullcaps to carpets and painted papyri. It's hard to avoid them, as vendors know every trick to lure innocent-looking tourists. Few have fixed prices, so the rule here, as elsewhere in Egypt, is to bargain hard, and you might well find some evocative souvenirs. The little statues of ancient Egyptian gods are a good choice, as are scarves (watch out for synthetic ones) and hand-woven cotton tablecloths from Akhmim. Another great buy is traditional clay cooking pots, sold at two stalls beside the police station. They can be used in the oven or on a hob, but need treating with a mixture of oil and molasses at a low heat for half an hour before use. If cooking is your thing, look out for cheap spices like cumin, chilli and black pepper. The bazaar is open in the morning until 1pm, and again from 5 to 9pm or later.

Alabaster

Alabaster is quarried 80km (50 miles) north of the Valley of the Kings and in workshops on the West Bank you can see how the stone is treated and polished. Several large shops sell kitsch statuettes and sphinx lamps, as well as beautiful unpolished alabaster vases or bowls in simple shapes, similar to those in the Egyptian Museum.

Bookshops

Luxor has some excellent bookshops stocking a wide selection of titles on Egypt, Arab culture and the Middle East, in several European languages. **Al Aboudi** (tel: 095-237 3390) in the tourist bazaar, next to the Winter Palace has an excellent children's section and several well-priced books on Egypt. It sells postcards too. Also next to the Winter Palace is **AA Gaddis** (tel: 095-237 0753), with books on modern and ancient Egypt, as well as postcards, Egyptian papyrus stationery and good-quality souvenirs.

Quality Crafts

Fine fabrics have been hand-woven in Akhmim for centuries, and the best selection of fabrics and table-cloths from there is available at the **Winter Akhmim Gallery** (tel: 095-238 0422) in the arcade of the Old Winter Palace Hotel. **Fair Trade Centre Luxor Outlet** (tel: 095-238 7015) on Sharia al Karnak is an excellent shop with a selection of crafts that have come from various NGO projects throughout Egypt, all of whom share in the profit. It sells hand-woven rugs from the Western Desert, pottery, Nubian baskets and plenty of other high quality souvenirs, all at fixed prices.

Where to...
Be Entertained

Luxor has so many monuments to visit that the only entertainment most tourists want at the end of the day is a dive in the pool, a cool drink, a good dinner and a soft bed. And that's just as well because there isn't really much else to do. But if you do still have the energy, you'll find listings of special events and exhibitions in the monthly magazine *Egypt Today*, available from bookshops.

Feluccas and Boats

Here, as elsewhere on the Nile, taking a *felucca* is a great way to wind down, once you've negotiated the price. The most popular destination is Banana Island, 4km (2.5 miles) upriver, where souvenir vendors await unwary tourists (so you might want to avoid it). Instead, take a boat for a few hours and just sail up the Nile, enjoying the beauty of the river and the landscape. It's particularly lovely around sunset. If there's no wind, you will be rowed – or it's an opportunity, perhaps, to take one of the small motorboats.

Horse-riding

Another way to relax is to rent a horse or camel from one of the stables. Try the **Nobi Horse Stable** (tel: 010-504 8558) or **Pharaoh's Stables** (tel: 095-231 0015), both behind the Mobil filling station on the West Bank. An hour-long circuit will take you through some lush countryside and then back along the Nile.

Swimming

Nearly all hotels will open their pools to non-residents, either for an entrance fee or for a minimum charge on drinks and snacks.

Nightlife

Luxor has a few discos in the hotels, but don't expect the latest dance music or a laser show. The liveliest discos are at the **Mercure Inn Hotel** and at the **Tutotel** on 1 Sharia Salah al Din, East Bank (tel: 095-237 7990). The **Mövenpick Hotel** has a good belly dance and folkloric show in its Fellah's Tent.

Sightseeing by Night

An excellent **Sound and Light Show** happens daily, in different languages, at Karnak Temple (▶ 84–87). Luxor Temple (▶ 88–90), dramatically floodlit at night and open until 10pm, makes for an unusual evening stroll.

Upper Egypt and Nubia

Getting Your Bearings

During the 19th century, as more and more archaeological discoveries were made, it became fashionable to spend the winter in Upper Egypt. Wealthy Europeans would rent a private *dahabiyya* (sailing houseboat) and set off on the river from Cairo, stopping to explore ruins and monuments.

Today, the best and most relaxing way to visit the sights along the Nile is once again by *dahabeyya*, some old ones were restored, some new ones are being built (➤ 122, panel). These old-fashioned sailing boats are more intimate (4–10 cabins) and often take a week to go from Esna to Aswan, taking in sights the big cruiseboats can't stop at. Luxury cruise ships run three- to five-day cruises between Luxor and Aswan that stop at the temples, but leave plenty of time to idle around on deck. The

Right: There seem to be temples and necropolises everywhere in Aswan

more adventurous can get even closer to the river on a three-or four-day *felucca* ride, sleeping under the stars. Several cruisers also offer a four-day trip on Lake Nasser, taking in rescued Nubian monuments, or fishing for the huge Nile perch.

Visitors travel only in a private vehicle from Luxor to Aswan in an armed police convoy, which leaves twice a day from both places, but doesn't stop at sights. Security concerns have also made travel by road from Aswan to Abu Simbel possible only in buses organised by tour operators and in a police convoy.

South of Luxor the landscape changes and the desert closes in on the Nile. The people change too, as many Nubian families who lost their land when the area was flooded after the Aswan Dam was built moved north to Aswan and beyond.

By the time you reach Aswan you know you've left the Mediterranean and the Middle East behind and entered a more exotic, more African environment. Aswan, with fewer important monuments than Luxor, is the perfect place to slow down and relax while enjoying views on the river and the islands.

Previous page and above: Sailing by *felucca* between Luxor and Aswan is an idyllic way to experience the temples

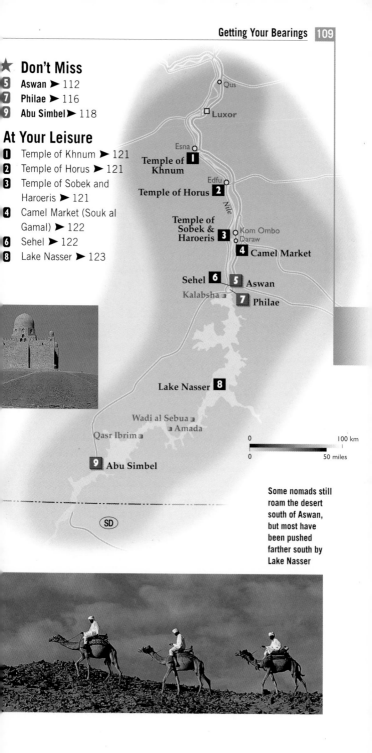

Qus

Luxor

Esna
Temple of 1
Khnum

Edfu
Temple of Horus 2

Nile

**Temple of
Sobek &
Haroeris 3**
Kom Ombo
Daraw
4 Camel Market

Sehel 6 **5 Aswan**
Kalabsha
7 Philae

Lake Nasser 8

Wadi al Sebua
Amada
Qasr Ibrim

0 ─────────── 100 km
0 ─────────── 50 miles

9 Abu Simbel

SD

Some nomads still
roam the desert
south of Aswan,
but most have
been pushed
farther south by
Lake Nasser

Enjoy the peaceful pace of Aswan and Lake Nasser, taking in the sites partly by taxi but mostly by motorboat or *felucca*. The light in the early morning and late afternoon is stunning, and the singing voices of Nubian children on the river before sunset are unforgettable.

Upper Egypt and Nubia in Three Days

Day One

Morning

Start early and hire a private taxi for a half day. Leave **⑤ Aswan** (► 112–115) along the road past the **Fatimid Cemetery** (► 114) and the **Unfinished Obelisk** on the outskirts of the town. Continue via the Old Aswan Dam to the Philae dock in Shallal to buy a ticket to the site and take a boat to the **⑦ island** (► 116–117). Spend about 90 minutes here, then drive on for a look at the **Aswan High Dam** (► 115) and return to Aswan via the Old Dam. Have a late lunch at the Aswan Moon restaurant (► 125).

Afternoon

From the terminal opposite the Egypt Air office, take a ferry out to Elephantine Island on the Nile to visit the **Aswan Antiquities Museum** and its peaceful garden for an hour or so (► 114). Stroll to the north of the island through the palm groves and Nubian villages. Back at the ferry landing, you can take a *felucca* around the islands. Have the *felucca* wait while you walk through the botanical garden on **Kitchener Island** (► 115) and then sail around the islands, past the **Aga Khan's Mausoleum** on the West Bank (► 115).

Evening

Finish the day with the Oriental show at the **Nubia House Restaurant** (► 126).

Day Two

Morning

Take a taxi for a round trip south to
8 Kalabsha Temple on Lake Nasser
(below left, ➤ 123). Depending on
the height of the lake you may have to
take a boat from the harbour.
Boatmen usually allow for an hour's
visit, which is enough. Return to
Aswan for lunch in one of the places
along the Corniche (➤ 125–126).

Afternoon

Stock up on water and good sun protection and take a *felucca* on a
two-hour round trip to **6 Sehel Island**
(left, ➤ 122). After returning to
Aswan, walk over to the **Nubia Museum**
(➤ 114) for a late afternoon visit. Stroll back to the Old Cataract Hotel for an
early evening drink on the terrace and dinner at the beautifully restored
Moorish restaurant (➤ 126).

Day Three

Morning

Having booked your return plane tickets in advance with a travel agent or
Egypt Air, take a half-day excursion to
the temples of **9 Abu Simbel** (right,
➤ 118–119), a flight of around
30–45 minutes. Head back to Aswan
for lunch in the Aswan Moon or one of
the other riverside cafés.

Afternoon

Relax by one of the hotel swimming pools (➤ 127) until late afternoon then
stroll over to the *souks* for some souvenir shopping and to take in the atmosphere as the sun goes down.

Evening

Take a cab to Philae for the *son et lumière* show (➤ 128, check with the tourist
office for times or online at www.sound-light.egypt.com).

5

Aswan

Aswan's setting on the Nile is both dramatic and idyllic. Here the river is squeezed in between the Eastern Desert and the Sahara. Its cool sparkling blue waters contrast starkly with the hot, golden desert sands, the pink granite boulders it flows around and the lush green islands in its stream. But the views over Aswan and the Nile are the real spectacle, particularly in the late afternoon.

The town of Aswan has been a frontier since ancient times, as Egypt's southernmost city and the gateway to Nubia and Africa. It has a sweet, exotic smell and its tall, dark Nubian population has more in common with the Sudanese than with other Egyptians. The climate is fabulous in winter – hot and dry – and the atmosphere is totally laid back. Aswan has fewer spectacular sights than Luxor or Cairo, so there's more time to hang out in the riverside cafés watching the sun set and the *feluccas* sail by, and to stroll in its quirky *souk*.

Nilometers

These instruments were used to record the annual flooding of the Nile, until it was controlled by the Aswan Dam. It was vital to know the accurate level of the Nile, as it formed the basis of tax calculations: the higher the waters rose, the bigger the harvest and therefore the higher the taxes.

Modern Aswan

Aswan is a relaxed and easy town to explore, and its attractive Corniche is lined with pleasant waterfront café-terraces. Sharia al Souk, the main market street, still retains an exotic air even though it's become increasingly touristy. At the southern end of the Corniche are the Ferial Gardens, a tranquil place to sit and watch the sunset if you can't get on the terrace of the Old Cataract Hotel (► 126).

Feluccas sail peacefully around the small islands on the Nile in Aswan

---

✚ 202 C3
✉ 215km (135 miles) south of Luxor
☎ 097-231 2811 (tourist office)

Aswan Museum/Nilometer/Ruins of Yebu
✉ Southern tip of Elephantine Island
🕐 Summer daily 8:30–6; winter 8–5
🚢 Ferry from opposite the Egypt Air office
🎟 Inexpensive

Fatimid Cemetery/Unfinished Obelisk
✉ 1.5km (1 mile) south of Aswan 🕐 Obelisk summer daily 8–6; winter 7–4 🎟 Moderate, tip at the cemetery

Nubia Museum
✉ Sharia Abtal al Tahrir, between the Old Cataract and Basma hotels ☎ 097-231 3826

🕐 Daily 9–1, 5–9 🚶 Walk or private taxi
🎟 Moderate

Botanical Garden
✉ Kitchener's Island 🕐 Summer daily 8–6, winter 8–5 🍴 Cafeteria (£) 🚢 Ferry from west side of Elephantine Island or rented boat or *felucca* 🎟 Moderate

Tombs of the Nobles
✉ West Bank, Aswan 🕐 Summer daily 8–5; winter 8–4 🚢 Ferry from northern end of Corniche, then hike uphill
🎟 Inexpensive

High Dam Pavilion
✉ A few kilometres south of Aswan
🕐 Daily 7–5 🎟 Tip for the guardian to open it 🎟 Inexpensive

Behind the hotel grounds is the **Nubia Museum**, a tribute to the culture and art of the people whose lands were flooded when the dams were constructed to create Lake Nasser. The museum's impressive collection, well displayed and labelled in English, traces the history of Nubia from prehistoric times.

About 1.5km (1 mile) south of Aswan is the vast **Fatimid Cemetery**, with domed mudbrick tombs from the 9th century, and the gigantic **Unfinished Obelisk** that was abandoned after a flaw was discovered. It's thought that it was intended to stand in Tuthmosis III's temple at Karnak (▶ 84–87).

Upriver from the First Cataract (▶ 122) is the Old Dam built in 1902, and farther on the High Dam, completed in 1971.

The *souk* in Aswan is very much an African affair – look out for charms, textile and exotic spices

Ancient Aswan

In ancient times the main town and temple area were on Elephantine Island, mid-river opposite modern Aswan, mainly on its southern tip which was known as Yebu (meaning "ivory" and "elephant"). The fortress of Yebu, protected by the turbulent waters of the Nile, was a perfect base for Egyptian expeditions into Nubia, Sudan and Ethiopia and an important cult place dedicated to Khnum – the god who controlled the Nile's level – his wife Satis and their daughter Anukis. During the Islamic period Yebu became an important trading post for the caravans of camels and elephants laden with ivory, gold, spices and slaves. Excavations of the extensive ruins of ancient Yebu are still underway, but so far you can see a small early Old Kingdom step pyramid, a gateway on which Alexander II is shown worshipping Khnum, and the 30th-Dynasty Temple of Khnum. Farther north there's a Nilometer with Greek, Roman, pharaonic and Arabic numerals.

Both the Nilometer and the ruins of Yebu now form part of the **Aswan Antiquities Museum**, which is housed in the villa of Sir William Willcocks, the British engineer who designed the Old Aswan Dam. The villa contains a huge collection of artefacts found on Elephantine, but it's a rather musty display of

Aswan Dams: Vital Statistics

- The Old Dam was the world's largest when built (1898–1902) and was raised twice.
- It's 50m (165 feet) high, 2km (1 mile) long, 30m (100 feet) wide at the base.
- The High Dam is 111m (365 feet) high, 3.8km (2.5 miles) long and 980m (1,072 yards) wide at the base.
- Lake Nasser, the world's largest reservoir, covers 6,000sq km (2,300sq miles).
- It's forbidden to take photos of the Aswan Dam.

Middle and New Kingdom pottery, jewellery and sculpture and a beautiful gilded statue of Khnum. If you've already been to the large museums in Cairo or Luxor, you might prefer to stroll through the Nubian villages on Elephantine, set amid lush, scented gardens.

The West Bank

The most visible landmark opposite Aswan on the Nile's west bank is the **Aga Khan's Mausoleum** (now closed to the public) where Aga Khan III, and his wife the Begum, are buried. Farther north, the tombs of the Princes of Elephantine Island, cut into the rock, are floodlit at night and command excellent views.

TAKING A BREAK

Café terraces along the Nile, particularly the **Aswan Moon** (▶ 125), serve delicious fresh juices and good, simple Egyptian food. Alternatively, the terrace of the **Old Cataract Hotel** (▶ 126) is the traditional place for an English tea and to watch the sunset, but it's closed to non-residents during busy periods.

Watch the sunset from the terrace of the colonial Old Cataract Hotel

ASWAN: INSIDE INFO

Top tips Take at least one *felucca* ride around the islands as there's nothing more relaxing, particularly around sunset when local children go out on their home-made boats and sing Nubian songs.
- Visit the sweet-smelling **Botanical Garden** on Kitchener Island, where General Kitchener planted shrubs imported from all over the world.

Hidden gems There's a good if tiring 30-minute walk across the desert from the tombs of Elephantine's nobles to the beautiful ruins of 7th-century **St Simeon Monastery** (open daily 8–5; admission moderate). A guardian will open the basilica and show you the place where St Simeon's beard was tied to the ceiling to stop him falling asleep during his prayers.

One to miss You can skip the simple tombs of the princes of Elephantine if you've been to the West Bank in Luxor.

7

Philae

The splendid Temple of Isis, set on an island surrounded by the blue waters of Lake Nasser, is one of Egypt's most romantic sights, especially as you arrive by boat. For more than 800 years, until AD 550, this temple to Isis and Osiris was one of the most important Egyptian cult centres.

Ptolemaic and Roman rulers, keen to identify themselves with this powerful ancient Egyptian cult, all added their mark, making for an interesting blend of styles. The worship of Isis as the Mother of the Gods eventually spread all over the Roman Empire, and early Coptic art clearly associates the Virgin Mary and baby Jesus with Isis suckling her infant son Horus.

Originally the Temple of Isis was built on the island of Philae (the "Island from the Time of Re") facing Bigah Island, which was believed to be one of the burial sites of Osiris. But Bigah was accessible only to priests, so all the religious festivities took place on Philae. With the building of the first Aswan Dam the temple was submerged for half the year. In the 1970s, when the High Dam threatened to submerge it completely, UNESCO and the Egyptian Antiquities Organisation painstakingly moved the entire complex to nearby Agilkia Island, which had been landscaped to resemble Philae.

Before Philae Temple was moved to the island of Agilkia, visitors toured it by rowing boat

Temple Highlights

Boats land near the oldest structure on the island, the Vestibule of **Nectanebo I**, beyond which lies a large court flanked by two elegant colonnades and the impressive **First Pylon** of the Temple of Isis. The small door to the left leads into a 3rd-century BC **Birth House**, whose outside back wall shows some lovely scenes of Isis nursing Horus in the marshes. The main gate, with two

Below: Some carvings are remarkably well preserved

✚ 202 C3
✉ Agilkia Island, between the Old Dam and the High Dam, 9km (6 miles) south of Aswan
🕐 Summer daily 7–5; winter and during Ramadan 7–4
🍴 Cafeteria (££)
🚖 Taxi to Shallal dock for a boat to the island
🎟 Moderate

granite lions, leads to the **Second Pylon**, opening up to a
Hypostyle Hall. The inner temple lost most of its decoration
when it was converted into a church around AD 553, but the
Sanctuary still contains Isis's sacred *barque*.

Near by, the **Temple of Hathor**, the cow goddess of music
(among other things), has a wonderful relief of the gods
playing musical instruments. And an elegant monument
here is the **Kiosk of Trajan** (used as a gateway to the temple
in Roman times), from where there are superb views across
the lake.

The lofty Kiosk of Trajan supported by 14 columns is locally known as the "Pharaoh's Bed"

TAKING A BREAK

There are a few simple cafés at the dock, and on the island
there is a cafeteria with a terrace, selling cold drinks, tea,
snacks and ice-cream.

PHILAE: INSIDE INFO

Top tips Check the official price list for boats at the docks before hiring one.
The price allows for a one-hour visit, but pay the captain extra if you want to
spend more time.

• The sound and light show at the Temple of Isis is often considered the best
in Egypt (➤ 128).

Hidden gem The Osiris Room on the upper floor, where Osirian mysteries
were enacted, has interesting reliefs illustrating the story of Isis and Osiris. It's
usually closed, but the guards may open the doors for some *baksheesh*.

9

Abu Simbel

The 13th-century BC rock-hewn Temple of Ramses II at Abu Simbel is the most impressive monument in Nubia, perfectly expressing the imperial ambition and audacity of the New Kingdom period. The four 21m-high (70-foot) seated figures of Ramses II that guard the temple's facade are among the largest sculptures in Egypt, and seem designed to warn the Nubians of Egypt's mighty power.

No modern Europeans had seen the temple at Abu Simbel until the Swiss explorer Jean Louis Burckhardt sailed past it in 1813. But by then the massive statues were buried up to their necks in sand and it took 20 days of digging in 1817 to clear the entrance, then under some 15m (50 feet) of sand. In the 1960s a different operation was underway, as the international community united to raise this wonderful temple high above the rising waters of Lake Nasser. The temple and the hillside into which it was cut were sawn into 1,050 blocks weighing up to 30 tonnes each, and painstakingly

---

🚻 202 A1   ✉ 280km (175 miles) south of Aswan, 40km (25 miles) from the Sudanese border
🕐 Summer 6–6, winter 6–5
🍽 Café (£)
🚌 Bus from Aswan in armed convoy
✈ Egypt Air flights from Cairo and Aswan. Flights from Aswan are sold as packages, including return trip and transfer to and from the site. This leaves you only about two hours to enjoy the site, which can be quite short, particularly if the outward flight is delayed
💰 Expensive including tour by a local guide

reassembled on higher ground beyond the reach of the lake. Before the salvage operation few people visited Abu Simbel, but today it's a major tourist attraction.

A Labour of Love

It took Ramses II about 30 years to build his "Temple of Ramses, Beloved of Amun". He dedicated it to Ra-Herakte, Amun-Ra and Ptah, but most of all to the deified image of himself. Next door he built a smaller temple for his favourite wife Nefertari, where she is identified with the cow goddess Hathor. The original temple was perfectly oriented so that the sun's rays would illuminate the statues deep in the sanctuary on Ramses II's birthday and on the day of his coronation. The relocated temple catches the rays a day later, and at dawn on 22 February and 22 October the sun's rays reach into the inner sanctuary of the Sun Temple and illuminate the remains of the four deities.

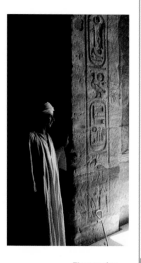

The massive doors to the temple are opened by an *ankh* key, the symbol of life

Left and below: Colossi of Ramses II front the main temple and also the temple dedicated to Queen Nefertari

The temple's facade is dominated by magnificent colossi of Ramses II, staring eternity in the face. The statues' heads and torsos are finely sculpted (but one lost its upper half during an earthquake in 27 BC), while the feet and legs seem rather crude. Members of the royal family, including Nefertari, Ramses' mother Muttuya and several of his children, stand at his feet.

Following the classic temple design, the interior reveals a series of increasingly smaller chambers with a floor that rises noticeably. The massive rock-hewn Hypostyle Hall contains eight 10m-high (33-foot) statues of the king as Osiris. The walls are decorated with scenes from his military campaigns, including the Battle of Qadesh which was fought against the Hittites, Libyans and Nubians. On the back wall he offers his captives to the gods. A smaller hall leads to a vestibule and the Sanctuary, with four statues of Ptah, Amun-Ra, the pharaoh-god Ramses II and Ra-Herakte.

The scale of the inner rooms of the Great Temple is progressively smaller as you approach the sanctuary

Queen Nefertari's Temple

To the north is the smaller temple of Nefertari, dedicated to Hathor. As with Ramses' temple, the rock was smoothed and angled to resemble a pylon, with six 10m (33-foot) colossi (four of Ramses and two of Nefertari) flanking the facade. Although smaller, this temple follows a similar plan, containing a hypostyle hall with carved Hathor images, a vestibule and small sanctuary.

TAKING A BREAK

There's only a small **café** on the site, with cold drinks and very little to eat, so bring a picnic to enjoy in the shade of the trees near the lake.

ABU SIMBEL: INSIDE INFO

Top tips Stay on board ship (if you're cruising) or at an Abu Simbel hotel and have the temple almost to yourself in the early morning or later afternoon. Sit on the left of the plane from Cairo or Aswan for a good view of the temple.
• There are several *son et lumière* shows daily starting at 6pm in winter and 8pm in summer (tel: 02-385 2880; www.sound-light.egypt.com).

Hidden gem Usually an ancient Egyptian queen was represented as a tiny figure coming up to her husband's knees only. Perhaps as proof of Nefertari's status, her own temple here in Abu Simbel is fronted by two statues of her husband Ramses II and four statues of herself at equal heights.

At Your Leisure

1 Temple of Khnum

The temple of Khnum at Esna is located 155km (96 miles) north of Aswan, the temple, rebuilt by Ptolemy VI (180–145 BC) on an older structure, was probably once as large as the one at Edfu (see below). Nowadays people come to see the temple's wonderful 1st-century AD Roman Hypostyle Hall – the only part that's been excavated. Here you get a true sense of what the hall was meant to represent. With 24 columns topped by various finely carved floral capitals, it really feels like a beautifully enclosed garden. The walls are decorated with carvings of various Roman emperors making offerings to Egyptian deities.

🚗 202 B4 ✉ Esna, 54km (34 miles) south of Luxor, 155km (96 miles) north of Aswan 🕐 Summer daily 6–5; winter 6–4 🚌 Bus or taxi from Luxor or Aswan 🚂 Trains from Luxor, Edfu or Aswan to Esna, then a *calèche* to the site 🎫 Inexpensive tickets from the riverside kiosk near the tourist bazaar

2 Temple of Horus

The Ptolemaic temple at Edfu (105km/65 miles north of Aswan), built from 257–237 BC, is the best preserved and one of the finest in Egypt. Built in classic pharaonic style, it gives a clear idea of the appearance and purpose of an Egyptian temple, as plenty of explanations are inscribed on the walls. The site was chosen because the falcon-headed god Horus fought here with Seth (➤ 12) for power over the world. Visitors now approach the temple from the back, but it's best to start from the First Pylon, fronted by two splendid falcons. Carvings on the inside walls record the annual Festival of the Beautiful Meeting, where the statue of Horus joined the statue of Hathor at her temple in Dendera (➤ 102). The annual festivals were celebrated in the Festival Hall, and recipes for incense and perfumes line the walls of a small side chamber. During the New Year festival, the statue of Horus was carried on to the roof to be revitalised by the sun. Outside the temple is the Birth House. Look at the carvings of Horus being suckled by his mother Isis.

🚗 202 C4 ✉ Edfu, 115km (71 miles) south of Luxor, 105km (65 miles) north of Aswan 🕐 Summer daily 6–5; winter 6–4 🍴 Café (£) 🚌 No public transport; cruise ships, *feluccas* or taxis 🎫 Moderate

3 Temple of Sobek and Haroeris

The remains of this Graeco-Roman temple at Kom Ombo, unusually dedicated to two deities,

Some of carvings are remarkably well preserved at the double temple of Kom Ombo

Dahabeyyas

A luxurious way to see the Nile is on a *dahabeyya* (➤ 108), a sailing boat with cabins. Some of the best are *Nour an Nil* with 10 cabins and *Assouan*, 8 cabins (tel: 010-657 8322/ 010-570 5341; http://nourel-nil.com), which offer 7-day cruises mooring at small islands on the way.

still look truly imposing, particularly from the river. The temple has two identical halves: the eastern part is devoted to the crocodile god Sobek, and the western to Haroeris, or Horus the Elder, the "Good Doctor", who attracted thousands of pilgrims hoping to find a cure for their illnesses. Its spectacular location on a bend of the river was responsible for the pylon and the forecourt eventually disappearing into the water, but much of the inner temple remains. The Chapel of Hathor near the entrance housed mummified crocodiles, while live ones swam in the well. A double entrance leads into the inner Hypostyle Hall, with elegant floral columns and two ceremonial paths leading into the symmetrical sanctuaries. Behind are seven chapels whose outer walls reveal a fascinating display of sophisticated instruments that were used to perform brain surgery.

➕ 202 C3 ✉ Kom Ombo, 45km (28 miles) north of Aswan 🕒 Summer daily 6–5; winter 6–4 🍴 Cafeteria just outside the temple (£) 🚌 Bus or taxi from Aswan in convoy
👁 Inexpensive

4 Camel Market (Souk al Gamal)

Egypt's largest camel market is a fascinating place, especially early in the morning when Sudanese traders go noisily about their business. Herdsmen walk the camels across the desert along the Forty Days Road from

Sudan, to somewhere north of Abu Simbel where they are driven to Daraw and sometimes to Birqash (35km/22 miles northwest of Cairo).
➕ 202 C3 ✉ Outskirts of Daraw, 5km (3 miles) south of Kom Ombo – ask or just follow the crowds 🕒 Sun 6:30–2 in winter (also Tue mornings, best before 10:30) 🍴 Cafés (£) 🚗 Service taxi from Aswan, private taxi taking in Kom Ombo in convoy

6 Sehel

This small island commands superb views over what was the white water of the First Cataract, where the Nile is channelled through dramatic outcrops of granite. Ancient Egyptians believed this to be the source of the Nile, from where the river flowed south into Nubia and north into Egypt. The Nile gods Hapy and Khnum were thought to live in a cave under the rapids from where they controlled the annual flood. Locals made offerings on Sehel for a good harvest and travellers prayed here for a safe return, as the area remained a danger for anyone travelling south until the Aswan dams were built.

These days the waters are less stormy and the *felucca* ride is the main attraction. However, two hills made up of granite boulders reveal more than 250 roughly carved ancient Egyptian inscriptions that record expeditions upstream. The Famine Stele, on top of one of the hills, relates how King Zoser (➤ 22) ended a seven-year famine by building a temple on Sehel Island.

On the other side of Sehel the Nubian villages, with their lovely gardens, are also worth exploring.
➕ 202 C3 ✉ 4km (2.5 miles) upriver from Aswan 🍴 Some villagers offer tea for *baksheesh* (£) 🚤 Accessible only by *felucca* or motorboat from Aswan (➤ 128)

○ Luxor

1
2
3
4
6 5
7
8
9

Cruises on Lake Nasser

Several luxurious cruise boats make three-, four- or seven-day tours from Aswan to Abu Simbel, stopping at the other Nubian temples. Happily, numbers have been limited. Choose between the stylish *Eugenie* (www.eugenie.com.eg) and *Qasr Ibrim* (www.kasribrim.com.eg) boats, run by Belle Epoque Travel (tel: 02-516 9653), or *Prince Abbas* (tel: 097-231 4660) or *Nubian Sea* (tel: 012-322 2065).

🄼 Lake Nasser

The building of the Aswan dams buried the Nubian Nile and created this, the world's largest reservoir, stretching more than 500km (310 miles) south of Aswan. The Nubian communities who lived along the Nile for thousands of years lost their homes, land and much of their rich culture to the dams and lake, but many of the ancient monuments were relocated to drier ground, with help from the international community. These include the little-visited Temple of Mandulis at Kalabsha. This healing temple, dedicated to the Nubian fertility god Marul (Mandulis in Greek), was mostly rebuilt during the Ptolemaic-Roman period, which is obvious from the blend of styles on the fine wall carvings. Next door is the photogenic Ptolemaic Kiosk of Kertassi and the small rock-hewn temple of Beit al Wali. This was built in honour of Ramses II, who is shown on the colourful reliefs in

A cruise on Lake Nasser offers a more peaceful and more relaxing alternative to the traditional Nile cruise

a battle with the rebellious Nubians. The interesting but more remote temple groups of Wadi al Sebua, Dakka and Amada and the fortress site of Qasr Ibrim can only be visited on a luxury cruise, although new roads are being built.

Fishing trips are increasingly popular on the blue waters of the lake, which is home to a few crocodiles, the elusive tiger fish and the Nile perch – one of the largest freshwater fish (► 128).

Kalabsha Temple/Beit al Wali
🗺 202 C2 ✉ Next to the High Dam
🕐 Daily 8–4 🚕 Private taxi, also rented boat from the harbour
💰 Inexpensive

Wadi al Sebua/ Amada/Qasr Ibrim
🗺 202 C2
🕐 Daily 6–6
🚢 Currently accessible by cruise boat only
💰 Inexpensive

Something for the Children

There are no attractions specifically for kids but they might enjoy:
• A *felucca* ride around the islands in Aswan
• The camel market in Daraw (► 122)
• Baby crocodiles in the *souk* (► 127)

Where to... Stay

Prices
The prices are for a double room per night.
£ under 400LE **££** 400–900LE **£££** over 900LE

ASWAN

Elephantine Island Mövenpick ££–£££

Apart from its ugly tower, which dominates Aswan's skyline, the Mövenpick is a comfortable hotel set in lush gardens on quiet Elephantine Island. The spacious rooms have good views of the Nile.

➕ 202 C3 ⊠ **Northern tip of Elephantine Island** ☎ 097-230 3455; www.movenpick-aswan.com

Happi £

This good budget hotel has 64 air-conditioned bedrooms, some with balconies and Nile views. Guests can use the rooftop pool at the Cleopatra Hotel on Sharia al Souk at a discount.

➕ 202 C3 ⊠ **Sharia Abtal at Tahrir** ☎ 097-231 4115; fax: 097-230 7572

Keylani Hotel £

This friendly, centrally located hotel with Internet café, has been popular with visitors for years. The rooms are spotless and comfortable, all with shower, air-conditioning or fan.

➕ 202 C3 ⊠ **25 Sharia Keylani, off main Sharia al Suq** ☎ 097-231 7332; www.keylanihotel.com

Nuba Nile £

This is another good budget option. It is situated near the train station, with simple, clean rooms, some with private bathrooms and air-conditioning. There is a popular café just next door.

➕ 202 C3 ⊠ **Just off Midan al-Mahatta** ☎ 097-231 3267; email: nubanil_hotel@hotmail.com

Old Cataract Hotel £££

Immortalised in the film of Agatha Christie's *Death on the Nile*, this is one of Egypt's most famous hotels. The splendid Moorish building is set in lush gardens and most rooms command stunning views. Some rooms are still impressive, as are the public areas of the hotel. For real indulgence, stay in one of the amazing suites with terraces over the river.

➕ 202 C3 ⊠ **Sharia Abtal al Tahrir** ☎ 097-231 6000; email: h1666@accor-hotels.com

Sarah Hotel ££

Well out of the centre, but quiet and with great views over the first cataract on the Nile and the Western Desert on the other side, this mid-range hotel offers great value for money. The rooms have little local flavour, but they are spacious and clean and some have big balconies. There is a swimming pool.

➕ 202 C3 ⊠ **On a cliff, 1km (0.5 mile) south of Nubian Museum** ☎ 097-232 7234; email: slasheen@menanet.net

ABU SIMBEL

Eskaleh ££

This delightful guesthouse is run by the charming Nubian musician and guide Fikri Kachif. There are just five simple rooms decorated with Nubian furniture, all with a terrace on the lake, a library with books on Nubia and a restaurant serving mostly produce from the organic garden. A totally relaxing atmosphere.

➕ 202 A1 ⊠ **On the waterfront Abu Simbel** ☎ 012-368 0521; email: fikrykachif@genevalink.com

Where to...
Eat and Drink

Prices
Expect to pay per person for a meal, excluding drinks and tips.
£ up to 100LE ££ 100–150LE £££ over 150LE

Don't expect grand cuisine in Aswan. It seems that most tourists visiting Aswan eat on board their cruise ships. Restaurants on the Corniche serve good but basic food, such as *kofta* and vegetable stews. Eateries in the *souk* specialise in cheap snacks such as kebab, *taamiya* or *fuul* sandwiches, and *koshari*. The food in international restaurants in the hotels can be a touch bland.

1902 Restaurant £££
The date refers to the opening of the Old Aswan Dam but the decor is less historical and more pure Oriental-Moorish fantasy, where you can dine in style under a huge dome. The four-course set menu prepared by a French chef is over-priced and not always very inspired, but with a good Oriental show and white-glove service, it makes for a memorable night out.

🕇 202 C3 ⊠ Old Cataract Hotel, Sharia Abtal al Tahrir ☎ 097-231 6000 ⊙ Daily 7pm–midnight, but can be closed to non-residents when the hotel is full

Aswan Moon £
The entrance through a mock castle gate may be alarming, but it gets a lot better after that. The restaurant has a floating extension, and there's also an attractive terrace for watching the sunset over the Nile while smoking a water pipe. By day it's the perfect place for fresh juice, breakfast or a light lunch in the shade. But at night it gets lively and the Nubian music is turned up. The food is simple Egyptian fare, but well prepared (often in earthenware pots), but no alcohol.

🕇 202 C3 ⊠ Corniche al Nil ☎ 097-232 6108 ⊙ Daily 8am–11pm (or until the last customer leaves)

Aswan Panorama £
The food is similar to that of the Aswan Moon, but the restaurant is a lot quieter. This is a good place for breakfast or to while away a lazy afternoon, sitting in the shade of some greenery and looking over Elephantine, with a cold drink and a delicious *roz bi laban* (milky rice pudding with a few drops of rose water). No alcohol is served.

🕇 202 C3 ⊠ Corniche al Nil, opposite the duty free shop ☎ 097-231 6169 ⊙ Daily 8am–11pm (or until the last customer leaves)

Biti Pizza £
Bright and shiny, this eatery serves a really good Egyptian pizza (*fateer*), sweet or savoury, as well as Italian-style pizzas.

🕇 202 C3 ⊠ Near the train station, Midan al Mahatta ☎ No phone ⊙ Daily all day

Chef Khalil ££
A lovely small restaurant, unassuming but popular, this place serves fresh fish from Lake Nasser and the Red Sea. Choose your fish, and after it is weighed, choose how you like it cooked. All fish dishes come with good french fries and salads.

🕇 202 C3 ⊠ Sharia al Suq ☎ 097-231 0142 ⊙ Daily lunch and dinner

Emy £

A popular place on a double-decker boat on the Nile, one of the few to still sell alcohol – perfect for a sundowner. This is also a good place to find the *felucca* captains who gather here at night, if you want to organise a *felucca* trip down the river. The menu features most backpacker's favourites from pancakes to spaghetti bolognese, as well as a few Egyptian stews, but the fresh fruit juices are excellent.

➕ **202 C3** ⊠ **Next to Aswan Moon, Corniche al Nil** 🕐 **Daily 9am–midnight**

Al Masry Restaurant £

Go local in this simple family restaurant that's famed for serving the best grilled *koftas* and kebabs in town. The décor is loud Islamic kitsch, with brightly coloured vinyl tablecloths, plastic flowers and Swiss mountain views on the walls. But the service is friendly and the delicious kebabs come with fresh bread, *tahina* and a good salad. The front room is for men only, but

women and mixed couples are welcome to eat in the family room at the back of the restaurant, which is very popular with locals. However, there is no alcohol.

➕ **202 C3** ⊠ **Sharia al Matar, off Sharia al Souk** ☎ **097-230 2576** 🕐 **Daily noon–11pm (or until the last customer leaves)**

Al Madina £

The Madina is a popular backpackers' dive serving good-value set meals of fish, *kofta* or kebab with salad, *tahina* and rice. No alcohol is served.

➕ **202 C3** ⊠ **Sharia al Souk, near the Cleopatra Hotel** 🕐 **Daily all day**

Nefartiti ££

Pleasant garden restaurant that offers a large buffet of well-prepared and sometimes unusual Egyptian dishes, such as quails, rabbit and pigeon stuffed with rice, and a few Nubian specialities. Make sure you keep some room for the desserts as the sweet pastries are a delight.

➕ **202 C3** ⊠ **New Cataract Hotel, Sharia Abtal al Tahrir** ☎ **097-231 6002** 🕐 **Daily 6:30–10pm**

Nubian House £–££

This delightful restaurant set in a traditional Nubian House overlooks the Nile. The food is mostly Nubian specialities, including meat and vegetable stews, as well as Egyptian dishes. If you can't get into the Old Cataract Hotel, then this is the place to watch the sunset, 700m (766 yards) south of the Nubia Museum on the Nile, while having the tea buffet (4–6pm) and listening to Nubian music.

➕ **202 C3** ⊠ **Corniche, 700m (750 yds) south of Nubia Museum** ☎ **097-236 6226** 🕐 **Daily 11–11**

Nubia House Restaurant ££

Try this for a Nubian night out. There's a three-course set menu followed by a folklore show of regional music and dance. The food is tasty – grilled meats and stews as usual – but this time done the Nubian way, which usually means with more spices. Be warned that it mostly seems to cater for tour groups. No alcohol is served.

➕ **202 C3** ⊠ **Essa Island, south of Elephantine; free shuttle boat from opposite the Egypt Air office** ☎ **097-230 2465** 🕐 **Daily 7–11:30pm**

Old Cataract Terrace ££

A legendary location, this splendid terrace, shaded by traditional Egyptian tent material, is a perfect place to watch the sunset. The view over the Nile, the peaceful garden and the boulders on the tip of Elephantine Island are spectacular, and the afternoon tea (Earl Grey, cakes and sandwiches) is a real treat. It's also a lovely place to while away the evening but beware of the steep minimum charge for non-residents from 4pm to dusk.

➕ **202 C3** ⊠ **Old Cataract Hotel, Sharia Abtal al Tahrir** ☎ **097-231 6000** 🕐 **Daily 8am–11pm, but can be closed to non-residents when the hotel is full**

Where to...
Shop

There's only one place to shop in this area and that's in the **Aswan souk** (market), smaller but certainly far more exotic than most Egyptian markets. The best time to shop is late afternoon, after the heat of the day. The *souk* is relaxed, and the colours, spices and amulets confirm that you are definitely in Africa.

Aswan is famous for *karkadeh*, dried hibiscus flowers which are soaked in boiling water to make a delicious blood-red tea, drunk hot or cold. You can also find good-quality **henna** powder, used by local women to paint their hands and feet, and *fuul sudani*, excellent roast peanuts, at good prices. If buying **spices**, stick to those used locally such as cumin, black pepper and chilli, as other spices are often fake.

The **Nubian baskets** make good wall decorations when you get home, and look out for the equally colourful handmade Nubian **skull-caps** that are worn by local men. Everywhere in the *souk* you can find brightly coloured, woven **scarves** that travel well but, contrary to what you'll be told, they may not be silk. In the *souk* you will find a selection of intriguing Nubian and Sudanese charms and sculpture, but the best selection of **African beads** and **crafts**, including old kaftans and Nubian baskets, is available from **Hanafy Bazaar** (41 Corniche al Nil; tel: 097-231 4083/212 6630), who specialises in genuine Nubian and Beshari products. For something very different visit **Atelier du Palmier** (16 rue al Berba, Ksar al Hagar; tel: 012-316 9547; atelierdupalmier@hotmail.com) where local artesan Amer Awadalla creates unique furniture and light shades from palm fronds. His workshop is open by appointment only, but definitely worth the effort.

Where to...
Be Entertained

Aswan is a quiet and pleasant provincial town. Most tourists are more than occupied with sight-seeing during the day, or lying by the hotel pool late afternoon. The best entertainment is probably to stroll along the Corniche and watch the parade of locals who come to do exactly the same thing, often dressed in their Sunday best. The Nile offers a shifting view at all times of the day, but is particularly spectacular at sunset or later at night when several sites are floodlit. The best place to go for a drink is one of the terraces beside the Nile.

Swimming

Aswan is often hot, and temperatures are even pleasantly warm in winter, so a dip in a pool is usually welcome. It's not advisable to swim in the Nile, not necessarily because of the crocodiles (although some have been spotted north of the High Dam), but because of the serious threat of bilharzia – a common yet chronic waterborne disease caused by parasitic flatworms.

Foreigners are not allowed in the public pool on the Corniche, so you'll have to resort to hotel pools. For a fee, non-residents can use the small rooftop pool at the **Cleopatra Hotel**, or the large but more expensive pools of the **Basma** and **Isis Island** hotels. At quiet times you might also get into the **Mövenpick**'s pool on Elephantine Island.

Felucca Trips

One of the best ways to enjoy Aswan and the islands on the Nile is to take a *felucca*, particularly just before sunset, when the light works its magic. Boats are moored all along the Corniche and you can just turn up and leave at once, after agreeing on a price. The usual trip sails around the islands of Elephantine and Kitchener and past the Mausoleum of the Aga Khan, but another slightly longer, and even more beautiful, trip goes to Sehel Island (▶ 122).

The most romantic way to get to Luxor from Aswan is to sail by *felucca* or *dahabeyya*. It's probably also more practical than travelling by road, because you don't have to travel in an armed convoy. The journey takes four to seven days, and you'll visit the temples of Kom Ombo, Edfu and Esna on the way, eating and sleeping on the boat.

The tourist office in Aswan lists official prices for all the different excursions and can help you arrange trips with reliable boat captains. Always take enough water and protect yourself from the sun. You'll also need to buy provisions from the food market around the railway station and Sharia al Suq.

Fishing

Fishing is popular on Lake Nasser (▶ 123), as it contains some of the largest freshwater fish in the world, including the Nile perch (which can weigh up to 200kg/440 pounds). **Lake Nasser Adventure** (tel: 012-240 5897; www.lakenasseradventure.com) is run by a Frenchman and a Nubian, both passionate about fishing and the area. They organise fishing safaris and trips into the rarely visited south of the Eastern desert. The **African Angler**, run by former Kenyan safari guide Tim Bailey, offers a range of outings, including week-long fishing safaris. Contact them through Abercrombie & Kent, Cairo (tel: 02-394 7735) or in Aswan (tel: 097-230 9748; www.africanangler.co.uk).

Sound and Light Show at Philae

There are two or three performances of the spectacular *son et lumière* at the temple of Philae per day, when a 60-minute tour leads through the dramatically floodlit temple to the tunes of a rather melodramatic soundtrack. The tourist office has a timetable of shows in several foreign languages, or you can check online at www.sound-light.egypt.com. You can buy tickets at the Shallal dock and also get a ferry across to the site (tel: 02-385 2880).

Music and Dance

Most live Nubian music is performed at Nubian weddings. As the singers and band are a major part of the wedding expenses, the bridegroom often invites plenty of friends and relatives, charging them about 10LE a head. Foreign guests are thought to bring good luck to the couple, so you may well be invited to join in the week-long celebrations. A similar offering of money will be more than welcome. But beware of occasional touts who invite foreigners to weddings in their village, get them drunk or stoned and then rob or cheat them.

The **Nubian Folk Troupe** performs at the austere-looking building of the Palace of Culture (tel: 097-231 3390) on the Corniche daily from 9:30 to 11pm from October until March, and all through Ramadan. The show, which is popular with locals, includes story-telling, Nubian stick dancing and traditional wedding and harvest songs. A nightly show of live Nubian music is also held at the Nubia House Restaurant (▶ 126).

The nightclubs at the **New Cataract Hotel** (Sharia Abtal al Tahrir, tel: 097-231 6002) and the **Elephantine Island Mövenpick Hotel** (Elephantine Island, tel: 097-231 4666) put on a floor show for tourists with Western and Nubian music, while the **Isis Hotel** (Corniche, tel: 097-232 4744) offers a nightly disco (except Mondays) which plays Western music.

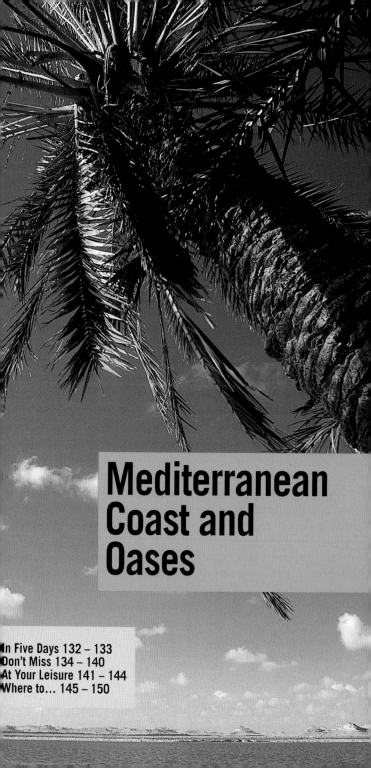

Mediterranean Coast and Oases

Getting Your Bearings

Although most foreigners left at the time of the Revolution in 1952, Alexandria retains something of its cosmopolitan flair. The city has been undergoing something of a cultural revival since the opening of the new Bibliotheca Alexandrina. The mix of the underlying ancient history and the vibe of a modern Arab Mediterranean city makes for a unique and pretty exciting place to spend a few days.

شارع الميناء الشرقية

RUE EL MINA EL SHARKIA

Because it's been inhabited continuously since antiquity, most historic monuments have disappeared beneath the sea or the modern city, so the National Museum of Alexandria is the best place to start a visit. Other layers will be revealed as you walk the downtown streets, which follow the ancient pattern.

The rest of the coast seems to have rejected its links to the Mediterranean and become 100 per cent Egyptian. What was a pristine sandy coastline has been developed into a string of mediocre resorts aimed at Egyptian holiday-makers. The Western Desert oases, some of which were important agricultural centres in Roman times, have their own idiosyncratic character because of their long isolation. Roads in the Western Desert are relatively recent. Before them, the oases – separated from each other by hundreds of kilometres of desert and cut off from the Nile Valley – were accessible only by camel caravans. Life in the oases is slow and traditions die hard. Siwa in particular has retained its very distinct character. A road was laid in the early 20th century, but it's only in the last few years that travellers no longer require a special permit to get there. But with the advent of television, the growth of desert tourism and the Egyptian government's plan to relocate people from the crowded Nile valley to the oases, change is at an alarming rate.

Alexandria's market behind Midan Tahrir offers a fascinating array of produce

Salum
Sidi Barrani
Marsa Matruh
4
Daba
Sidi Abd
al Rahman
al Alamein **3**
ALEXANDRIA
2
Rashid
Damanhur
Tanta
Benha
**Wadi Natrun
Monasteries** **1**
Giza **CAIRO**
Qara
▼ -133m
Qattara Depression
Siwa
5
Siwa Oasis
Faiyum
Oasis
Faiyum
Beni Suef
Nile
0   150 km
0   100 miles
al Bawiti
Harra
6 **Bahariya
Oasis**
Maghagha
Beni Mazar
Minya
Mallawi
W   e   s   t   e   r   n
Qasr Farafra **7** **Farafra Oasis**
Asyut
D   e   s   e   r   t
Tahta
Sohag
Nile
al Qasr
Mut **8**
**Dakhla
Oasis**
Kharga
Mahariq
9 **Kharga Oasis**

**Colourful fishing boats
in Alexandria's Eastern
Harbour**

★ **Don't Miss**
2 **Alexandria** ➤ 134
5 **Siwa Oasis** ➤ 138

At Your Leisure

This is a tour of two extremes. Enjoy the pleasures and delights of the ancient and modern city of Alexandria for two days, then experience the freedom of the desert and the tranquillity of the oasis of Siwa.

Mediterranean Coast and Oases in Five Days

Day One

Morning
Our first stop in **2** **Alexandria** (➤ 134–137) must be the **National Museum of Alexandria** (➤ 136) as only here and at the Roman Odeon (➤ 136), in the city centre, can you really get a feel of what the city once was. Take a taxi or walk along the Corniche to the **Bibliotheca Alexandrina** (➤ 137) for a visit and have a light lunch at the Hilton Café on the site.

Afternoon
Hire a taxi for two hours to visit the Serapeum and **Pompey's Pillar** (➤ 136) and the nearby catacombs of **Kom al Shuqafa** (➤ 135). Back in downtown Alexandria, stroll through the streets admiring the grand facades of 19th-century buildings or sniffing out antiques in the **Attarin junk shops** (➤ 149). Have a drink in the Sofitel Alexandria Cecil Hotel lounge (➤ 145) and walk along the Corniche to one of the fish restaurants. The dome of Abu al Abbas Mosque is pictured below.

Day Two

Morning
Leave by car or taxi to **4** **Marsa Matruh** (➤ 142), a journey of about three hours, and stop for a simple lunch and then a swim in the brilliantly clear sea at the small resort of Sidi Abd al Rahman.

Afternoon
Continue to Marsa Matruh and visit the little town on foot, or check out the nearby beaches of Cleopatra or Agiba before returning to Marsa Matruh for dinner at the Beausite Restaurant on the beach.

Day Three

Morning

Drive to **5 Siwa** (pictured above and right, ► 138–140), a journey of about four hours through the desert, and arrive in time for lunch at the Kenooz restaurant (► 149).

Afternoon

A half-hour walk through splendid palm groves leads to **Aghurmi** where Alexander the Great consulted the Oracle (► 140). Continue to Cleopatra's Bath, where you can stop for a drink at the cafeteria. A further 10 minutes through the palms is Gebel Dakrur, with wonderful views over Siwa. Return by foot along the first dirt road for about half an hour, and back in town climb up to Shali (the old town) for some more superb views.

Day Four

Morning

Visit on foot the **Traditional Siwan House** (► 139), then take the Matruh road out of town and continue walking for about 30 minutes to the tombs of **Gebel al Mawta** (► 140). Have lunch back in town.

Afternoon

Take an organised tour into the desert around Siwa for a chance to see the sand dunes and explore the saltwater lakes and hot-water pools.

Day Five

Take a bus or taxi back to Alexandria (about seven hours), stopping *en route* for lunch and a swim in Marsa Matruh.

❷

Alexandria

Modern Alexandria may be a little worn, but its name still conjures up some dazzling images. Alexander the Great founded the city in AD 331; beautiful Cleopatra had her passionate love affair with Mark Antony here; the Alexandrian Library was the intellectual centre of the ancient world; while the lighthouse, the Pharos, was one of the seven wonders of the world.

The city's wealth and glory slowly vanished after the Arab conquest of AD 641, but in the 19th century Alexandria regained some of its wealth and grandeur, growing rich from trading in cotton and adopting the cosmopolitan air evoked in Lawrence Durrell's series of novels, the *Alexandria Quartet*.

But in spite of all its history and legends, modern Alexandria reveals very little of its past. Fragments of Cleopatra's Palace and the Pharos have recently been found in the Mediterranean, but for centuries rulers and archaeologists have searched in vain for Alexander the Great's tomb.

Kom al Dikka held about 800 spectators

Alexandria Tourist Office
✚ 200 A5 ✉ Midan Saad Zagloul ☎ 03-485 1556 🕐 Daily 8:30–6

National Museum of Alexandria
✉ 110 Tariq al Hurriya ☎ 03-483 5519 🕐 Daily 9–4; public holidays 9–3 💵 Moderate

Kom al Dikka (Roman Odeon)
✉ Behind Cinema Amir, Sharia Salman Yusuf ☎ 03-486 5106 🕐 Daily 9–5 💵 Inexpensive

Pompey's Pillar
✉ Sharia Amud al Sawari, Karmouz 🕐 Daily 9–4 🚋 Tram 16 from Ramla 💵 Inexpensive

Bibliotheca Alexandrina
✉ Corniche al Bahr ☎ 03-483 9999; www.bibalex.org 🕐 Sun–Thu 11–7, Fri–Sat 3–7 💵 Moderate; separate charge for all museums

Kom al Shuqqafa Catacombs
✉ Off Sharia Amud al Sawari, Karmouz ☎ 03-484 5800 🕐 Daily 9–5 💵 Inexpensive

Cavafy Museum
✉ 4 Sharia Sharm al Sheikh, off Sharia Sultan Hussein, Downtown ☎ 03-486 1598 🕐 Tue–Sun 10–4 💵 Inexpensive

Fort Qaytbey
✉ Western end of the Corniche ☎ 03-486 5106 🕐 Closed for restoration until further notice 🚋 Tram 15 from Ramla

Graeco-Roman Museum
✉ Sharia Mathaf al Romani ☎ 03-486 5820/487 6434; www.grm.gov.eg 🕐 Daily 9–5, closed Fri 11:30–1:30 💵 Moderate

The Corniche curves around the Bay of Alexandria

Watch Your Step

You may not see so much of it, but Alexandria's past is always beneath your feet, and every construction site reveals new sections of the hidden city, yielding the remains of buildings, statues and pottery. Elsewhere, holes suddenly appear in the city's roads, leading to the discovery of underground treasures. Egypt's largest Roman burial site, the eerie catacombs of **Kom al Shuqafa**, were discovered when a donkey fell through a hole in the ground. These 2nd-century AD catacombs are decorated in a uniquely Alexandrian blend of Egyptian, Greek and Roman motifs, even including some bearded serpents, images of Medusas and the Egyptian gods Anubis and Sobek dressed as Roman legionnaires.

City Highlights

At first, modern Alexandria, a sprawling and overpopulated town, may seem disappointing, but time spent discovering its hidden splendours is well rewarded. The fascinating **National**

Could Alexandria's founder, Alexander the Great, be resting under this busy street?

Below: A gem from the National Museum of Alexandria.
Bottom: A sphinx guards the giant granite column of Pompey

Museum of Alexandria clearly illustrates the city's history from antiquity until the modern period, through well-displayed artefacts. The museum is laid out chronologically over three floors: the basement is devoted to the pharaonic period, the ground floor to the Graeco-Roman period, which includes a sphinx and other sculptures found in the Eastern Harbour, and the top floor covers Coptic, Muslim and modern Alexandria.

The old **Graeco-Roman Museum** has one of most comprehensive collections of Graeco-Roman art in the world, so typical for Alexandria, with more than 40,000 objects. The collection of *tanagra*, very realistic terracotta figures from the Hellenistic period, alone is worth a visit, and so are the three heads of Alexander the Great, the city's founder, and the massive basalt Apis bull.

Kom al Dikka ("Pile of Rubble"), a short walk away from the National Museum, has an elegant 2nd-century AD Roman Odeon with a marble seating area and the remains of a mosaic floor. A Graeco-Roman street nearby passes late-Roman ruins. The Roman Villa of the Birds has been uncovered, with large floor mosaics (charge: inexpensive).

In the Karmouz neighbourhood is **Pompey's Pillar**, a 27m (88-foot) pink granite column, from around AD 295. Crusaders attributed it to Pompey, but the pillar probably supported a statue of Emperor Diocletian (AD 284–305). Two granite sphinxes and statues are the only other remains of the fabled Serapeum on Rhakotis, the settlement Alexander the Great developed into Alexandria. The Serapeum housed the magnificent temple of Serapis and the Second Alexandrian Library, containing Cleopatra's private collection of 200,000 manuscripts. Until destroyed by Christians in AD 391, this was an important intellectual centre.

ALEXANDRIA: INSIDE INFO

Top tips Take time to explore the back streets downtown and in **Attarin** (➤ 149), to catch glimpses of history both in the monuments, the people and the junk shops.
• Escape the urban sprawl in the **Muntazah Gardens** east of downtown, or in the elegant **Antionadis Gardens**.

Hidden gems Underwater archaeology has revealed that much of ancient Alexandria lies submerged near Fort Qaytbey and in the Eastern Harbour. There were vague plans for the world's first underwater museum but in the meantime a small company **Alexandria Dive** (tel: 03-483 2042; www.alexandria-dive.com) offers diving tours in both of these sites.

Ones to miss If time's short skip the **Naval Museum** in Qaytbey and the five very faded tombs from 250 BC in the Anfushi Necropolis.

Downtown Alexandria

Alexander's city had two main streets – Canopic and Soma – which survive in the downtown streets of al Hurriya and Nabi Danyal. The area opposite the old-style Sofitel Alexandria Cecil Hotel (➤ 145) was the site of the Ptolemies' palaces and of the Caesareum, Cleopatra's monument to Mark Antony. Fragments of a royal palace, perhaps Cleopatra's, were discovered in the waters of the Eastern Harbour. The impressive modern building of the new **Bibliotheca Alexandrina** (Alexandrian Library) is intended to be an international centre of knowledge like its ancient ancestor, designed to hold 8 million books in many languages. The book collection is far from complete yet, but the complex includes a good manuscript collection, a small antiquities museum, a concert hall and a planetarium.

The **Nabi Danyal mosque** on Sharia Nabi Danyal houses the tombs of Danyal al Maridi and Lukman the Wise, and some believe Alexander's tomb is in the crypt. Nearby, the former home of Greek poet Constantine Cavafy (1863–1933) has become the **Cavafy Museum**, a place of pilgrimage for his many fans. At the western end of the Corniche, 15th-century **Fort Qaytbey** and the Naval Museum covers the site of the 125m (410-foot) high Pharos, built in 279 BC by Sostratus for Ptolemy II, and destroyed by earthquakes in the 11th and 14th centuries. Underwater excavations have revealed fragments of the Pharos.

Mashrabiya windows at the Abu al Abbas Mosque on the Corniche

Taking a break in downtown Alexandria

TAKING A BREAK

Downtown Alexandria is a great place to stroll or hang out in one of the excellent pâtisseries or bars immortalised in Durrell's *Alexandria Quartet* and Cavafy's poems.

5

Siwa Oasis

The oasis of Siwa is one of the most remote and idyllic places in Egypt, where lush palm groves and gardens appear like a mirage from the surrounding desert of rocks and sand. Here you'll find freshwater springs and natural hot pools, salt lakes and the dangerous sand dunes of the Great Sand Sea.

In late antiquity Siwa was famous for its Oracle of Amun, whose predictions were sought by people all over the ancient world. It was important enough for the Persian emperor Cambyses to send an army of 50,000 to conquer the oasis and destroy the Oracle. The troops were subsequently lost in the desert, thus enhancing the Oracle's reputation. In 331 BC the young Alexander the Great, having conquered Egypt, travelled eight days from Alexandria to consult the Oracle, hoping to confirm his divine birth.

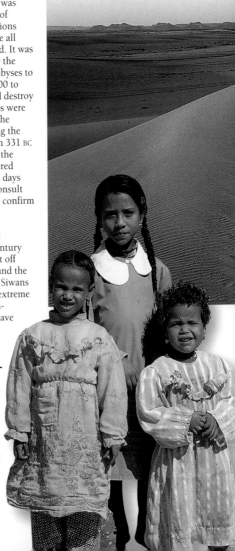

Splendid Isolation

Until the late 19th century Siwa was virtually cut off from the Nile valley and the rest of the world and Siwans had a reputation for extreme hostility towards non-Muslims. They still have their own language, Siwi, and their own customs and their own rituals.

✚ 198 A4
Siwa Tourist Office
✉ At beginning of Tariq Meisa Matrouh, Siwa Town ☎ 046-460 1338
🕐 Sat–Thu 9–5

Traditional Siwan House
✉ Siwa Town
🕐 Sat–Wed 10–noon
💲 Inexpensive

The impressive medieval Shali, founded by a Berber tribe, still dominates Siwa town

Change came quickly in the 1980s with a new road from Marsa Matruh and the arrival of electricity and, therefore, television. This and the advent of tourism have made dramatic changes to the villages of Siwa, and unfortunately not always for the best. Siwans now welcome foreigners, but they are proud of their traditions and keen to preserve them.

In and Around Siwa

Siwa town is still a sleepy and laid-back place, even though much of its old mudbrick architecture has been replaced by shabby breeze-block structures and hotels. The **Traditional Siwan House**, in a traditional mudbrick building, contains a beautiful collection of silver jewellery and costumes.

The new town is overshadowed by the ruins of **Shali**, the fortified hilltop town founded in 1203 and inhabited until

1926, when a heavy rainstorm caused serious damage and forced the inhabitants out. Shali's melting labyrinth of houses, storerooms and passages disintegrates more with every rainfall.

Just outside the town is **Gebel al Mawta** ("Mountain of the Dead"), a sculpted rock formation pitted with ancient Egyptian and Graeco-Roman tombs, only four of which are open to the public. To the south is **Aghurmi**, an older fortified settlement under which Siwans believe a large amount of treasure is buried. The 6th-century BC **Temple of the Oracle**, built over an older temple dedicated to Amun, is where Alexander the Great sought confirmation that he was Zeus or Amun's son, but he died before revealing what the Oracle told him.

A walk through the palm groves, past **Cleopatra's Bath**, leads to **Gebel Dakrur** where rheumatics are buried in the hot sands to help ease their condition. A few kilometres from Siwa is the edge of the **Great Sand Sea**, stretching more than 800km (500 miles) south and with dunes up to 150m (500 feet) high.

TAKING A BREAK

The best restaurants in Siwa are **Kenooz** (➤ 149) and **Abdu's** (➤ 148). These are also good places to meet desert guides or to find an organised tour into the desert.

Below: Siwans waiting for hot pitta bread at the bakery and sweet shop

SIWA OASIS: INSIDE INFO

Top tips The oasis is still very **traditional**, so dress modestly out of respect for local customs. Women in particular should keep arms and legs covered and avoid wearing bikinis in the local baths. Also, avoid shows of affection in public.
• Don't bring **alcohol** into the oasis.
• The **best time to visit** is during spring and autumn when the climate is most pleasant. In winter the days are usually fine enough but the nights can get very chilly, while from May onwards it's just hot, hot, hot.
• Around the full moon in October there's a big **harvest festival** on Gebel Dakrur that lasts for three days.
• Friday is **market day** in the main square.

In more depth The Great Sand Sea, 800km (500 miles) of amazing sand dunes, starts just outside Siwa and it is a sight to behold. **Take a tour** with one of the desert guides who will slide down the dunes in his four-wheel drive or take you to one of the cool lakes or hot water springs. One of the best is Abdallah Baghi, who is passionate and very knowledgeable about Siwa and the desert (tel: 03-460 1111; email: shali55@hotmail.com).

At Your Leisure

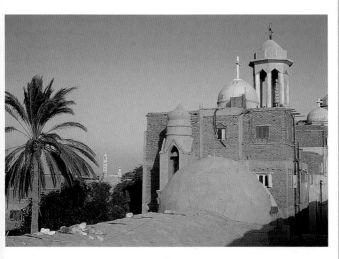

1 Wadi Natrun Monasteries

Wadi Natrun played an important role in Egypt's Coptic Church, as for more than 1,500 years its popes have invariably been elected from these monasteries. The monastic tradition runs strong in the Coptic religion, and many educated Coptic men choose to retreat at some time during their life. One of Wadi Natrun's earliest monks was St Bishoi (AD 320–407), and more than 100 monks and hermits now live at his monastery. Deir al Suryani, originally inhabited by Syrian monks and formerly the home of the current Pope Shenouda III, has superb frescoes in its Church of the Virgin. Here also is St Bishoi's Cave where the saint's hair was tied to the ceiling to keep him standing. The church of the remote Deir al Baramus has a beautiful iconostasis, while Deir Abu Maqar (closed to the public) is the resting place of many Coptic popes.

🕂 200 B4 ⊠ Valley off Cairo–Alexandria desert road ☎ Deir Anba Bishoi: 02-592 4448; Deir al Baramus: 02-592 2775; Deir al Suryani: 02-572 3658 🕔 Daily 9–6 (Deir al Baramus

The Wadi Natrun monasteries are often a place of retreat for Coptic professionals

Fri–Sun 9–5). Lent restrcitions 🍴 Wadi Natrun Resthouse on desert road (£–££) 🚌 Cairo–Alexandria bus via desert road stop at Resthouse, then pick-ups to the monasteries 🖑 Donations welcome

3 Al Alamein

This tiny coastal village was the site of the battle in 1942 that changed the course of World War II. Winston Churchill claimed "Before Alamein we never had a victory. After Alamein we never had a defeat". More than 70,000 soldiers were wounded and 11,000 killed in the battle between the German Afrika Korps under Field Marshal Rommel and Field Marshal Montgomery's British Eighth Army. The Commonwealth War Cemetery, overlooking the battlefield, is an eerie and moving place containing more than 7,000 graves. The smaller German and Italian cemeteries lie farther west. The War Museum houses a small collection of artillery, uniforms, maps and models related to the North Africa Campaign and the Battle of al Alamein.

🔲 198 C5 ✉ 106km (65 miles) west of Alexandria 🕐 Museum daily 9–4 ☎ 046-410 0031; Commonwealth War Cemetery daily 9–4 🍴 Alamein Resthouse (£) 🚌 Alexandria–Marsa Matruh buses stop near the War Museum, but there's no public transport to the cemeteries 💰 Museum inexpensive, cemeteries free

❹ Marsa Matruh

Egypt's entire northern coast is being developed into an unattractive sprawl of resorts for Egyptian holiday-makers, and the once sleepy fishing village of Marsa Matruh has not escaped. During the summer its fantastic beaches are overcrowded with Egyptian families, fully dressed even in the water. And without sufficient services to cope with this influx, both beach and sea are polluted. Slightly cleaner is Rommel's Beach, where the World War II Field Marshal known as the Desert Fox reputedly took a dip.

The nearby Rommel

Museum has some of his memorabilia, including his coat. The best beaches are farther out of town. Cleopatra's (or the Lovers') Beach has some interesting rock formations and, according to legend, Cleopatra's Bath is where the exotic queen took a dip with her lover Mark Antony. Agiba (Miracle) Beach seems to deserve its name for the beauty of its dazzling turquoise water.

🔲 198 B5 ✉ 290km (180 miles) west of Alexandria, 512km (318 miles) from Cairo ☎ Tourist office: 046-493 1841 🍴 Beausite Restaurant (££) 🚌 From Cairo, Alexandria and Siwa ✈ From Cairo 🚆 From Cairo

Great Natural Wonders in the Oases

- Surreal sculptures in the White Desert
- Acres of palm trees and gardens in Siwa
- Sand dunes near Mut in Dakhla
- Hot springs in all the oases

❻ Bahariya Oasis

In ancient times Bahariya was a considerable agricultural centre, famous for its wines, but with the decline of the Roman Empire in the 4th century AD the rich fields and vineyards turned to desert. Nowadays several villages make up the oasis, but the main town is al Bawiti, with over 30,000 inhabitants. Over the last few years the town has seen a huge increase in tourism.

In 1996 a donkey dropped into a hole near the temple of Alexander the Great, and thus uncovered the "Valley of the Golden Mummies", a vast cemetery with probably over 10,000 mummies. So far about 250 Graeco-Roman mummies have been excavated, and 10 of them are on show at the new **museum**. The mummies are richly decorated but what is stunning are the realistically painted masks that cover the faces, like the famous Fayoum paintings.

The **Oasis Heritage Museum** has a display of local costumes, clay figures representing scenes of traditional oasis life and a small shop selling local crafts.

Towards the Roman well of Ain Bishnu are the mudbrick houses of Bawiti's old quarter. Hot water (30°C/86°F) flows into the palm-filled gardens. Farther along is the old settlement of al Qasr, which was built over the ancient capital. Notable are the ruins of the Temple of Bes (664–525 BC) and a Roman triumphal arch.

A trip into the desert, to the hot springs in the surrounding Black Desert, or the amazing rock formations in the White Desert, is a must.

🚰 198 C4 ✉ 330km (205 miles) southwest of Cairo ☎ Tourist office 02-847 3835 ⏰ Museum daily 8–2; sites 8–2, but no fixed hours 🍴 Popular Restaurant (£) 🚌 Buses daily from Cairo; from Farafra Sat, Mon and Thu 💰 Moderate: one charge for all sites

A farmer working in the fields near Bahariya Oasis

🟦 Farafra Oasis

This is the most isolated of Egypt's oases. Known as the "Land of the Cow" in ancient times, Farafra's cows look uncannily like those depicted in tomb paintings. Qasr Farafra is the only settlement in this beautiful oasis, and its only sight is Badr's Museum, a pretty mudbrick structure built by the eponymous local artist. Farafra's main attraction is its peace and quiet, especially in the palm groves and gardens, and its location near the spectacular White Desert, with its bizarre, eroded, white rock formations, shaped like moon craters or icebergs. Ain Besai, 15km (9 miles) from town, has ancient rock tombs and a cold freshwater spring.

🚰 198 B3 ✉ 180km (112 miles) south of al Bawiti, Bahariya ⏰ Museum 8:30–4, inexpensive 🍴 El Badawiyya Hotel restaurant (£–££) 🚌 Buses from Cairo, Bahariya and Dakhla daily except Wed

🟦 Dakhla Oasis

Recent excavations have shown that the lush oasis of Dakhla has been inhabited continuously since prehistoric times, when it was the site of a vast lake. Mut, the ancient and

The medieval city of al Qasr at Dakhla Oasis

Rock formations rise from the White Desert

modern capital, has an old citadel, hot sulphur pools and a small Ethnographic Museum with scenes of oasis life. West of Mut are the colourful ancient Muwazaka Tombs, with mummies intact, and the 1st-century AD Roman temple of Deir al Haggar.

Dakhla's medieval capital, al Qasr, is a charming place lined with mudbrick houses. The 12th-century mosque of Nasr al Din has an unusual mudbrick minaret. Next to the pottery factory you can see how mudbricks are still made in the ancient way.

The picturesque village of Balat, on the way to Kharga, also retains its medieval Islamic charm. Farther along this road, just beyond Teneida, are strange rock formations with prehistoric rock paintings of antelopes, fish and giraffes.

➕ 198 C2 ✉ 310km (193 miles) southeast of Farafra ☎ Tourist office: 092-782 0407 🕐 Museum Sat–Thu 8–2 🍴 Ahmad Hamdy (£) 🚌 Daily buses from Cairo, Asyut, Kharga, Farafra and Bahariya 🎟 Mostly free or inexpensive

🟑 Kharga Oasis

Kharga Town, the capital of the New Valley, has unfortunately retained little of its original character and charm, but there are still several individual attractions. The New Valley Museum houses a small collec-

tion of well-labelled archaeological finds from local excavations. North of town is the ancient capital Hibis, its 6th-century BC temple built by the Persian emperor Darius I and dedicated to Amun. The nearby Roman Temple of Nadura commands fabulous views over the oasis and the desert, while the impressive Bagawat Necropolis has finely decorated mudbrick Christian tombs dating from the 3rd to the 7th centuries. The ruins of the monastery of Deir al Kashef overlook the crossroads of two major caravan routes.

➕ 199 D2 ✉ 195km (121 miles) east of Dakhla ☎ Tourist office 092-921 206 🕐 Museum daily 8–4; Bagawat Necropolis daily 8–5 🍴 Pioneers Hotel (£–££) 🚌 Daily from Cairo, other oases and Asyut, Minya and Beni Suef

Where to... Stay

Prices
The prices are for a double room per night.
£ under 400LE **££** 400–900LE **£££** over 900LE

Alexandria has some wonderful old-style and sumptuous new hotels, but accommodation elsewhere along the coast is usually basic. Some oasis hotels are set in luscious palm groves, but most are simple.

ALEXANDRIA

Four Seasons Alexandria £££
The new Four Seasons hotel (opened summer 2007) has dramatically change the hotel scene in Alex. With more than 100 spacious rooms overlooking the Mediterranean, it is by far the most luxurious hotel in town. There are nine superb restaurants to choose from, a huge European spa, a state-of-the-art fitness centre and a private cleaned-up beach.
✠ 200 A5 ⊠ San Stefano Mall, 2nd floor, 388 Tariq al Geish, Zizinya
☎ 03-469 0141;
www.fourseasons.com/Alexandria

Hotel Union £
This excellent budget option has very clean rooms, all with bathrooms and some with a balcony offering great views of the Eastern Harbour. Breakfast is included. Book ahead as this is a popular choice.
✠ 200 A5 ⊠ 164 Sharia 26 July
☎ 03-480 7312

Le Metropole ££–£££
Not so long ago the Metropole was a cheap-and-cheerful alternative to the Cecil Hotel, but it is today a four-star establishment with all modern amenities. Overlooking the old harbour and the Mediterranean Sea, the beautiful art-deco building retains a colonial feel with large, cosy rooms decorated in a sumptuous style. The hotel is well situated in the heart of Alexandria, and has an art collection with paintings by local and international artists, as well as antiques.
✠ 200 A5 ⊠ 52 Sharia Saad Zaghloul
☎ 03-486 4465;
www.paradiseinnegypt.com

Sofitel Alexandria Cecil Hotel £££
For a long time the grandest hotel in Alex and still an institution, the Cecil was immortalised by Lawrence Durrell in his *Alexandria Quartet* novels. It's no longer a celebrity hangout and the renovation was insensitive, but with all that history, the occasional old waiter to tell a story and magnificent sweeping views over the bay, it's still worth the stay. The mirrored tearoom and Monty's bar are a must, but you can give the restaurants a miss, with the selection of better restaurants near by.
✠ 200 A5 ⊠ 16 Midan Saad Zaghloul ☎ 03-487 7173;
www.sofitel.com

SIWA

Adrere Amellal £££
This splendid eco-lodge, on the edge of Siwa Lake, is built in mud and salt against the magical backdrop of the White Mountain. The rooms are simple, but comfortable and really stylish, decorated with local furniture and lit by oil lamps and lots of candles (there is electricity only in the kitchen and

lobby). Drinks are served on the terrace with great views over the lake, and the wonderful chef creates some of the best food in Egypt, fresh from the hotel's own organic oasis' gardens. The pool is a natural spring set in a palm grove.

Activities such as horse-riding, desert safaris and swimming in hot-water pools in the middle of the desert, are all included in the room rate. Rooms must be booked at the Cairo office, so no money is needed within the desert resort.

➕ 198 A4 ⊠ Near the White Mountain, Sidi al-Jaafar, 18km (11 miles) from Siwa Town
☎ 02-736 7879/735 9976;
www.adrereamellal.net

Shali Lodge £–££

In this beautiful mudbrick hotel, set in a lovely palm grove, there are only eight rooms surrounding a small pool. The large rooms are decorated with local furniture, and are pleasant and comfortable. The staff are friendly, and the restaurant Kenooz (▶ 149) is excellent value.

➕ 198 A4 ⊠ Sharia Subukha, Siwa
☎ 046-460 1299; email:
info@eqi.co.eg

OASES AND ELSEWHERE

Aquasun Farafra £–££

Hisham Nessim runs a wonderful hotel in Farafra with 21 chalet-style rooms set in a garden. Every room has its own shady veranda made from palm fronds. The water in the swimming pool comes from the Bir Sitta well, the restaurant serves food from the organic garden, and Hisham organizes interesting tours into the desert, including a search for the lost army of the Persian ruler Cambyses.

➕ 198 B3 ⊠ Bir Sitta, Farafra
☎ 012-211 8632/337 2898
www.eg-westerndesert.com

Desert Lodge ££

Delightful lodge in traditional oasis style, overlooking the old town of al Qasr and the desert. This is definitely the best accommodation in this oasis, and the nicest part of the oasis to be.

➕ 198 C2 ⊠ al Qasr, 29km from Mut, Dakhla ☎ 092-772 7061;
www.desertlodge.net

Nature Camp £

At the foot of the Gebel Dist mountain is this pleasant eco-friendly camp, with candle-lit huts over-looking the desert, and adjacent to the spring of Bir Ghaba. The food is excellent and the owner Ashraf organises great tours into the desert.

➕ 198 C4 ⊠ Bir al Ghaba
☎ 02-347 3643/012-337 5097
email: naturecamps@hotmail.com

Pioneers Hotel £££

One of the few more luxurious options in the oases, this modern rather uninspiring-looking, salmon-pink hotel provides a comfortable base for visitors travelling in the desert. There's a good swimming pool for a cooling dip. The bedrooms are surprisingly spacious and air-conditioned, and have many facilities, including satellite television if you're missing your favourite programmes from back home.

➕ 199 D2 ⊠ Near the temple of Hibis, Kharga ☎ 092-792 7982;
fax: 092-792 7383;
www.solymar-hotels.com

Qasr el Bawity ££–£££

Set at the foot of the black Gebel al Ingleez mountain, and in the middle of a lush palm grove, is this friendly eco-lodge built in tradi-tional oasis style. There are 24 spacious rooms and 4 suites built in local stone, furnished with textiles from the oases and in the garden is a spring-fed swimming pool as well as a hot spring where you can bathe under the stars.

➕ 198 C4 ⊠ At the foot of Gebel al Ingleez, 6km (4 miles) from al Bawiti, Bahariya ☎ 02 847 1880;
www.qasrelbawity.com

Where to...
Eat and Drink

Prices
Expect to pay per person for a meal, excluding drinks and tips.
£ up to 100LE ££ 100–150LE £££ over 150LE

Alexandria may no longer have glamorous restaurants where the likes of the Aga Khan entertained international politicians and famous movie stars, but there are still some pleasant and fun places. Many specialise in fish and shellfish and the cuisine is generally more Greek-Mediterranean or Levantine than Egyptian. Some city bars have a typical port atmosphere with a mixed crowd of locals and visiting sailors. Food along the rest of the coast and in the oases is mostly standard Egyptian fare. In Kharga the only places to eat are in the hotels, the best of which is probably at the Pioneers Hotel (▶146), but even here the food is mediocre.

ALEXANDRIA

Cap d'Or £
This small but delightful art nouveau bar-restaurant is one of a kind. Cap d'Or is probably the type of bar you'd come across in a back street of Marseilles, serving cold beers and tasty, sizzling dishes of shrimps, casseroles and squid stew to the tunes of aged Euro-pop music. The patron races horses, and his clients are mostly laid-back Egyptians and expat residents.

🚩 200 A5 ☒ 4 Sharia Adib, off Sharia Saad Zaghloulm ☎ 03-483 5177 ⓒ Daily noon–2am

Coffee Roastery £–££
Lively and incredibly popular Western-style café-restaurant where you can get a good coffee, fresh juices, sandwiches and salads as well as grilled meats. Large MTV screens and good music attract young Alexandrian students and families, and the place seems to hop all day. A great place to watch new Alexandria in the old part of town.

🚩 200 A5 ☒ 48 Sharia Fuad, Downtown ☎ 03-483 4363 ⓒ Daily 7am–2am

Fish Market ££
Literally on the sea, this is the city's most upmarket fish restaurant with great views over the Med and a huge counter of the latest catch to choose from. Service is efficient and all fish and seafood comes with *mezze* and Oriental rice. Delicious Oriental pastries can be bought from the bakery downstairs.

🚩 200 A5 ☒ Beside the Kashafa Club, Corniche al Bahr ☎ 03-480 5119 ⓒ Daily noon–2am

Greek Club (Club Nautique Hellenique) £–££
As Mediterranean as it gets, the Greek Club has a flair of old Alexandria with a large terrace overlooking the sweeping bay of Alexandria. The food is OK, equally very Mediterranean with fish and fried calamari, but the best thing is to come for a sundowner, cold beer with *mezze*.

🚩 200 A5 ☒ Sharia Qasr Qaytbay, Anfushi ☎ 03-554 4512 ⓒ Daily noon–11pm and serves some relatively expensive, but well-prepared standards such as pasta dishes and chicken and rice to weary desert travellers.

➕ 198 B3 ⊠ Farafra ☎ 092-510 060 ◉ Daily breakfast, lunch and dinner

Beausite Restaurant ££

The menu offers old-fashioned Graeco-Mediterranean food of the sort that once dominated Alexandrian cuisine. This beachside restaurant is spacious, a bit like a very large domestic dining room, and one member of the family of patrons is usually around to welcome newcomers, or to chat to the many returning regulars.

➕ 198 B5 ⊠ Sharia al Shati, Marsa Matruh ☎ 03-493 8555 ◉ Daily breakfast, lunch and dinner

Dunes £

A very relaxed restaurant-bar, Dunes offers a large, interesting menu including vegetable stews, stuffed pigeon, pastas and

➕ 198 A4 ⊠ Siwa Town ☎ 046-460 1243 ◉ Daily breakfast, lunch and dinner

Ahmad Hamdy £

Another popular backpackers' meeting place, serving not only the usual roast chicken, kebabs and vegetable stews, but also delicious fresh lime juice and ice-cold beers.

➕ 198 C2 ⊠ Sharia al-Saura, Mut, Dakhla Oasis ☎ 092-820 767 ◉ Daily 24 hours

Aquasun Farafra £

At this pleasant outdoor restaurant, freshly prepared Egyptian and Western dishes are served. Ingredients are mostly from the restaurant's own organic garden.

➕ 198 B3 ⊠ Bir Sitta, Farafra ☎ 010-667 8099 ◉ Daily 8am–11pm

Al Badawiyya Hotel Restaurant £-££

By far the best option in town, the Badawiyya has a shady courtyard

Qadoura ££

A popular fish restaurant, partly indoors, partly street terrace, this place is often considered to be the best in town, but no alcohol is served. Choose your fish or seafood from the counter and decide how you want it cooked. Specials include crab stew, clams with spaghetti and crayfish. The dishes come with *mezze* and salads.

➕ 200 A5 ⊠ Shari' Bayram et-Tunsi, al-Anfushi ☎ 03-480 0405 ◉ Daily 9am–3am

Seagull Restaurant ££-£££

Worth a trip from the centre of town, this excellent seafood restaurant is in a mock castle on the beach. The fruit and vegetables have been picked from the Seagull's own farm, and the fish is also really fresh. Meat, chicken and pizzas also feature on the menu.

➕ 200 A5 ⊠ Al-Agami Road, off the desert road to Cairo, between al-Max and Agami ☎ 03-440-5575; www.seagullegypt.com ◉ Daily lunch and dinner

Spitfire Bar £

This popular 1970s watering hole caters mainly for a few locals, expats and visiting American marines. The walls are covered with pictures of warships, favourite customers and other memorabilia, the atmosphere is thick with smoke and the music is pure rock and roll. For an unusual Egyptian souvenir, you can buy a Spitfire T-shirt over the counter.

➕ 200 A5 ⊠ 7 Sharia al Bursa al Qadima, off Sharia Saad Zaghloul ☎ 03-480 6503 ◉ Daily noon–1am

THE OASES

Abdu's £

If you're on a tight budget, this simple restaurant is the best in Siwa. It serves traditional Egyptian dishes and vegetable stews, as well as couscous and pizzas, and the yoghurt and pancakes are particularly recommended for breakfast. You might also pick up some useful tips about the oases here.

couscous – some specialities need to be ordered in advance. Most of the day people hang out, drink tea and play backgammon, while puffing on a *sheesha* (water pipe). Sometimes there are performances of live Siwan music at night.

✚ 198 A4 ⊠ **Just off the central square, on Gebel Dakrour road, Siwa town** ☎ 010-653 0372 ⏺ **Daily all day**

Kenooz £

Palm trees feature quite highly in this restaurant. It is set in a shady palm grove so you can eat in the shade of palm trees, and a palm tree grows up through the middle of the interior. The menu features well-prepared, authentic Egyptian and Siwan dishes and good grills, as well as fruit juices and drinks. Go for tea and a water pipe on the delightful roof terrace.

✚ 198 A4 ⊠ **Shali Lodge, Sharia Subukha, Siwa** ☎ 046-460 1299 ⏺ **Daily 8am–midnight**

Popular Restaurant £ (also known as Bayyumi's)

This is the only restaurant outside the hotels in this oasis. Bayyumi, the owner, serves a basic selection of meat and vegetable stews, bread, omelettes, rice and soup. The restaurant is something of a meeting place for both locals and tourists and is the place to go for a cold beer.

✚ 198 C4 ⊠ **Main intersection of al Bawiti, Bahariya** ⏺ **Daily 5:30am–10pm**

Talaa Ranch £

Have dinner in a Bedouin tent, or stay in one of the ranches' 6 beautiful rooms. Sherif organises wonderful camel trips in the surrounding desert while his wife cooks up 4-course meals in Egyptian-Bedouin style. Gorgeous star-watching after dinner, but call ahead as they are not always there.

✚ 198 A4 ⊠ **Gebel Dakrour** ☎ 010-588 6003 ⏺ **Dinner only**

Where to... Shop

ALEXANDRIA

Alexandria has a small *souk* off Midan Tahrir selling cheap clothes, shoes and plastic kitchen tools. Alternatively, the **Attarin Market** has an amazing variety of antiques and junk shops, crammed into a maze of alleys. Many items were left behind by Alexandria's wealthy European families who fled after the Revolution in 1952 (▶ 27). Dealers know the value of their stock, but there's still the occasional bargain. And if not, it's an atmospheric neighbourhood to explore.

THE OASES

Most handicrafts sold in the Western oases are made of camel hair. **Ganoub Traditional Handicrafts**

on Sharia Misr in Bawiti, has a selection of good crafts from the oasis, and the **al Badawiyya Hotel** in Farafra sells camel-hair hand-knitted socks and sweaters made by the locally nick-named "Dr Socks".

Siwa has a rich craft tradition, but most of the older pieces and family heirlooms were sold to foreign collectors long ago, so most of what's on sale is new. Siwans traditionally wear large, heavy silver jewellery, including a wedding ring worn on the middle finger, which covers half the hand. The oasis is also famous for its embroidery, with green, red, orange and black thread. The Adrere Amellal (▶ 145) has a shop where the best and the priciest of Traditional Siwan crafts are sold, but for something more authentic try Siwa Original Handicrafts, next to Abduh's restaurant (▶ 148) and even better Siwa Traditional Handicraft around the corner on the main market square (tel: 010-304 1191) which has really good quality embroidered clothes and shawls as well as other crafts.

Where to be... Entertained

ALEXANDRIA

Alexandria's efforts to sustain a cultural life on a par with Cairo are slowly paying off. The old Sayyid Darwish Theatre (22 Sharia al Hurriya; tel: 03-486 5106) has been beautifully restored, and now houses the small *bijou* **Alexandrian Opera House** with performances of opera and classical concerts. The **Bibliotheca Alexandrina** (▶ 137) is the most important cultural venue in town, hosting international festivals of music, art and culture, as well as major international concerts. The **Alexandria Centre of Arts** (1 Sharia al Hurriya; tel 03-495 6633) has regular exhibitions and weekly concerts. **L'Atelier** (8 Sharia Victor Bassili; tel: 03-482 0526) has regular films, lectures and exhibitions, as

does the British Council (11 Sharia Mahmoud Abou al Ela, Kafr Abdu, Rushdi; Tel: 03-545 6512) and the **Centre Culturel Français** (30 Sharia Nabi Danyal; tel: 03-391 8952). For listings of events and exhibitions check the monthly *Egypt Today*.

Beyond that, nightlife is pretty minimal, although it does perk up in summer. Several hotels offer a belly dance show, the best and most lively being at the **Helnan Palestine** or the nearby **Muntazah Sheraton**.

Most Alexandrian families hang out in one of the city's shopping malls, which offer cafés, restaurants, cinemas and other entertainments.

For the more active, the **Delta Hash House Harriers** organise weekly runs and walks in the countryside around Alexandria on Fridays at 2pm from September to

June. Everybody is welcome and the meeting point is at the Portuguese Cultural Centre, Sharia Kafr Abdu, Rushdi. You can get more information from www.geocities.com/deltahhh and Howard Wellman tel: 03-545 4364.

THE OASES

Nights can be long in the oases, but if you're lucky you may find a cool beer on a café terrace, a water pipe to smoke in the company of locals or a light bright enough to read by. The only daytime entertainment, apart from quiet walks in the palm groves and outings to the desert, is bathing in the hot springs. But springs in town should be avoided, especially by women, as they're too public. More isolated springs are often delightful, but women are not advised to visit these alone. To get to some springs you'll need your own transport or you can join a trip organised by local restaurants

or hotels, on which you'll see some spectacular desert scenery as well. Most will also offer overnight stays in the desert, which are recommended.

If you want to see more of the desert, you'll need careful planning, an experienced desert guide and a four-wheel drive vehicle. A number of reliable and experienced guides have set up travel companies: **Amr Shannon**, has been taking small groups through the Egyptian deserts for more than 20 years. He has his own four-wheel drive and camping equipment, and can also take food for the trip (tel: 02-519 6894). **Egypt Off Road** (tel: 010-147 5462; www.egyptoffroad.com) is a reputable desert operator. The owner Peter Gaballa has taught many expat desert fans how to drive in the desert, and he organises the most fabulous desert tours, including a two-week trip to the Gilf al-Kebir. The experienced rally driver **Hisham Nessin** (tel: 010-188 1368; www.eg-westerndesert.com) arranges some great desert tours of up to two weeks into the Western Desert.

Red Sea & Sinai

Getting Your Bearings

The main attractions of the Red Sea and Sinai are underwater: whatever their experience, there isn't a diver in the world who wouldn't want to explore these crystal waters. The Red Sea is home to some of the world's most amazing coral reefs, with about 1,500 different fish species and 150 types of coral. Much of the coastline of Sinai and the mainland is being developed, partly to exploit the diving possibilities, but also because of the area's year-round sunshine and beautiful beaches. Most resorts have a wide range of accommodation, and internationally accredited dive clubs.

In contrast to the hedonism along its coast, Sinai also has its spiritual side and is holy to Jews, Christians and Muslims. This was where Moses received the Ten Commandments and led the Hebrews across the parted Red Sea. The Holy Family also passed this way after fleeing Herod's wrath. For millennia Christian hermits have settled near Wadi Feiran and Muslim pilgrims have passed by on their way to Mecca.

Surrounding the deep blue waters of the Red Sea is the harsh desert and barren, rugged mountains that inspired Egypt's early Christians to build the first monasteries – St Anthony's and St Paul's. Since ancient times people have also come in search of the gold that is found around Wadi Hammamat, turquoise from mines around Serabit al Khadem and more recently phosphates, which are mined in the Eastern Desert.

The Suez Canal separates Africa and Asia and, although the canal cities have lost most of their lustre, historic Ismailiya and Port Said still make a pleasant change from the rest of the coast.

Sinai's coastline is slowly being developed, except for the wilder shores of Ras Mohamed

Previous page: St Catherine's Monastery is a haven in a harsh landscape

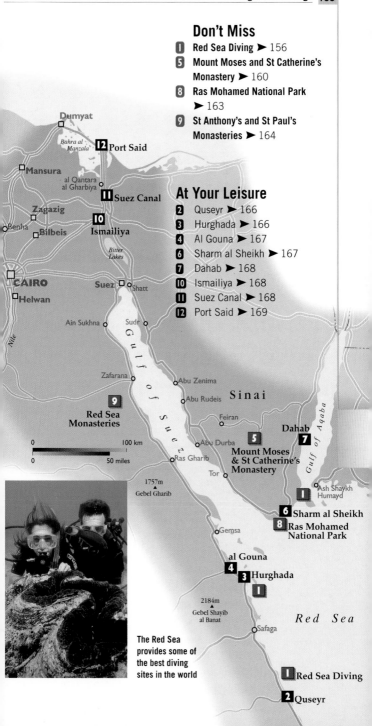

Don't Miss

At Your Leisure

Dumyat
Bahra al Manzala **12** Port Said
Mansura
al Qantara al Gharbiya
11 Suez Canal
Zagazig
10 Ismailiya
Benha
Bilbeis
Bitter Lakes
CAIRO
Helwan
Suez Shatt
Ain Sukhna Sudr
Nile
Zafarana Abu Zenima
Abu Rudeis
S i n a i
9
Red Sea Monasteries
Feiran
Dahab
7
0 ___ 100 km
0 ___ 50 miles
Abu Durba
5
Mount Moses & St Catherine's Monastery
Gulf of Aqaba
Ras Gharib
Tor
Ash Shaykh Humayd
1757m ▲ Gebel Gharib
I
6 Sharm al Sheikh
8 Ras Mohamed National Park
Gemsa
al Gouna
4 **3** Hurghada
I
2184m ▲ Gebel Shayib al Banat
R e d   S e a
Safaga

The Red Sea provides some of the best diving sites in the world

I Red Sea Diving
2 Quseyr

Besides the wonderful diving and snorkelling opportunities, the mountains in the Sinai interior and along the Red Sea coast also have their attractions. From early Christian monasteries to a fantastic barren landscape, they form a perfect contrast to the dazzling colours of the underwater world.

The Red Sea and Sinai in Five Days

Day One

Morning

From your base in **6 Sharm al Sheikh** (➤ 167), hire a car or book a taxi for the day and make the 30-minute drive to **8 Ras Mohamed National Park** (➤ 163). Stop at the Visitors' Centre for a video show of the park's highlights. Divers can take a boat to the Shark Reefs or The Mushroom, while others can snorkel at Anemone City or the Mangrove Channel. You can have lunch at the Visitors' Centre, but the park also has some great places to picnic.

Afternoon

Late afternoon, return to Naama Bay in Sharm al Sheikh (above) for a stroll along the beach walkway and then dinner at the Hilton's fish restaurant.

Day Two

Morning

Once again arrange a car and start with a 90-minute or so drive to **7 Dahab** (➤ 168) where you can stop for a swim or snorkel at the **Canyon** (➤ 157) a bit farther up the coast. Have lunch at one of the numerous beach restaurants that line the bay of Asilah in Dahab.

Afternoon

After lunch drive inland for about two hours to the St Catherine area and start your ascent of **5 Mount Moses** (➤ 160, also known as Mount Sinai) at around 5pm (earlier in winter) in time to watch the spectacular sunset over the desert mountains. Take the long and easy route up the camel path (about three hours) and descend by the muscle-wrenching Steps of Repentance, which will take about 90 minutes. Stay at the monsatery's auberge (➤ 171).

Day Three

Morning

If you missed the sunset, you can see the even more spectacular sunrise by rising very early (check with the monastery for exact times). Later visit **5 St Catherine's Monastery** (below, ➤ 160), and admire its amazing icon collection.

Afternoon

Drive back to Sharm al Sheikh for a late lunch and a swim, then catch the 6pm ferry to Hurghada in time for dinner and an overnight stop.

Day Four

Morning

Pack a picnic for lunch and get a car or taxi for the two-hour drive into the desert to **9 St Paul's Monastery** (➤ 164–165), around 200km (125 miles) north. It's then another 82km (51 miles) to **St Anthony's Monastery**.

Afternoon

After lunch drive back towards Hurghada and stop at Gouna (about 20km/ 12 miles north of Hurghada) for a swim and dinner later in Gouna Town before heading back to Hurghada for the night.

Day Five

Morning

Spend the morning diving in the area (➤ 156–159), or visit **3 Hurghada**'s Red Sea Aquarium (➤ 166) and take a trip in the **Sindbad Submarine** (➤ 166). Have lunch in Hurghada Town, perhaps swapping stories with divers in Papa's Bar (➤ 174).

Afternoon

After lunch it's a six-hour drive to Cairo so that you can arrive there in time for dinner.

Red Sea Diving

For many divers and snorkellers the Red Sea is sheer paradise. Its easily accessible coral reefs are among the most fascinating in the world, with deep coral walls, lagoons and submerged gardens teeming with a variety of sealife. The sun shines most of the year, the sparkling waters are warm and the visibility is generally crystal clear.

The Red Sea lies along the northern section of the Great Rift Valley, which runs from the Jordan Valley, through the Dead Sea, across Kenya and Tanzania and down to Mozambique. The Red Sea is about 1,930km (1,200 miles) long and can reach a depth of 1,850m (6,070 feet).

The Nature of Coral

The sea's tropical reefs are built from corals – primitive animals closely related to sea anemones. Each coral is made up of a mass of minute polyps that grow together in a colony. When a colony dies, another one grows on top of its skeleton, so only the outermost layer of the reef is alive. Corals grow very slowly, around 1–10cm (0.5–4 inches) a year, but the size of a colony can vary from a few centimetres to a few metres. Some are hundreds of years old. The most prolific coral growths are found in shallow, well-lit waters that are warm enough (at least 18.5°C/65°F) to allow zooxanthellae (microscopic plants on which corals depend) to thrive.

The following are among the better-established and more reputable diving centres.

Sharm al Sheikh
✚ 201 F2
Anemone ✉ Pigeon Hotel ☎ 069-360 0999; email: anemone@sinainet.com.eg
Camel Dive Club ✉ Naama Bay ☎ 069-360 0700; www.cameldive.com
Oonas Diving Centre ✉ Naama Bay ☎ 069-360 0581; www.oonasdivers.com
Red Sea Diving College ✉ Naama Bay ☎ 063-360 0145; www.redseacollege.com
Sinai Divers ✉ Ghazala Hotel ☎ 069-360 0697; www.sinaidivers.com

Dahab
✚ 201 F3
Fish & Friends ✉ Masbat ☎ 069-364 0720; www.fishandfriends.com
Nesima Diving Center ✉ Nesima Hotel ☎ 069-364 0320; www.nesima-resort.com

Hurghada
✚ 201 E1
Aquanaut ✉ Shedwan Golden Beach Hotel ☎ 065-354 9891; www.aquanaut.net
Easy Divers ✉ Corniche, al Dahar ☎ 065-354 7816; www.easydivers-redsea.com
Jasmin Diving ✉ Jasmin Village ☎ 065-346 0475; www.jasmin-diving.com

Protecting the Reefs

Egypt's coral reefs have suffered both at the hands of hotel builders and the tourists, so it's extremely important to protect them:
• Don't touch the corals and certainly never stand on them.
• Avoid kicking up sand, as it smothers the corals.
• Don't fish or feed the fish.
• Don't collect or buy any shells, corals or other marine souvenirs.

Three types of reef are found in Egypt. Fringing reefs lie in shallow water near land. Barrier reefs, much larger, grow along the edges of islands and continental shelves and tend to be separated from the shore by a lagoon. Patch reefs are mounds of coral that grow out of the sandy seabed. The area between the shore and the seaward reef, the back reef, is a mixture of sand, coral colonies and rubble.

Sinai's Top Five Diving and Snorkelling Sites

• **Blue Hole** (a few kilometres north of Dahab). This large lagoon on top of a 300m (984-foot) vertical shaft features hard corals and a variety of fish on the outer reef. Beware that diving deep down is extremely dangerous and has claimed many lives.
• **The Canyon** (near the Blue Hole, Dahab). This narrow, extremely beautiful canyon has plenty of corals and a range of reef fish that can even be seen by new divers. But only experienced divers should attempt the deep exit out of the canyon.
• **The Islands** (near the Laguna Hotel, Dahab). A magnificent seascape covered with the most diverse and well-preserved corals in the area, with an amazing variety of fish. The added attraction here is a large amphitheatre, halfway along the reef, where schools of barracudas are common. It's also excellent for snorkelling.
• **End of the Road Reef** (north of Sharm al Sheikh). This submerged island has some of the best corals in Egypt and an abundance of fish.
• **Ras Ghozlani** (Ras Mohamed, ► 163). The most beautiful spot on the south coast features plenty of small reef species and well-preserved corals.

Top Mainland Spots for Diving and Snorkelling

• **Shaab Abu Ramada** (The Aquarium), about 15km (9 miles) south of Hurghada. This shallow reef is home to the tiniest reef fish, stingrays, barracuda, tuna and grey sharks.

• **Carless (Careless) Reef**, 5km (3 miles) north of Giftun Island. Divers from all over the world come to see the population of semi-tame moray eels, untamed sharks and jacks.

• **Green Hole**, 59km (37 miles) north of Quseyr. Excellent for both snorkelling and diving, this stunning coral growth is home to dolphins and blue-eagle rays.

• **Beit Goha**, 20km (12 miles) north of Quseyr. An exceptional and very shallow coral labyrinth harbours elaborate canyons and exquisite coral gardens.

• **Sirena Beach Home Reef**, Mövenpick Sirena Beach Hotel, Quseyr. Off the hotel's jetty is a fantastic reef with a variety of corals and fish (➤ 171).

Spectacular Sealife

Even on the patchiest corals you might find small gobi, snappers, triggerfish, emperors and sea urchins, as well as bottom-dwelling species burrowing in the sand. In protected lagoons you might see wonderful varieties of seaweed and seagrasses. Most divers head straight for the reef fronts, with their spectacular features and variety of marine life. The top 20m (65 feet) attracts many of the brightest-coloured species, including damselfish, butterflyfish, clownfish and snappers. Even sharks are known to thrive here.

Try a Dive

Most hotels in Sinai and along the coast have a diving centre (or arrangements with one), with boats, equipment and experienced instructors (➤ 156) and snorkelling equipment for rent or to buy. Egypt's diving centres are a relatively inexpensive way to learn open-water diving and earn a PADI (Professional Association of Diving Instructors) or CMAS (Confédération Mondiale des Activités Subaquatiques / World Underwater Federation) certificate, which enables you to dive anywhere in the world. Around Sharm al Sheikh and along most of the mainland coast diving is done offshore from a boat. But beyond Dahab and Nuweiba you can easily swim out to the reefs, and Sinai in particular offers some interesting snorkelling opportunities along almost the entire coast. In Hurghada, most snorkelling and diving sites are accessible only by boat. The most popular day trip is to Giftun Island with snorkelling before and after lunch.

RED SEA DIVING: INSIDE INFO

Top tip The best time to dive is spring or autumn. In summer, temperatures below the surface are pleasant, but out of the water it can be unbearably hot. From March to June, the *khamsin*, a hot desert wind bringing dust and sand, may blow. During the winter the water can be too cold for snorkelling without a wetsuit.

Hidden gems The hundreds of kilometres of coast south of Hurghada, particularly past Quseyr, are still mostly untouched, with spectacular unpolluted reefs.

TAKING A BREAK

Ras Mohamed National Park has some good spots for a picnic, and Hurghada and Dahab have plenty of eating places and watering holes.

Left: Royal angelfish
Below: A large shoal of anthias

5

Mount Moses and St Catherine's Monastery

For centuries pilgrims have climbed Gebel Musa (Mount Moses or Mount Sinai) to visit the site where Moses is believed to have received the Ten Commandments. Some make the ascent for the spectacular mountain views, while others search for a more spiritual experience.

Mount Moses rises 2,285m (7,500 feet) above sea level and can be climbed via two routes. The easiest (and longest) follows a camel path and takes about three hours. The other route, known as Sikkat Sayyidna Musa (Path of our Lord Moses), takes 90 minutes but is far more exhausting because it leads up the 3,750 steep Steps of Repentance, hewn by monks.

The monks of St Catherine hold closed services in the small Greek Orthodox chapel on top of Mount Moses

Deir Sant Katrin (St Catherine's Monastery)

At the foot of Mount Moses is the remarkable 6th-century Greek Orthodox monastery of Christian martyr St Catherine of Alexandria, built on the supposed site of the Burning Bush. In AD 337 the Byzantine Empress Helena built a chapel over the Burning Bush, which had already attracted many pilgrims and hermits. Emperor Justinian then enlarged and fortified it in the 6th century. About 20 monks, mostly from Mount Athos in Greece, now live at the monastery. However, the rapid expansion of tourism along the coast and the many day trippers threaten the peace of the monastery.

The entrance to the monastery is a small gate in the massive granite walls, near Kléber's Tower. To the right is Moses' Well,

✚ 201 E3
✉ Sinai interior, 450km (280 miles) from Cairo, 140km (90 miles) west of Dahab ☎ 02-482 8513 (Cairo); email: sinai@teolata.net.eg
◉ Mon–Thu and Sat 9–noon; closed public holidays; phone in advance to check 🍴 Café/restaurant (£)
🚌 Buses from Cairo, Sharm al Sheikh, Dahab and Nuweiba to St Catherinevillage (al Milga), 2km (1 mile) from the monastery
✈ Egypt Air flights to Sharm al Sheikh 🎟 Free

The Ten Commandments

According to the scriptures (Exodus 3), God revealed himself to Moses as a flame of fire in the Burning Bush (also associated with Sinai), and told the prophet to lead the people of Israel out of Egypt to escape hardship under the pharaoh. The people fled to Sinai and Moses spent 40 days on the mountain, where God communicated the Ten Commandments to him, which were written on two stone tablets. Sinai is sacred to the Jewish community, Christians and Muslims because the Ten Commandments became the basis of Christian and Jewish religion, and the incident is also recounted in the Quran.

where the prophet met his future wife Zippora, while a left turn leads to an enclosure with a thorny bush, a cutting from the Burning Bush – the original is inside the chapel.

The granite Basilica of St Catherine, entered through beautiful original cedar-wood doors, has 12 magnificent pillars for each month of the year, each decorated with an icon of a saint. The

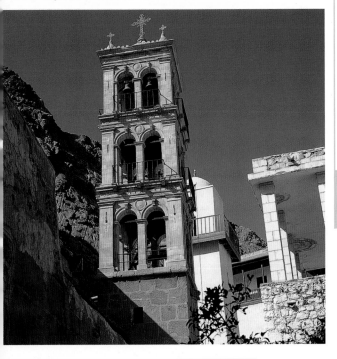

A Christian Martyr

Born in AD 294 to an Alexandrian family, St Catherine was tortured for her faith on a spiked wheel, which broke and beheaded her. This later inspired the Catherine wheel firework and heraldry symbol. Her remains are said to have been taken to Sinai by angels.

The basilica of St Catherine dominates the monastery compound iconostasis (altar screen) is 17th century, but the sanctuary beyond it houses the Mosaic of the Transfiguration (AD 550–600), a masterpiece of Byzantine art. The icon collection is unique and covers 1,400 years, including the period between 746 and 842 when the monks in this isolated monastery were unaware of the injunction banning Byzantine Christians from painting the Holy Family or saints. The monastery also has a precious collection of rare and early manuscripts, not on public display.

A 6th-century Byzantine mosaic of the Transfiguration

TAKING A BREAK

Bedouins often sell tea at the top of the mountain (pictured right), but don't count on it –
take your own food and drink. Al Milga village
has restaurants and little shops where you can
stock up for a picnic. Simple meals are included
if you're staying at the monastery's hostel.

MOUNT MOSES & ST CATHERINE'S MONASTERY: INSIDE INFO

Top tips The **climb up Mount Moses** is spectacular, both at dawn and dusk, and you can take in both by bringing a sleeping bag and staying outdoors in Elijah's Basin, near the summit. You can leave your luggage in the monastery's storeroom.
• **Take lots of water** for the intense heat, but also come prepared with suitable gear, as it can snow here in winter. **Temperatures drop dramatically** at night, even in summer.
• **Dress modestly** when visiting the monastery.

In more depth You need **special permission** to see the Chapel of the Burning Bush.
• The St Catherine Protectorate publishes a good **guide to the monastery**, as well as some excellent walking guides to the surrounding area (tel: 069-347 0032).
• Visitors to the mountains **must be accompanied by a Bedouin guide**, which can be organised through Mountain Tours' office at al Milga, Sheikh Mousa (tel: 010-641 3575; email: sheikmusa@yahoo.com).

⑧

Ras Mohamed National Park

Egypt's first national park was created in 1988. Only 12 per cent of it is open to the public, and it can get crowded with day trippers from nearby Sharm al Sheikh. Nevertheless, so far the project has been extremely successful in protecting the area's outstanding ecosystem.

The park's underwater area has some of the Red Sea's most remarkable coral reefs, including the rich growth of spectacular Anemone City. On land too there's a lot of wildlife, including foxes, gazelles and ibexes, and the mangroves are a valuable breeding ground for migratory birds. Children love the warm shallow waters of Mangrove Channel and the Crevice Pools. The Visitors' Centre has free telescopes, wildlife videos and information on the park trails.

The modern entrance to Ras Mohamed National Park

✚ 201 F2
✉ 30km (19 miles) northwest of Sharm al Sheikh   ⓣ Daily 8–5
🍴 Restaurant at Visitors' Centre (£–££). Sat–Thu 10–5
🎫 Moderate, camping permits available from the Visitors' Centre

---

RAS MOHAMED NATIONAL PARK: INSIDE INFO

Top tips Take your passport to go through the **UN checkpoints**; Israelis and foreigners without a full Egyptian visa (only the Sinai visa) should expect delays.
• You can rent **diving equipment** at Ras Mohamed, but it's safer to get it from a diving centre in Sharm al Sheikh.

9

St Anthony's and St Paul's Monasteries

The monasteries of Deir Anba Antunius and Deir Anba Bula (St Anthony and St Paul), hidden in the barren Red Sea mountains, are the oldest Christian monasteries in Egypt, perhaps in the world. Monastic rituals were more or less invented here, where the daily life of the Coptic monks has barely changed in 1,600 years. The hermit St Anthony found refuge here in the silence of the desert, but silence can be hard to find when the tours arrive from Hurghada.

St Anthony's Monastery

St Anthony (► 24) moved to the desert in AD 294, settling first in a spot with palm trees. But when things became too crowded he moved to a cave in the mountain, where he lived for 25 years until his death at the age of 105. The monastery dedicated to him was founded around AD 361 by his disciples, who lived an ascetic life in a community. Surrounded by 12m-high (40-foot) walls, the monastery compound is dramatically located beneath a ridge of cliffs in the Wadi Araba, at the foot of St Anthony's Cave, covered in centuries of graffiti and supplications left by pilgrims. The views from the top are fantastic, and well worth the steep climb up 1,200 steps. The monastery itself is home to about 65 monks and looks similar to an Egyptian village, with houses, churches and gardens. The oldest building is the Church of St Anthony, which contains the saint's tomb and beautiful 13th-century murals.

Top right: St Anthony's monastery contains some beautiful stained-glass windows.

Right: The peaceful Monastery of St Anthony was at the foot of the mountain where the saint went into retreat

St Paul's Monastery

St Paul the Ascetic (not to be confused with the apostle) settled here before St Anthony, and lived in his cave for 90 years until his death at the age

✚ 201 D3 ✉ St Anthony's: 50km (30 miles) west of Zafarana; St Paul's: 40km (25 miles) south of Zafarana ☎ 02-590 0218 ⏰ St Anthony's: daily 7–5, St Paul's: 8–3. December and Lent: Fri, Sat and Sun. Closed Holy Week 🚌 Take a taxi or tour (► panel 165). Buses from Suez to Hurghada stop 26km (16 miles) south of Zafarana; then walk 13km (8 miles) to St Anthony's. To get to St Paul's stop at the turn off on the Suez–Hurghada road, near the Zafarana lighthouse, then walk for 14km (9 miles).

of 113. He met St Anthony at the end of his life and recognised his spiritual superiority. The dilapidated monastery, built around his cave by St Paul's followers, is overshadowed by its larger neighbour. The Church of St Paul, filled with candles and murals, encloses the saint's cave. The 17th-century Church of St Michael has an icon of the Virgin attributed to St Luke (AD 40).

TAKING A BREAK

Both monasteries have cafés and St Paul's also has a grocery, but consider taking a picnic.

ST ANTHONY'S AND ST PAUL'S MONASTERIES: INSIDE INFO

Top tips The easiest, although perhaps not the most satisfying, way to visit both monasteries is by taking an organised tour from Cairo or Hurghada.
• At both monasteries there is an English-speaking monk who can give a guided tour (free, but donations welcome).
• The guesthouse at St Paul's only accommodates pilgrims (tel: 02-590 0218), but both monasteries have a small cafeteria with drinks and snacks.
• Take plenty of water while visiting the monasteries and the mountains.

In more depth Experienced walkers can hike along a trail in the hills between the two monasteries in about two days. Maps are available from St Anthony's.

At Your Leisure

2 Quseyr

You can enjoy some of the best snorkelling along the coast at this sleepy fishing town. The beaches here are beautiful, and the peace and quiet make this an agreeable alternative to Hurghada. Until the 10th century Quseyr was the largest port on the coast and even in the 19th century there was regular traffic. The remains of a 16th-century fort, built by Sultan Selim, are a reminder of the town's former significance.

➕ 199 E3 ✉ 80km (50 miles) south of Hurghada 🍴 Mövenpick Quseir (£££) 🚌 Daily buses from Cairo, Qena, Suez, Hurghada and Marsa Alam

3 Hurghada

Since about 1980 al Ghardaqa (Hurghada) has grown from a tiny fishing village into Egypt's largest resort, and it's still expanding along the coast. The sprawling town and *souk* have little character, but the offshore reefs are a diver's delight and the beaches, with a warm sea for most of the year, offer all manner of watersports. The Sindbad

Mahmiya Island, off the Hurghada Coast

Submarine (tel: 065-344 4688 to book) and the small Red Sea Aquarium (6 Sharia al Corniche, ad-Dahar; tel: 065-354 8557) give an enjoyable insight into reef life.

➕ 201 E1 ✉ 529km (330 miles) southeast of Cairo, 299km (185 miles) northeast of Luxor ☎ 065-344 4420 (tourist office) 🍴 Several 🚌 Regular buses from Cairo, Luxor, Aswan and Suez

The beach resort of Sharm al Sheikh

Bedouin Life

The Bedouin of Sinai used to be split into tribes, each of which roamed its own patch of territory to graze its herds. But as Sinai's coastline is developed, the dwindling Bedouin community is being settled into windswept concrete villages inland. Very few Bedouin remain semi-nomadic – many work in tourism, as builders or taxi drivers. The largest Bedouin settlement is in al Arish in northern Sinai, which has an interesting market on Thursdays.

✈ Flights daily from Cairo, three per week from Luxor, and weekly from Sharm al Sheikh and St Catherine ⛴ Ferry from Sharm al Sheikh several times a week (tel: 065-344 7571)

❹ Al Gouna

The mainland's most stylish resort is built on a series of islands and lagoons. Wealthy Cairenes own villas here, while tourists stay at the beautiful luxury hotels. The complex also includes an 18-hole golf course, a private airport (➤ 37), aquarium and a small museum with replicas of ancient Egyptian treasures.

➕ 201 E1 ✉ 30km (19 miles) north of Hurghada 🚍 Taxis from

Hurghada ✈ Flights to Cairo with SunAir (tel: 02-335 7440; www.sunair-eg.com)

❻ Sharm al Sheikh

The Israelis developed Sharm al Sheikh during their occupation of Sinai (1967–82), both for military purposes and as a holiday resort. But since the Egyptians returned Sharm has become one of the Red Sea's most popular and high-quality resorts. The highest concentration of hotels and restaurants is at Naama Bay, which is known for its excellent watersports facilities, but hotels have now also spread into the neighbouring bays. On the cliff north of Naama Bay is Sharm's residential area, with villas and condominiums mostly inhabited by staff working at the hotels. Here also is the first Ritz hotel in Africa. Most of Sharm's treasures are under water – the only sight on land is Ras Kennedy, a rock vaguely resembling the face of former US president John F Kennedy.

➕ 201 F2 ✉ 470km (290 miles) from Cairo 🍴 Several 🚍 Buses from Cairo, Dahab, Nuweiba, Suez and Taba ✈ Domestic flights from Cairo, Luxor and Hurghada ⛴ Ferry from Hurghada several times a week (tel: 069-260 0190; www.intlfastferries.com)

5 Things for the Kids

- See the corals and fish from the **Sindbad submarine** in Hurghada (➤ 166).
- **Red Sea Aquarium**, Hurghada, with colourful local fish and corals (➤ 166).
- **Camel rides** in Naama Bay, Gouna or Hurghada beach.
- **Fun Town Amusement Park**, Naama Bay (tel: 069-360 2556).
- Children between 8 and 11 years old can **learn to dive** in swimming pools. From the age of 10, they can do an open-water diving course at the Red Sea scuba schools in Hurghada and Sharm al Sheikh (tel in the UK: 0870 2201 777; website: www.regal-diving.co.uk).

7 Dahab

Dahab, which means "gold" in Arabic, has superb beaches and some of Sinai's best dive sites near by (➤ 157), although the town itself is a bit of a mess. It's divided into three distinct parts: the Bedouin settlement of Asilah; the hotel area of al Mashraba; and Al Masbat, which is made up of cheap campsites and hotels, where old hippies and young backpackers rave and hang out. The strip of seafront bars and restaurants serve typical backpacker staples such as spaghetti, milkshakes and banana pancakes. Young Egyptians associate Dahab with drug culture but, although things may appear relaxed, the Egyptian police

The main street in Dahab's Bedouin village

are taking a tougher line and penalties are severe. The real attractions here as elsewhere along the coast are underwater, particularly the dangerous Blue Hole, the Canyon and other nearby reefs. Alternatively, Bedouin organise camel treks into the spectacular desert interior.

🚹 201 F3 ✉ 100km (60 miles) northwest of Sharm al Sheikh 🍴 Bars, restaurants in the bay of Asilah (££) 🚌 Buses from Sharm al Sheikh, Taba, Nuweiba, Cairo and St Catherine

10 Ismailiya

Ismailiya's renovated and tree-shaded old town, built at the same time as the Suez Canal, makes for a pleasant walk. Start on Muhammad Ali Quay at the Swiss-style house of Ferdinand de Lesseps, the canal's French architect. Near by is the Ismailiya Museum's collection of ancient artefacts. Around Lake Timsah (Crocodile Lake) are several good beaches and restaurants. One of the best views of the canal is from Nemra Setta, a lovely garden suburb with colonial villas.

🚹 201 D4 ✉ 120km (75 miles) east of Cairo, 85km (53 miles) from Port Said ☎ 064-332 1078 (tourist office in Governorate Building, Sharia Sheikh Zayeed) 🎫 Ismailiya Museum Sat–Thu 8–4, closed Fri 11:30–1:30; to visit de Lesseps House check with the tourist office 🍴 George's (££; ➤ 174) 🚌 Buses from Cairo, Hurghada and Port Said, Sinai

11 Suez Canal

Before the 167km (104-mile) Suez Canal opened in 1869, linking the Mediterranean to the Red Sea, European

Port Said's harbour at the entrance of the Suez Canal

ships had to sail around southern Africa to reach the East, so it halved the distance between Europe and Asia.

The concept wasn't new. The idea of a canal cutting through the desert had already occurred to the 7th-century BC pharaoh Necho II, but an oracle dissuaded him from completing the project. A century later the Persians dug a small canal, but it fell out of use over the centuries.

Work on the Suez Canal began in 1859, under the supervision of Frenchman Ferdinand de Lesseps. It took 10 years and 25,000 workers to finish and is still one of the world's greatest feats of engineering. When President Nasser (➤ 27) nationalised the Suez Canal in 1956 in response to the West's refusal to help finance the Aswan High Dam, Britain, France and Israel retaliated by bombing the area. The canal cities suffered further damage during the Arab-Israel wars (1948 to 1973), when the canal was closed and the city of Suez more or less levelled (it has yet to recover). Since the Suez Canal reopened in 1975, it has been Egypt's second-largest source of revenue, after tourism.

➕ 201 D5 ✉ Between Bur Said (Port Said) and Ismailiya 🚌 Buses from Cairo, Hurghada, Port Said and Ismailiya

🔟 Port Said

Brothels and hashish dens have long disappeared from the free port of Bur Said (Port Said), once dubbed "the wickedest town in the East", but a hint of its former seedy atmosphere lingers in the back streets. This relaxed town is a popular, cheap shopping destination for Egyptians as its bazaar sells international brands. It's also a stopover for Mediterranean cruise liners, but there are few sights apart from the Suez Canal, which is best viewed from the free ferry across to Port Fuad. In the early evening the locals stroll along the Corniche to watch the vessels on the canal. A new Suez Canal Museum is being built on Sharia Safia Zaghloul. The Military Museum (Sharia 23 July) illustrates the Suez Canal's troubled history.

➕ 201 D5 ✉ 225km (140 miles) from Cairo, 85km (53 miles) north of Ismailiya ☎ 066-323 5289 (tourist office) ⏰ Military Museum Sat–Thu 9–4 🍴 Galal Seafood (£; ➤ 173) 🚌 Buses from Cairo, Suez, Ismailiya and Hurghada

The Statue of Liberty

New York's most famous landmark was originally intended to stand at the entrance to the Suez Canal, at Port Said. Inspired by the colossi of Ramses II (➤ 100), the French sculptor Bartholdi (1834–1904) designed a huge woman representing "Egypt carrying the light of Asia". Khedive Ismail (viceroy of Egypt 1863–79) loved this grand idea, but later decided it was too expensive, so the statue was presented to the USA.

Where to... Stay

Prices
The prices are for a double room per night. **£** under 400LE **££** 400–900LE **£££** over 900LE

Since the 1980s Sinai's coast has developed rapidly. Sharm al Sheikh in particular has seen a boom in hotels, most resembling small villages and part of international chains for package tourists. Budget options are rare, but there's a range of inexpensive hotels up the coast in Dahab.

SHARM AL SHEIKH

Amar Sina ££
Away from the Naama Bay hubbub, the Amar overlooks the turquoise sea and pink mountains and is designed to look like an Egyptian village. Rooms are pleasant and comfortable, often covered with a dome, and always stylishly decorated. The hotel's owner (and designer) lives on site and ensures service with a smile. The Amar Sina has a great pool, gym and Jacuzzi as well as a farm and an Oriental café with water pipes.

✚ **201 F2** ⊠ **Ras Umm al Sid**
☎ **069-366 2222;**
www.minasegypt.com

Four Seasons Sharm al Sheikh £££
The Four Seasons Sharm al Sheikh is the most stunning five-star hotel in town with unequalled levels of service and comfort. Built in a Moorish style overlooking the Straits of Tiran, the Four Seasons offers large suite-size rooms with fabulous views. The hotel has a great pool and all watersports are available.

✚ **201 F2** ⊠ **North of Naama Bay**
☎ **069-360 3555;**
www.fourseasons.com/sharmelsheikh

Pigeon House £
The only viable budget option in Naama Bay, accommodation ranges from simple huts with fans to "superior" air-conditioned rooms with bathrooms. It's in a quiet area, but across the road from the beach.

✚ **201 F2** ⊠ **Northern edge of Naama Bay** ☎ **069-360 0996;**
fax: 069-360 0965

Sanafir ££
One of the older hotels in town, the Sanafir has white domed rooms, decorated in traditional Egyptian style, set on several levels around a lagoon-shaped pool. There's also a waterfall and several lounge terraces with Bedouin sofas. Service is particularly friendly, attracting a young crowd that likes the nightlife and does not mind the noise. The Sanafir's diving centre is renowned.

✚ **201 F2** ⊠ **Naama Bay** ☎ **069-360 0197; www.sanafirhotel.com**

DAHAB

Nesima ££
This stylish and wonderfully relaxed hotel is one of the few in Sinai to be specifically aimed at the individual traveller. The very comfortable, well-designed domed rooms overlook a beautiful swimming pool. The hotel is popular with divers of all levels and has an excellent diving centre offering equipment and tuition.

✚ **201 F3** ⊠ **Al Mashraba**
☎ **069-364 0320;**
www.nesima-resort.com

ST CATHERINE

Auberge St Catherine £–££

The obvious place to stay in St Catherine is this refurbished hostel at the monastery, which offers 150 beds in single, double or triple accommodation, with breakfast and evening meal included. Rooms overlook an orchard just below the monastery. You can leave your luggage here while you climb Mount Moses.

✚ 201 E3 ☒ St Catherine's Monastery ☎ 069-347 0353; email: moussaboulas@yahoo.com

Basata £

Farther north on Sinai's eastern coast is a place like no other in Egypt. Basata is extremely popular with Europeans, Egyptians and Israelis who come to enjoy a relaxed and peaceful stay in this camp of simple beach huts and bungalows. Facilities are generally basic, but there is a desalination plant. The owner cares about the environment, so the preservation of the coral reef is a much-discussed topic at the simple, healthy communal meals. Drugs, alcohol and loud music are not allowed.

✚ 201 F3 ☒ Ras al Burg on the Taba–Nuweiba road, 42km (26 miles) south of Taba ☎ 069-350 0480; www.basata.com

ISMAILIYA

Mercure Fursan Island ££

The most luxurious accommodation in Ismailiya (part of the French-owned chain) is on Fursan Island in the middle of the lake. The hotel is popular with families who visit at weekends, attracted by a private beach and the promise of quiet nights. Rooms are comfortable though uninspiring, and have all modern amenities. Some have lake views. A variety of watersports is available.

✚ 201 D4 ☒ Fursan Island, north-east of Ismailiya ☎ 064-391 8040; www.accor.com

GOUNA

Dawar al Omda ££

The Dawar al Omda (Mayor's House), built on a man-made island in a lagoon, is an inventive mix of modern architecture and traditional Egyptian features. The stylish interior is simply decorated with regional antiques and locally made furniture. The pool is small but there's good swimming near by in the lagoons.

✚ 201 E1 ☒ Kafr al Gouna, Gouna ☎ 065-354 5060

Miramar Sheraton £££

A luxury American-designed hotel, the Miramar is a pastel, postmodern mirage covering several islands. The spacious rooms, overlooking either the sea or a lagoon, are decorated in Mediterranean style, some with balconies. All watersports facilities are available, as well as a golf course.

✚ 201 E1 ☒ Gouna ☎ 065-354 5606; www.starwoodhotels.com/sheraton

HURGHADA

Giftun Beach Resort ££

One of the oldest resorts in town, Giftun is popular with divers and windsurfers for its excellent facilities, friendly staff and whitewashed beach chalets. At the lively bar divers exchange the stories of the day.

✚ 201 E1 ☒ Resort strip, Hurghada ☎ 065-346 3040; www.giftunbeachresort.com

QUSEYR

Mövenpick Sirena Beach £££

Inspired by traditional village architecture, the simple, comfortable domed rooms are in a pleasant garden. This resort is perfect for a peaceful holiday, with excellent service, good food and a large pool. It has some of Egypt's best snorkelling and diving from its private beach, and there's also a dive centre.

✚ 199 E3 ☒ al Quadim Bay, Quseyr ☎ 065-333 2100; www.moevenpick-quseir.com

Where to...
Eat and Drink

Prices

Expect to pay per person for a meal, excluding drinks and tips.
£ up to 100LE ££ 100–150LE £££ over 150LE

ST CATHERINE

Places to eat in St Catherine are rare, but the best option is probably the **Auberge St Catherine**. In the nearest village of al Milga there are a few basic eateries, including **Katrien Rest House** and **Ihlas**. Your best bet is to visit the bakery and local shops and enjoy a picnic in this wonderful landscape.

SHARM AL SHEIKH

Sharm al Sheikh, and particularly Naama Bay have no shortage of restaurants and bars, but most are in hotels, so food is expensive. However, in Sharm itself you can find cheaper places popular with Egyptians. As the majority of tourists in Sharm al Sheikh are Italian, you should have no problem finding good pizza or excellent pasta, although you can just about eat your way around the world here now. Even the Hard Rock Café has arrived, as have McDonald's, KFC and Pizza Hut.

Al Fanar £££

Delightful upmarket Italian restaurant on the waterfront with delicious pizzas, the freshest fish and seafood and calming views over the sea.

➕ 201 F2 ⊠ Ras Um Sid ☎ 069-366 2218 ◎ Daily 10am–10.30pm

The Fish ££–£££

One of the older restaurants in Sharm and just off the beach, it serves a good selection of fresh fish and seafood from its shrimp pond. The restaurant occupies a covered terrace, with nets and marine paraphernalia draped over pillars and walls. The cooking is excellent, but the service can be painfully slow.

➕ 201 F2 ⊠ Hilton Fayrouz ☎ 069-360 0136 ◎ Daily lunch and dinner

Il Frantoio £££

This excellent and refined Italian restaurant has a lovely alfresco dining area, perfect on a warm evening. The food is inventive, using only the best ingredients – try the fresh raviolis, or grilled stuffed sea bass.

➕ 201 F2 ⊠ Four Seasons Hotel, north of Naama Bay ☎ 069-360 3555 ◎ Daily lunch and dinner

La Luna £££

At this award-winning Italian restaurant with the best dishes from various regions in Italy, the chef flies in the best ingredients with which to prepare inventive dishes. The signature dish is pasta stuffed with cream and dried beef, as well as osso bucco and sea bass. As you would expect of a restaurant in the Ritz Carlton, the courteous and faultless service perfectly complements the meal.

➕ 201 F2 ⊠ Ritz Carlton, 0m as Sid ☎ 069-366 1919 ◎ Daily 6:30–10.30pm

Little Buddha ££–£££

The sister venue of the famous Paris Buddha Bar, this is definitely one of the places to be seen in Sharm. The massive lit up sweeping bar, the dark red walls, the classic Buddha Bar sounds, and a giant gold Buddha all set the tone, but the food is equally impressive. Sit at the bar and watch the delicious sushi being prepared, or dine at one of the tables and taste the inventive French-Asian fusion cuisine. Later in the night when the beat gets turned up, there is room to dance, or hang out on the Japanese futons.

➕ 201 F2 ⊠ Naama Bay Hotel, Naama Bay ☎ 069-360 1030; www.littlebuddha-sharm.com
🕒 Daily 6pm–3am

Pirates Bar £-££

One of the oldest drinking haunts in town, Pirates still draws the crowds, particularly divers. The terrace is set in a kitsch but charming garden, lit by fairy lights at night, with bridges over little ponds.

➕ 201 F2 ⊠ Hilton Fayrouz, Naama Bay ☎ 069-360 0136 🕒 Daily from 2pm

La Rustichella ££-£££

Sharm's many Italian residents and tourists love this charming Italian

restaurant, where you can eat pasta almost as *la mamma* cooks it. Besides fresh pasta there is also plenty of fresh fish and seafood on the menu.

➕ 201 F2 ⊠ Behind Naama Bay ☎ 067-360 1154 🕒 Daily lunch and dinner

Safsafa £-££

The original Safsafa in Sharm town is really old and has only eight tables, but the new family-run restaurant is a much more upmarket eatery. The accent is still on fresh fish and seafood but, although stylish, it is low on atmosphere.

➕ 201 F2 ⊠ Naama Centre, Naama Bay ☎ 069-360 0150 🕒 Daily lunch and dinner

Sala Thai £££

If you are looking for something special, other than the all available Egyptian or Italian food, then this is the place to head for. The classical Thai/Asian food at the Hyatt's restaurant is exquisite and the

interior is peacefully Asian with lots of teak wood and a pleasant terrace overlooking the sea.

➕ 201 F2 ⊠ Hyatt Regency Hotel ☎ 069-360 1234 🕒 Daily lunch and dinner

Sinai Star £-££

This simple eatery serves the best-value seafood in Sharm. The place is popular with Egyptians working in Naama Bay, so the majority of customers are men. The décor is spartan, but the atmosphere is real.

➕ 201 F2 ⊠ Shopping arcade behind bus station, Sharm al Sheikh ☎ 069-366 0323 🕒 Daily lunch and dinner

TamTam ££

In this very popular café and restaurant serving all the traditional Egyptian dishes such as *mezze*, salads, *meloukhiya* (soup made from a spinach-like vegetable, served with chicken or rabbit), *kushari* (macaroni, rice, onions, chickpeas and lentils topped with tomato sauce) and meat grills, the

atmosphere is laid-back and joyous. Digest your food as the Egyptians do, with a strong mint tea and a water pipe.

➕ 201 F2 ⊠ Ghazala Hotel, Naama Bay ☎ 069-360 0150 🕒 Daily lunch and dinner

DAHAB

Carm Inn £

One of the better waterfront places with freshly prepared Western, Egyptian and Indian dishes, favoured by the local expats.

➕ 201 F3 ⊠ Masbat ☎ 069-364 1300 🕒 9am–10pm

Nirvana Restaurant £-££

Arguably the best in Dahab, this beach-side restaurant has tables literally on the beach. It serves excellent Indian food, and a wide selection of vegetarian dishes.

➕ 201 F3 ⊠ At the Lighthouse on the boardwalk, Masbat ☎ 069-364 1261; www.nirvanadivers.com
🕒 Daily lunch and dinner

ISMAILIYA

George's ££

Cairenes have been known to cross the desert just to eat at this pleasant Greek-run fish restaurant. The atmosphere is agreeable and intimate, while the owner's fresh seafood is famous. There is also a well-stocked bar.

☐ 201 D4 ☒ Sharia Sultan Hussein ☎ 064-391 7327 ⏰ Daily lunch and dinner

GOUNA

Kiki's Café ££

A popular hang-out in Gouna, Kiki's has good Italian food, friendly service, funky music and a relaxed atmosphere. Delicious home-made pastas and copious salads are served on two small open-air terraces with views over the town and lagoons.

☐ 201 E1 ☒ Above the museum in Kafr al Gouna ☎ 065-354 2407 ⏰ Daily dinner only

Sayadeen Fish Restaurant ££

Fresh seafood is an obvious speciality of this beach restaurant situated in a pavilion built over the sea with fantastic views. The menu focuses on a different national cuisine each month, so you can have your fish simply grilled or cooked the way it's done somewhere else in the world. Oriental dishes are also served.

☐ 201 E1 ☒ Mövenpick Hotel, beach ☎ 065-354 4501 ⏰ Daily lunch and dinner

Le Tabasco ££

Imported from the capital, Cairo's hottest bar/bistro in the heart of Kafr al Gouna, is just as trendy and lively. It has three terraces, the same relaxed atmosphere, cool tastefully designed interiors, excellent music and great food. The bar is on the second floor.

☐ 201 E1 ☒ Between the museum building and El Khan hotel, Kafr al Gouna ☎ 065-354 5516 ⏰ Daily late afternoon–2am

HURGHADA

Felfela £–££

Part of the popular Cairene chain (▶ 75), this atmospheric restaurant in a cliff-top location overlooking the Red Sea and harbour. It serves Egyptian dishes, from a variety of *mezze* to delicious roast pigeon stuffed with *fireek*.

☐ 201 E1 ☒ Sharia Sheraton ☎ 065-344 2410 ⏰ Daily lunch and dinner

Liquid Lounge £–££

This popular and ultra-relaxed beach bar serves snacks, good Western dishes and a slightly more elaborate dinner menu.

☐ 201 E1 ☒ Sharia Sheraton ☎ 010-512 9051 ⏰ 9am–3am

Da Nanni ££

The chefs, a couple, are Italian and they know how to make a delicious pizza. Da Nanni is considered by many to make the best pizzas in town. Homemade pasta also served.

☐ 201 E1 ☒ Sharia al Hadaba, Sigala ☎ 065-344 7018 ⏰ Daily lunch and dinner

Papa's Bar £

This lively bar is particularly popular with dive instructors and other temporary residents in Hurghada. Some nights the music gets turned up and the party is on.

☐ 201 E1 ☒ Next door to Pizza Rossi, Sigala ☎ 010-512 9051; www.papasbar.com ⏰ Daily all day until late

Portofino ££

Fresh Italian fish and seafood dishes are a speciality and the home-made pasta is the best in town. The fondues are also popular. There's an enjoyable atmosphere because the décor is simple and the service friendly; the owner likes to chat to guests in the evening.

☐ 201 E1 ☒ Sharia Sayed al Qorayem, al Dahar ☎ 065-354 6250 ⏰ Daily lunch and dinner

Where to...
Shop

Most resorts on the Red Sea and in Sinai were tiny fishing hamlets or Bedouin settlements until recently, so there are no authentic *souks* or *bazaars*. The American-style shopping malls here have no local flavour. Most shops sell cheap tourist souvenirs but a minority sell better quality produce such as Bedouin embroidery, local weaving and pottery.

It is alarming to see the corals, shells, starfish and even stuffed sharks on sale. Avoid buying these as it's damaging to the coral reefs.

The Red Sea Coast

The sprawling bazaar area in **Hurghada's al Dahar** has hundreds of shops and street vendors selling the usual tourist tat. In general the quality of merchandise is quite poor, but prices are reasonable enough if you're prepared to haggle. As Hurghada has become popular with Russian and Eastern European tourists, you may also find products from these countries.

Tax-free goods are available at the **Egypt Free Shop** opposite the Egypt Air office or at the pyramid-shaped shopping mall in Sigala.

Gouna has several top-quality shops. The boutique **Queeny** sells the best of European fashion labels. For something more ethnic head for **Malaika** with fantastic Egyptian cotton embroidered *galabeyas* and great sleep wear. **Al Nol** makes Bedouin-style *galabeyas* and scarves in bold ethnic colours. The **Egyptian Women's Handicrafts** supports several fair trade projects all over the country: Moqattam's recycled paper

and notebooks from Cairo, Bedouin embroidered pillows and purses from Sinai and other handicrafts from all over Egypt. All these stores are in Abu Tig Marina.

Sinai

Sharm al Sheikh's ever-expanding bazaar area sells the usual tourist souvenirs, including silver jewellery, copies of ancient statues and papyri, cotton T-shirts printed with Red Sea fish. A few shops stand out, however. **Aladin**, at the Falcon al Diar Hotel in Naama Bay (tel: 069-360 0828), sells lovely Egyptian glass, Bedouin textiles, woodwork and beads. **Baraka Carpets**, in front of the Sanafir Hotel (tel: 012-218 1597/227 2363) has a great selection of woollen and silk carpets, Bedouin rugs and patchwork carpets from all over Egypt, as well as other handicrafts. The best bookshop in Sharm is the **al Ahram Bookshop**, on the road to Sharm in Naama Bay, with a good selection of English-language books, papers and magazines.

Every Thursday a **Bedouin market** is held in the old part of al Arish on the north coast of Sinai, where veiled Bedouin women sell their beadwork, silver jewellery and traditionally embroidered dresses. The market is mostly geared towards tourism, as their best pieces probably go directly to the shops in Cairo, but it's still a colourful sight.

Most hotels have their own shopping malls. The best places for Egyptian cotton clothes are **Mobaco** at the Sanafir, **Hilton Fayrouz** in Naama Bay, and **Pyramisa Hotel** at Shark Bay in Sharm al Sheikh; the **Shirt Shop** (Mövenpick Jolie Ville) has men's shirts, as has the franchised **New Man** (Sanafir and Pyramisa hotels).

Suez Canal

Port Said is a duty-free port and therefore popular with Egyptians looking for a bargain; you can buy almost anything here. Most of the shops selling brand names, cheap electronics and designer jeans are on and around Sharia al Gumhuriya.

Where to...
Be Entertained

Listings of what's on in Sinai are in the monthly *Sinai Today* and *Egypt Today*, (check the websites www.sharm-el-sheikh.com and www.elgouna.com). For the Red Sea there's *Hurghada Bulletin* and *Red Sea Life*.

Scuba-diving/Snorkelling

All Red Sea and Sinai resorts have excellent dive centres offering equipment rental, boat excursions and diving courses (▶ 156–159).

Glass-bottom Boats/Submarines

Most resorts, both in Sinai and along the Red Sea coast, offer daily trips by glass-bottom boats that give non-swimmers the chance to explore the wonders of the coral reefs. Contact **Sindbad Submarines** (tel: 065-344 4688) in Hurghada; **Aquascope** is at the Hoi Palace in Hurghada (tel: 065-344 3710) and at the al Kheima Resort in Sharm al Moya (tel: 065-344 3710).

Nightlife

Sharm al Sheikh is lively at night around the bars and discos of hotels, especially **Bus Stop** and **Pacha** at the Sanafir Hotel (▶ 170) and **Little Buddha Bar** (▶ 172) at Naama Bay Hotel. **Pirates Bar** (▶ 173) is popular in the early evening when there's a happy hour. Naama Bay has a **Hard Rock Café** (tel: 069-360 2665), with the usual rock 'n' roll memorabilia. The **Black House Discotheque** at the Rosetta Hotel in Naama Bay (tel: 069-360 1888) gets crowded later on, and the music's a real mish-mash of Euro-pop. In high season several music bars along the beach can also be good for a dance. In Hurghada most of the larger hotels have discos, also open to non-residents, with the **Dome** at the InterContinental a favourite. A few other places are worth checking out. **Papa's Beach Club** (tel: 065-344 4146) often has wild parties with DJs from abroad. **Liquid Lounge** (▶ 174) is the most popular beach bar, with dance parties on Thursday, Friday and Saturday nights. **Black Out Disco** in the Ali Baba Palace on the Sharia al Hadaba (tel: 012-221 7734) does Ibizan-style parties with smoke and foam.

Alternatively, you can try your luck at the **Casino Royale** in the Mövenpick Jolie Ville in Naama Bay (tel: 069-360 0100). The **InterContinental** in Hurghada has a casino for late-night gambling.

Sports

All the Red Sea resorts offer watersports, including sailing lessons, banana boats, windsurfing and parasailing. The best windsurfing places in Hurghada are **Three Corners, Giftun** and **Jasmin Village**. In Sinai, **Moon Beach Hotel** (Ras Sudr; tel: 02-336 5103; www.moonbeachretreat.com) is renowned for its windsurfing facilities.

Most resorts also offer horse-riding in the desert, camel rides on the beach or longer trips into the mountains with Bedouin guides.

Hot-air Balloons

German-run **Cast Ballooning** in Hurghada organises spectacular one-hour trips over the desert, returning by four-wheel-drive. There's also breakfast at a Bedouin camp (for more information tel: 065-344 4929).

Jeep Safaris in the Desert

Both the Red Sea Mountains and Sinai offer spectacular landscapes to explore, as well as Bedouin camps. In Sinai there are trips from Dahab, Nuweiba and St Catherine's Monastery to colourful and picturesque wadis like the Coloured Canyon and Ras Abu Gallum.

Walks & Tours

1 MEDIEVAL CAIRO

Walk

The only way to discover the splendours of Cairo's medieval city is to walk its streets and alleys, lined with stunning mosques, amazing palaces and intriguing *wikalas* (merchant's houses). Many ancient monuments are still intact, but others have collapsed. The backdrop seems medieval, but the modern world is close by.

DISTANCE 4km (2.5 miles) **TIME** 3 hours to look at buildings, but a day to visit the major sights
START POINT Ibn Tulun Mosque, Sharia Saliba (minibus 54 from Midan Tahrir to Sayyida Zeinab, but a taxi is easier) 197 D3
END POINT Sharia al Azhar 197 E4

Early morning or late afternoon is the best time to go. On Sundays the bazaar is closed and things are much quieter, so it's a good time to take a closer look at the architecture.

1–2

Turn left out of the mosque of **Ibn Tulun** (▶ 68) towards the main street, Sharia Saliba, then turn right. Sharia Saliba follows the medieval main street known as the Qasaba, lined with palaces and mosques most of which have been restored after the earthquakes in the 1990s. On the left is the 15th-century late Mameluke mosque-*madrasa* of **Amir Tagri Bardi**, followed by the very ornate but lovely 19th-century *sabil* (public fountain) of **Umm Abbas**. Farther on, facing each other, are the tall walls of a *khanqah* (Sufi convent) to the right and a mosque to the left, both built by **Amir Shaykhu** in the 14th century. Note the unusual pharaonic cornice above the entrance gate and the beautiful ceiling of the sanctuary *iwan*. Outside turn right and walk about 150m (165 *yards*) to the impressive

The Aqsunqur Mosque is also called the Blue Mosque

Map labels

Bab al Futuh
Bab al Nasr
Qaytbey Wikala
Sultan Baybars Khanqah
Amir Qarasunqur Madrasa
Oda Bashi Sabil-Kuttab
SHARIA HARB AL TAHAR
AL MUIZZ LI DIN
7
Gamal ad Din al Ustadar Mosque-Madrasa
Ahmad Pasha Sabil-Kuttab
al Husayn Mosque
MIDAN AL HUSAYN
6
Khan al Khalili
SHARIA AL AZHAR
al Ghuri Mosque
SHARIA AL MUIZZ LI DIN
al Ghuri
8
al Azhar Mosque

King Farouk is buried in the Mosque of al Rifai

assassinated because of his cruel ways. Just past the mosque walk left along the citadel walls and turn off at the tree-shaded Bab al Wazir, the third street on the left. A farther 250m (275 yards) to the right is the 14th-century mosque of **Aytmish al Bagasi**, and just

Salih Talai Mosque

Gamia al Ishaqi
Mosque

al Mihmandar
Mosque
④

Katkhuda
Mustahfizan
Sabil-Kuttab

SHARIA TABBANA

Altinbugha
al Maridani Mosque

Aqsunqur Mosque

Alin Aq Palace

Kathkuda
al Razzaz Palace

Umm al Sultan
Madrasa

al Sharifi Mausoleum
& Sabil-Kuttab

③

Khayrbak
Mosque-
Mausoleum

SHARIA BAB AL WAZIR

Aytmish al Bagasi
Mosque

Mahmud Pasha Mosque

al Rifai Mosque

Sultan Hasan
Mosque

②

MIDAN SALAH
AL DIN

Citadel

SHARIA SALIBA

Sultan Qaytbay
Sabil-Kuttab

Amir Shaykhu
Mosque

Amir Shaykhu
Khanqah

Amir Tagri Bardi
Mosque-Madrasa

SHARIA SALIBA

Ibn Tulun
Mosque

①

0   500 metres
0   500 yards

It's easy to pass the unassuming window of the **Khan Misr Touloun** (▶77; tel: 02-365 2227, Mon–Fri), opposite the Ibn Tulun Mosque. But inside is a spacious shop selling some of the best crafts in Egypt. Prices are fixed and the staff are friendly.

Mameluke *sabil-kuttab* (fountain-Quranic school) of **Sultan Qaytbay** with an extremely handsome red, white and black entrance portal. At the fork take the street to the left past one of Cairo's most notorious prisons before arriving on Midan Salah al Din, a large square overlooked by the **Citadel** (▶68), and the mosques of **Sultan Hasan** (▶69) and **al Rifai**.

2–3

Cross the square towards the striped 16th-century mosque of **Mahmud Pasha**, a governor of Cairo who was north of it are the remains of the mausoleum and *sabil-kuttab* of **Tarabay al Sharifi** from the late Mameluke period. Farther along Sharia Bab al Wazir on the right is the entrance to the ruins of the once-impressive **palace of Alin Aq** and the early 14th-century mosque-mausoleum built for **Khayrbak**, a Mameluke *amir* who became the first Ottoman viceroy of Egypt.

3–4

Farther on the right is the mosque of **Aqsunqur**, which is also known as the **Blue Mosque** because of the beautiful turquoise Iznik (that is, ancient Nicaea, in northwest Turkey) tiles lining its interior. The street here is known as Sharia Tabbana. About 70m (75 yards) farther along on the left is the grand entrance to the 14th-century *madrasa* of **Umm al Sultan**, and next door the huge but rambling 15th-century palace of **Katkhuda al Razzaz**. Farther along the street on the left is one of the very finest monuments in the area, the 14th-century mosque of **Altinbugha al Maridani** – with a beautifully carved *qibla* (showing the direction of Mecca) behind a stunning *mashrabiya* (wooden lattice) screen. Still on the left is the 14th-century mosque of **al Mihmandar**, decorated with lovely calligraphic verses of the Quran, which adjoins a much later Ottoman *sabil-kuttab* of Katkhuda Mustahfizan.

The traditional tentmakers now also apply their skills to more decorative wall hangings

4–5

Where the street bends, its name changes to Darb al Ahmar. At the intersection the mosque of **Qajmas al Ishaqi** has fine marble decoration. On the left, just before Bab Zuwayla is the late Fatimid mosque of **Salih Talai** and beyond it the covered **Tentmakers' Bazaar** (al Khiyamiya ▶ 77).

5–6

Walk through the splendid restored **Bab Zuwayla** gate adjacent to the Sultan al Muayyad Mosque, and along the market street of **Sharia al Muizz li Din Allah** (▶ 56–58) until you reach Sharia al Azhar. At the end are the beautifully restored mosque and mausoleum of al Ghuri. Turn right along Sharia al Azhar to the **al Azhar Mosque** (▲ 70). Use the underpass to Midan al Husayn and at the mosque of the same name take the small alley to the left into **Khan al Khalili** (▶ 70–71). The first alley left again brings you to **al Fishawi Café** (▶ 75).

6–7

After a stroll in the bazaar return to the mosque of **al Husayn** (closed to non-Muslims), and turn left along its western wall into a street lined with various states of decay, along the street. Most are commercial centres for spices and coffee, but a few of them are still lived in.

7–8

Just before you reach the gate of Bab al Nasr, on your left is the large **wikala of Qaytbey**, built in 1481, with the typical plan of a large central courtyard surrounded by shops and storerooms on the ground floor and rooms for the traders upstairs. **Bab al Nasr** (Gate of Victory) with the two square towers is part of the Fatimid fortifications. Walk outside the gate left to **Bab al Futuh** (▶ 57) and walk back through the gate along Sharia al Muizz li Din Allah to Sharia al Azhar where you can pick up a taxi.

Taking a Break

Stop in Khan al Khalili (▶ 70–71) and smoke a water pipe or have a drink at the café al Fishawi (▶ 75), or in the Naguib Mahfouz Café (▶ 76) on the main street of the bazaar. The restaurant part of the Naguib Mahfouz also serves good *mezze* and Oriental dishes. There are also several cafés along Sharia Bab al Wazir.

mosque-*madrasa* of **Gamal ad Din al Ustadar**, built at great cost by the powerful prince who gave his name to this area, al Gamaliya. On the opposite corner stands the handsome 17th-century *sabil-kuttab* of **Oda Bashi** with lovely tiled panels, and next door is his *wikala* (merchant's hostel) which was one of Cairo's main trade centres for coffee and spices in the 18th century. Farther to the right is the *madrasa* of **Amir Qarasunqur** who was polo master to Sultan Qalawun; two polo mallets can be seen above the window of the mausoleum. On the next corner is Cairo's oldest surviving *khanqah*, built in 1306 by Sultan Baybars II. It has superb marble panelling in the mausoleum and a typical early Mameluke minaret. There are several more *wikalas*, in

Never a dull moment in Cairo's bustling Khan al Khalili Bazaar

vendors selling prayer beads and incense. To the left is the 19th-century **Sabil-Kuttab of Ahmad Pasha**, now partly occupied by a sweet vendor. Turn left where the street bends, then immediately right and continue along Sharia Habs al Rahaba. To the left is the 15th-century

2 AROUND THE THEBAN NECROPOLIS

Cycling Tour

DISTANCE 16km (10 miles)

TIME 1 day (start early, particularly in summer when it's too hot to ride in the midday sun)

START POINT/END POINT Ferry terminal on the West Bank, Luxor (either ride round and cross over the bridge south of Luxor, or put the bike on the local ferry opposite Luxor Temple)

⊞ 202 B4

Cycling is the best way to explore the amazing tombs and mortuary temples of the Theban necropolis and you'll also get a stronger sense of the Egyptian countryside. This tour passes beautiful villages where life is still traditional, many of the houses painted with motifs marking a pilgrimage to Mecca. You'll see people working in the field or children going to school, who might wave or give you a big smile. Take it easy and enjoy a rhythm very much in tune with the region.

You can rent bikes from several shops along Sharia al Mahatta (Station Street) on the East Bank, but better, more expensive ones are available from hotels, including the Sheraton, Mercure Inn

and Windsor. Make sure you check the bike before renting it and always insist on a pump as the standards of the roads and tracks aren't always high.

In summer it might be too hot to do this tour, but even in winter you need a hat and good sunscreen. It's particularly important to drink lots of water to avoid dehydration.

The Colossi of Memnon are locally known as "Timthileen"

1–2

Once on the West Bank cycle straight ahead for 10–15 minutes to the ticket booth on the crossroads before Deir al Madina. On the way, immediately past the al Fadliya canal to the right, note the village of **New Gurna**. This beautiful village, built by the Egyptian architect Hasan Fathy, was a failed attempt to relocate the villagers from Old Gurna, whose houses sit on top of the ancient tombs. Farther to the right are the **Memnon Colossi** staring across the sugarcane fields. These gigantic 14th-century BC statues of Amenhotep III are all that's left of his mortuary temple. At the ticket kiosk, just left at the crossroads, buy tickets for all the places you intend to visit.

2–3

Return towards the colossi, take the first road to the right along a little canal, then right again to the entrance of the vast **Temple of Madinat Habu** (▶ 98).

3–4

Turn left on leaving the temple and, after 100m (110 yards), continue along the dirt track towards the ticket office and main crossroads. Follow the signpost for **Deir al Madina** (▶ 99).

4–5

Cycle back to the crossroads and turn left to visit the **Tombs of the Nobles** (▶ 96–97). Leave the bike in the site's car-park, opposite the Ramesseum. Walk back across the road towards the **Ramesseum** (▶ 100–101), where you can relax and picnic under the trees, or have a simple Egyptian lunch at the Marsam Hotel, just past the temple.

5–6

Turn right (north) on to the road and then take the first road on the left towards the **Deir al Bahari** (▶ 94–95).

6–7

Back on the main road, take a left to the next crossroads then turn right. The domed house on top of the hill belonged to Howard Carter who found the treasures of Tutankhamun. Temple enthusiasts can stop at the mortuary temple of Seti I, which has exquisite wall carvings, or take a look at the peaceful cemetery across the road. Continue along the same road until the canal then turn right. At the New Gurna crossroads turn left back to the ferry.

Taking a Break

Stop for a drink at the Maratonga café opposite Madinat Habu temple, or at the café near the Tombs of the Nobles.

Luxor

□ Luxor Temple

The now-abandoned market area at New Gurna, designed by Egyptian architect Hasan Fathy

3 DESERT DRIVE IN SINAI

Tour

DISTANCE About 492km (305 miles)
TIME Preferably two days to stop over at St Catherine's Monastery to see the sunrise at Mount Moses **START POINT/END POINT** Sharm al Sheikh, but you could also start in Dahab or Nuweiba
⊞ 201 F2

The gentle way up to Mount Moses, via the camel path

The road across the mountains of the Sinai peninsula is one of the most beautiful in Egypt, perhaps even in Africa. There are plenty of tours from Sharm al Sheikh, but they tend to be rushed and don't allow you to stop where you like, to take in a view or walk in the desert. It's a long drive, best done over two days, and a highlight of any trip to Egypt.

Although this tour follows a regularly used route, you are crossing a desert so make sure you have enough petrol and water. Be careful when leaving the main road, as there are still thousands of unexploded mines in Sinai, a legacy of the Arab-Israeli wars – do not enter any fenced-off areas. Watch out for camels that sometimes wander across the road.

Renting a car can be something of a lottery, so inspect it thoroughly before you agree to take it and make sure you know who to call if you have a problem.

occasional car or bus, the chances are you will have the place to yourself, although, depending on the season, you might see Bedouin camps. The road drops down to the coast again as you come to a police post (87km/54 miles). From here you can drive into Dahab (8km/5 miles) for a swim and a drink, or keep going north into the desert towards Nuweiba. At the major intersection, about 130km (80 miles) from Sharm al Sheikh, take the left turn towards St Catherine's Monastery.

2–3

The drive through the Sinai desert to St Catherine's Monastery (122km/76 miles) follows a good road through beautiful if stark landscape. The driving is generally easy and there are plenty of places to stop and admire the great *wadis* (dry riverbeds) that cut through the peninsula. Wadi Ghazala, some 10km (6 miles) after the Dahab police post, is accessible and if you feel adventurous you could follow it some way,

1–2

Leave Sharm al Sheikh by the road, heading north to the airport and Dahab. After about 8km (5 miles) the road splits; take the left-hand fork to Dahab. From here the road then cuts farther into the mountains, which are coloured in many places with veins of minerals. The desert here is mostly rock and scrub, the defining features being the bare mountains and the valleys and plains in between. Apart from the

Wherever they are, Muslims observe prayer time

Map labels:

- Dahab
- Gulf of Aqaba
- St Catherine's Monastery
- Sharra Pass
- Watia Pass
- al Milga
- 2285m Mount Moses (Gebel Musa)
- Feiran
- Wadi Feiran
- Sinai
- 226m Gebel Sabbagh
- 1459m Gebel Sahara
- Naama Bay
- Sharm al Sheikh
- Ras Mohamed National Park
- Hurghada
- Gebel Musa
- Hammam Sayyidna Musa
- Tor
- Gulf of Suez
- Abu Durba
- 30 km / 20 miles

became sufficiently important to warrant a bishop. The ruins of the cathedral and ancient settlement are being excavated at the oasis of Feiran. You can visit the small convent near by (ask if it's open at St Catherine's Monastery, or just ring the doorbell), and the mountains are dotted with the caves and shelters of hermits.

Taking a Break

Sharm al Sheikh, Dahab and the St Catherine area all have plenty of options for eating and drinking and you'll also find refreshments at Wadi Feiran.

though your car probably wouldn't like it. Also on this road is the MFO checkpoint, the multi-national force that observes the peace between Egypt and Israel.

There are several places to visit near St Catherine, starting with the monastery (▶ 160–162). The climb up to Mount Moses, where Moses is said to have obtained the Ten Commandments, is strenuous but worthwhile for its atmosphere and views over the mountains. The area around St Catherine is a protectorate where several walking trails have been laid out. The official office (by the monastery car-park) has details.

3–4

The road out of St Catherine continues through broad *wadis* for some 45km (28 miles), where the mountains close in again. This is the beginning of the palm-lined Wadi Feiran. Early Christians iden-tified this with the exodus of Moses and it

The main roads in Sinai are well kept and accessible to all vehicles

Having crossed the desert, 45km (28 miles) beyond Feiran is an intersection with the west Sinai coast road. Turn left here, following signs for Tor, along the road back to Sharm al Sheikh, some 160km (100 miles) away. Heading south, the road cuts through a wide, barren plain with 2,000m-high (6,600 feet) mountains to your left. Some 57km (35 miles) from the intersection a road leads right, through a small oasis, to the **Hammam Sayyidna Musa** ("Bath of Our Lord Moses"), a hot spring that's long been used for its healing proper-ties. The farm here produces food for St Catherine's

Monastery. Farther on is Tor, once the gulf's main port and quarantine station for pilgrims returning from Mecca. **Ras Mohamed National Park** (▶ 163) is a farther 87km (54 miles), and Sharm al Sheikh 27km (17 miles) from there.

For more detailed itineraries in Sinai look for *The Red Sea Coasts of Egypt*, by Jenny Jobbins (AUC Press, available in Egypt).

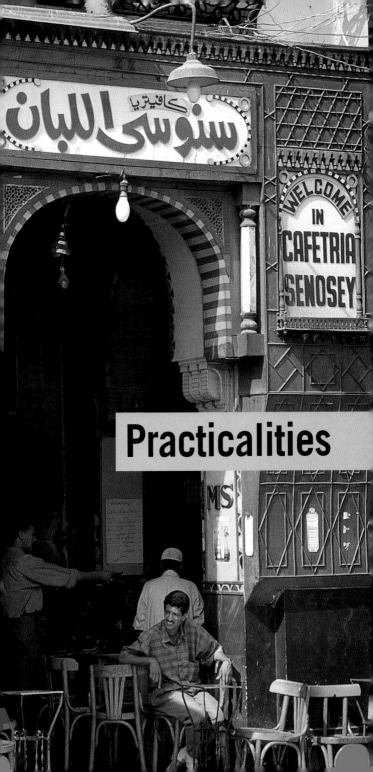

Practicalities

GETTING ADVANCE INFORMATION

Websites

● www.touregypt.net
Excellent official site of
Egypt's Ministry of Tourism.

● www.sis.gov.eg
General information on

Egypt, tourism and culture .

● www.yallabina.com
What's on in Cairo,
including entertainment,
restaurants and nightlife.

In the UK and Ireland
Egyptian House
3rd Floor, 170 Piccadilly
London W1
☎ 020 7493 5283;
www.gotoegypt.com

BEFORE YOU GO

WHAT YOU NEED

	UK	Germany	USA	Canada	Australia	Ireland	Netherlands	Spain
Passport/National Identity Card	●	●	●	●	●	●	●	●
Visa (tourist visa – available from airport on arrival)	●	●	●	●	●	●	●	●
Onward or Return Ticket	▲	▲	▲	▲	▲	▲	▲	▲
Health Inoculations (tetanus and polio)	○	○	○	○	○	○	○	○
Health Documentation	▲	▲	▲	▲	▲	▲	▲	▲
Travel Insurance	○	○	○	○	○	○	○	○
Driver's Licence (national)	●	●	●	●	●	●	●	●
Car Insurance Certificate (if own car)	●	●	●	●	●	●	●	●

● Required
○ Suggested
▲ Not required
△ Not applicable

Entry requirements differ depending
on your nationality and are also subject
to change without notice. Check prior to
a visit and follow news events that may
affect your situation.

WHEN TO GO

Cairo

High season — Low season

JAN	FEB	MAR	APR	MAY	JUN	JUL	AUG	SEP	OCT	NOV	DEC
18°C	21°C	23°C	27°C	32°C	34°C	35°C	35°C	32°C	30°C	23°C	18°C
64°F	70°F	73°F	81°F	90°F	93°F	95°F	95°F	90°F	86°F	73°F	64°F

☀ Sun

⛅ Sun/Showers

Temperatures are the **average daily maximum** for each month but differ greatly
between night and day, and over the country. The Mediterranean coast is always
cooler, while Cairo is extremely hot from June to September. The air becomes
drier towards the south, but although Upper Egypt is always hot, the nights can
be cold. March and April can bring the *khamseen*, a strong, hot wind that
carries sand from the Sahara. The winter months can be quite cold, often with
rain around Christmas. The tourist season is from November to February but
Cairo and Luxor are chilly then, and hotels are overbooked. The best time to
visit is May, or in October or November after the long, hot summer has ended.

GETTING THERE

By air There are direct scheduled flights to Cairo from New York and Los Angeles, and from many European capitals. You can also fly there from the Middle East and most of the adjacent African countries. Some international scheduled flights also land in Luxor, Alexandria and Aswan. Charter flights are available to Luxor, Hurghada and Sinai. When leaving Egypt, remember to reconfirm your flight 48 hours beforehand.

By sea There are twice weekly ferries May–November from Port Said to Limassol in Cyprus. Tickets and info are available from Canal Tours in Port Said (tel: 066-332 1874/ 012-798 6338; canaltours@bec.com.eg). Also in Port Said is Mena Tours (tel: 066-322 5742/323 3376) which sells tickets for the erratic ferries between Port Said and Beirut or Antalya (Turkey). There are excellent fast ferries between Nuweiba in Sinai and Aqaba in Jordan, tickets are sold at the Nuweiba harbour on the day of departure. Several ferry companies operate boats from Hurghada to various ports in Saudi Arabia.

By bus Buses from Tel Aviv, Jerusalem and Eilat in Israel go to Sinai and Cairo, crossing the border at Rafah or Taba, but at the time of writing the border crossing at Rafah was closed. Frequent buses also connect Cairo with Tripoli and Benghazi in Libya. You cannot obtain a visa at the Egyptian border if you enter by land, and there are likely to be long delays at border crossings.

By car Complicated bureaucracy means that entering Egypt by car is one of the least popular options. You should be allowed to bring a car into Egypt for three months if you can show an *international triptyque* or a *carnet de passage de douane* issued by the automobile club in the country where the car is registered.

TIME

Egypt is 2 hours ahead of GMT, or 3 hours ahead from the start of May to the start of October. But remember that time is a loose concept in Egypt.

CURRENCY AND FOREIGN EXCHANGE

Currency The basic unit of currency is the Egyptian pound (LE, *guineh* in Arabic). This is divided into 100 piastres (PT, *irsh* in Arabic). There are **notes** for 5, 10, 20, 25 and 50 piastres and 1, 5, 10, 20, 50, 100 and 200 pounds, as well as **coins** of 10, 20 and 25 piastres. Small denominations are useful for *baksheesh*. Egypt is still generally a cash economy, so ensure that you carry sufficient money for your needs.

Travellers' cheques, preferably in US$, can be changed in all banks and exchange bureaux but it can be complicated and there is a transaction charge.

Credit cards are widely accepted at banks, hotels and some restaurants, but it is wise to check first. Smaller establishments and shops are likely to prefer cash.

ATMs More and more five-star hotels and banks in tourist resorts have automatic cash dispensing machines. In most cities there are several ATM cash machines that will dispense cash to most Western-issued cards, with PIN.

TIME DIFFERENCES

GMT 12 noon	Egypt 2pm	USA (East) 7am	USA (West) 4am	Europe 1pm	Australia (East) 10pm

WHEN YOU ARE THERE

CLOTHING SIZES

UK	International	USA	
36	46	36	Suits
38	48	38	
40	50	40	
42	52	42	
44	54	44	
46	56	46	
7	41	8	Shoes
7.5	42	8.5	
8.5	43	9.5	
9.5	44	10.5	
10.5	45	11.5	
11	46	12	
14.5	37	14.5	Shirts
15	38	15	
15.5	39/40	15.5	
16	41	16	
16.5	42	16.5	
17	43	17	
8	34	6	Dresses
10	36	8	
12	38	10	
14	40	12	
16	42	14	
18	44	16	
4.5	38	6	Shoes
5	38	6.5	
5.5	39	7	
6	39	7.5	
6.5	40	8	
7	41	8.5	

NATIONAL HOLIDAYS

1 Jan	New Year's Day
7 Jan	Coptic Christmas
Mar/Apr	Sham al Nessim
25 Apr	Liberation Day
1 May	Labour Day
18 Jun	Liberation Day
23 Jul	Revolution Day
6 Oct	Armed Forces Day
24 Oct	Suez Victory Day

Egypt also observes Muslim feast days and the month of fasting, Ramadan. Dates follow the lunar calendar and move back by 11 days a year.

OPENING HOURS

○ Shops ● Offices ● Banks ● Post Offices ● Museums/Monuments ● Pharmacies

☐ Day ☐ Midday ☐ Evening

All times given may vary. In tourist areas shops tend to remain open all day until late at night, especially in high season. Banks in tourist areas often stay open all day until late at night. Banks at Cairo airport and the Marriott and Nile Hilton hotels in Cairo are open 24 hours. Museums and monuments close between 11 and 1 on Friday for prayers. Post offices are open from Saturday until Thursday. Pharmacies are often open until 9pm or later.

During Ramadan, everything tends to open an hour later and close an hour or two earlier, but shops and some offices reopen from 8 to 10pm.

POLICE 122

TOURIST POLICE 126/02-395 9116 (Cairo)

FIRE 180

AMBULANCE 123

ANGLO-AMERICAN HOSPITAL IN CAIRO 02-735 6162

PERSONAL SAFETY

Petty crime is rare in Egypt but like everywhere else you should watch your belongings in busy tourist areas and on full buses.

- Leave valuables in the hotel safe. Carry only what you need.
- There is a crackdown on drugs, with fines for possession, and life imprisonment or hanging for anyone convicted of dealing or smuggling.
- Foreigners travelling between cities in Middle and Upper Egypt usually have to move in a police-protected convoy.

Tourist Police assistance:
☎ **126**

ELECTRICITY

The power supply is 220 volts. Sockets take two-round-pin plugs. British and US visitors will need an adaptor. North American visitors should check whether appliances need a voltage transformer.

TELEPHONES

Until recently, international calls could only be made from specified Telephone and Telegraph offices but Egypt now has an extensive network of payphones, operated by Menatel and Nile Communications. These can be used for local, national and international calls. Phonecards, available in values of LE10, 20 and 30, can be bought from telephone exchanges as well as shops and kiosks displaying stickers with the Menatel logo. It is still possible to make local calls from coin-operated phone boxes, shops, hotels and kiosks, but these tend to be more expensive than calls made on Menatel phones.

POST

Buy stamps at post offices, souvenir shops and hotel newsagents. Airmail letters take about a week to arrive: post them at your hotel or at a post office; avoid street letterboxes. Cairo's main post office (open 24 hours) is on Midan al Ataba.

TIPS/GRATUITIES

Tips are expected and may be a person's sole or main source of income. As a general guide:

Restaurants	✓	8–10% (if no service included)
Cafés / Bars	✓	10%
Tour guides	✓	LE10–20
Car parking	✓	LE2–5
Taxis	✓	Agree price first, 5–10%
Hotel workers	✓	LE10–15
Lavatories	✓	PT50–LE1

UK	USA	Ireland	Australia	New Zealand
☎ 02–794 0850	☎ 02-797 3300	☎ 02-735 8547	☎02-575 0444	☎ 02-574 9360

HEALTH

Insurance Egypt has well-qualified doctors and good hospitals, particularly in Cairo and Alexandria. Taking out travel insurance which covers medical care is a must. Keep all receipts and medical bills for a refund back home.

Dental Services In an emergency contact your embassy for a list of English-speaking dentists. Make sure you are covered by medical insurance. English-speaking dentist in Cairo: Dr Sabri Karnouk, Sharia Talaat Harb, opposite Cinema Metro, tel: 02-575 8392.

Weather Use a high-factor sunblock, cover up with light cotton clothes, and wear sunglasses and hat when in the sun. Coffee and alcohol are dehydrating; instead drink at least 3 litres (6 pints) of water a day.

Drugs Pharmacists (*saydaliya* in Arabic) usually speak English and can recommend treatment for minor ailments. A wide range of drugs is available over the counter and they are cheap. Check the expiry date and the leaflet to see if it is what you need. Most main cities or resorts have an all-night pharmacy.

Water It is fairly safe to drink tap water in cities but buy bottles of mineral water elsewhere. Avoid ice cubes in drinks.

CONCESSIONS

Students and Youths
Museums and sights offer a 50 per cent reduction on tickets and there are also reductions on rail and airline tickets for students who have an official student card. An ISIC Student Card can be issued at the Egyptian Student Travel Services, 23 Sharia al Manyal, Roda Island, Cairo (tel: 02-531 0330; www.estsegypt.com. You need to bring one passport photo and proof that you are a student.

Senior Citizens
There are no concessions for senior citizens.

TRAVELLING WITH A DISABILITY

There are no special facilities for visitors with disabilities. Visiting the major sites can be quite a challenge although Egyptians will be ready to help. **Egypt for All** (tel: 02-311 3988; www.egyptforall.com) specialises in making travel arrangements for visitors with mobility problems.

CHILDREN

Children are welcome everywhere, and often attract a great deal of admiring attention. Some of the better hotels organise high chairs, cots and babysitters. but don't expect much in the way of baby-changing facilties.

LAVATORIES

Public lavatories vary between sitting, squatting and standing-up types, but they are often filthy. Instead of paper, a bucket of water or squirter is provided. For a more comfortable experience, use lavatories in quality hotels and restaurants.

WILDLIFE SOUVENIRS

Importing wildlife souvenirs sourced from rare or endangered species may be illegal or require a special permit. Before purchase you should check your home country's customs regulations.

SURVIVAL PHRASES

The official language in Egypt is Arabic, but English is taught in schools. People are always happy, and proud, to practise their foreign languages, but even if you only speak a few words in Arabic you will generally meet with an enthusiastic response. The following is a phonetic transliteration from the Arabic script. Words or letters in brackets indicate the different form that is required when addressing, or speaking as, a woman.

GREETINGS AND COMMON WORDS

Yes **Aywa, na'am**
No **Laa**
Please **Min fadlak (fadlik)**
Thank you **Shukran**
You're welcome **Afwan**
Hello *to Muslims* **As salaamu alaykum**
Response **Wa alaykum as salaam**
Hello *to Copts* **Saeeda**
Welcome **Ahlan wa sahlan**
Response **Ahlan bik(i)**
Goodbye **Ma'a salaama**
Good morning **Sabaah al kheer**
Response **Sabaah en nur**
Good evening **Masaa al kheer**
Response **Masaa en nur**
How are you? **Izzayak (Izzayik)**
Fine, thank you **Kwayyis(a) il hamdulillaah**
God Willing **Inshallah**
No problem **Ma feesh mushkila**
Sorry **Ana aasif (asfa)**
Excuse me **An iznak (iznik)**
My name is... **Ismee...**
Do you speak English? **Bititkallim(i) ingileezi**
I don't understand **Ana mish faahem (fahma)**
I understand **Faahem (Fahma)**
I don't speak Arabic **Ana mish aarif (arfa) arabi**

NUMBERS

0	**sifr**	14	**arbahtaashar**
1	**wahid**	15	**khamastaashar**
2	**itnayn**	16	**sittaashar**
3	**talaata**	17	**sabahtaashar**
4	**arbah**	18	**tamantaashar**
5	**khamsa**	19	**tisahtaashar**
6	**sitta**	20	**ashreen**
7	**sabaa**	21	**wahid wa-ashreen**
8	**tamanya**		
9	**tesah**	30	**talaateen**
10	**ashara**	40	**arbaeen**
11	**hidaashar**	50	**khamseen**
12	**itnaashar**	100	**miyya**
13	**talataashar**	1000	**alf**

EMERGENCY! Taari!

Help! **el ha'nee!**
Thief! **Haraami!**
Police **Shurta; bulees**
Fire **Hareea**
Hospital **Mustashfa**
Go away **Imshee**
Leave me alone! **Bass kifaaya!**
Where is the lavatory? **Feyn it twalet?**
I'm sick **Ana ayyaan(a)**
We want a doctor **Ayzeen duktoor**

SHOPPING

Shop **dukkan**
I would like... **Ayyiz (Ayza)**
I'm just looking **Batfarrag bass**
How much...? **Bi kaam?**
That's my last offer **Aakhir kalaam**
That's too expensive **Da ghali awi**
I'll take this one **Aakhud da**
Good / bad **Kwayyis / mish kwayyis**
Cheap **Rakhees**
Big / small **Kabeer(a) / sughayyar**
Open / closed **Maftooh / makfool**

DIRECTIONS AND TRAVELLING

I'm lost **Mush aarif ana feen**
Where is...? **Feyn...?**
Airport **Mataar**
Boat **Markab**

DAYS

Today	**innaharda**
Tomorrow	**bukra**
Yesterday	**imbaarih**
Tonight	**innaharda bileel**
Morning	**issubh**
Evening	**massa**
Later	**bahdeen**
Monday	**youm al itnayn**
Tuesday	**youm at talaat**
Wednesday	**youm al arbah**
Thursday	**youm al khamees**
Friday	**youm al gumah**
Saturday	**youm is sabt**
Sunday	**youm al hadd**

Bus station **Mahattat al autubees**
Church **Kineesa**
Embassy **Sifaara**
Market **Souk**
Mosque **Gaama; masgid**
Museum **Mathaf**
Square **Midaan**
Street **Shaari**
Taxi rank **Mahattat at taxiyat**
Train station **Mahattat al atr**
Is it near / far? **Da urayyib / baeed?**
How many kilometres? **Kaam keelu?**
Here / there **Hinna / hinnaak**
Left / right **Shimaal / yimeen**
Straight on **Ala toul**
When does the bus leave / arrive?
  Al autubees yisaafir / yiwsal emta?
I want a taxi **Ayyiz / ayza taks**
Stop here **Hina kwayyis**
Return ticket **Tazkara raayih gayy**
Passport **Basbuur**
Bus **Autubees**
Car **Arabiya**
Train **Atr**

RESTAURANT: Al matam

I would like to eat... **Ana ayyiz aakal...**
What's this? **Eeh da (di)?**
Alcohol / beer **Khamra / beera**
Bread **Aysh**
Coffee / tea **Qahwa / shay**
Meat **Lahma**
Mineral water **Mayya madaniya**
Milk **Halib**
Salt and pepper **Malh wa filfil**
Wine red / white **Nabit ahmar / abyad**
Breakfast **Fitaar**
Lunch **Ghada**
Dinner **Asha**
Table **Tarabeeza**
Waiter **Raees**
Menu **Cart / menu**
Bill **Al hisab**
Bon appetit **Bi l hana wa shiffa**

MONEY: Filoos

Where is the bank? **Feen al bank?**
Egyptian pound **Guineh masri**
Half a pound **Nuss guineh**
Piastre **Irsh**
Small change **Fakka**
Post office **Bosta**
Mail **Barid**
Cheque **Cheque**
Travellers' cheque **Travellers' cheque**
Credit card **cart**

GLOSSARY TO THE TEXT

Ahwa café, coffee house
Amir military leader of the Mamelukes
Baksheesh alms, tip or bribe
Barque a ship with three masts
Beejou estate car communal taxi
Cartouche a group of hieroglyphs representing the name of a leader, often carved into a wall or tablet
Calèche horse-drawn carriage
Caliph leader during the Islamic Fatimid Dynasty (10th-12th centuries)
Caravanserai lodgings for travellers and animals, around a courtyard
Corniche coastal road
Faience ceramic glaze, sometimes on a minaret
Felucca Egyptian sailing boat
Fuul ubiquitous fava bean stew
Hypostyle part of the temple supported by pillars
Iwan vaulted space around a courtyard of a mosque or *madrasa*
Khanqah Sufi monastery
Khedive the viceroy of Egypt under 19th-century Turkish rule
Kushari spicy mix of pulses, pasta and rice
Kuttab Quranic school for boys
Madrasa Quranic school
Mamelukes slave-soldiers who established a Muslim dynasty from 13th–16th centuries
Maristan (Islamic) hospital
Mastaba grave, burial place
Mezze small plates of food, appetisers
Midan square
Mina ferry terminal
Moulid religious festival, often on the anniversary of a holy figure's birth
Ptolemics rulers of Egypt, 323–30 BC
Pylon temple gateway formed by two truncated pyramidal towers
Sabil public water fountain
Sahn courtyard
Sharia street
Shawarma meat roasted on a spit
Sheesha water pipe i.e. pipe for smoking (flavoured) tobacco that draws smoke over water to cool it
Souk market
Taamiya deep-fried, spiced ground fava beans
Tarboush fez, a traditional red, conical flat-topped hat with a black tassel, worn by some Islamic men
Vizier governor

Atlas

Marsa Matruh

Alexandria

Port Said

CAIRO
196/197

Suez

Siwa

200/201

al Bawiti

Minya

Asyut

Hurghada

198/199

Qasr Farafra

Quseyr

Mut

Kharga

Luxor

202 Aswan

To identify the regions, see the map on the inside of the front cover

Regional Maps

—·—·—	International boundary	☐	City
═══════	Major divided highway	▫	Major town
──────	Main road	◎	Large town
──────	Other road	○	Town, village
	Built-up area	▪	Place of interest
	Cultivated area	✈	Airport

City Plan

– – –	Riverbus	🄸	Information
──────	Rail line	●	Metro station
∿∿∿∿∿	City wall	▨	Important building
		▪	Featured place of interest

197

Cairo

SHARIA RAMSES   **D**   **SHARIA BUR SAID**   **E**   **SAKAKINI**   **SHARIA ABBASIYA**   **F**

airo Railway
tation

GHAMRA

5

SHARIA AL ZAHIR

MIDAN
AL ZAHIR

Pont Limoun
Station
Mubarak (Ramses)

MIDAN
RAMSES

SHARIA KAMIL SIDQI

Fatimid Walls

SHARIA BAB AL BAHR

SHARIA AL GHEISH

SHARIA HUSEINIYA

SH. MASNA AL TARABISH

EZBEKIYA

Bab al Futuh

Mosque of
al Hakim

Bab al Nasr

SHARIA

SHARIA CLOT BEY

Ataba
Ezbekiya
Gardens

MUSKI

Sulayman Agha
al Silahdar
Mosque

Qaytbey Wikala

AL GAMALIYA

SHARIA SALAH SALEM

MIDAN
ATABA

OPERA

Sultan Barquq
Madrasa
Khanqah

Beit al Suhaymi

al Aqmar
Mosque

QAYTBEY

entral
ost Office

SHARIA AL GHEISH

SHARIA BUR SAID

SH. BEIT AL QADI

SHARIA AL MU IZZ LI DIN ALLAH

Sultan Qalawun
Madrasa-Mausoleum

Qasr Amir Bashtak

4

SHARIA
ABD AL AZIZ

SHARIA AL AZHAR

Sultan Barsbay
Madrasa

Khan al Khalili
al Husayn Mosque

SHARIA AL MANSURIYA

MIDAN AL HUSAYN

SHARIA
QALA

al Ghuri
Mosque &
Mausoleum

SHARIA AL AZHAR

al Azhar
Mosque

Islamic Art
Museum

MIDAN
AHMED
MAHIR

SH. AHMED MAHIR

Sultan al Muayyad Mosque
Bab Zuwayla

Abdin Palace

Tentmakers'
Bazaar

Qajmas al Ishaqi
Mosque

BAB AL KHALQ

Altinbugha al
Maridani Mosque

SH. TABBANA

SH. AL MUZAYIN

SHARIA BUR SAID

AL DARB
AL AHMAR

Aqsunqur
Mosque

Alin Aq Palace

SHARIA AHMED OMAR

SHARIA AL HILMIYA

BAB
AL WAZIR

3

AL HILMIYA

al Rifai
Mosque

Sultan Hasan
Mosque

MAGID AL LABBAN

Military
Museum

Carriage
Museum

SHARIA

AL MUQATTAM

Sultan Hasan
Mosque

SHARIA AL
GALIBA

MIDAN
SALAH AL DIN

Citadel

National Police Museum

Muhammad Ali
Mosque

an Nasir
Mosque

Gayer-
Anderson
House

SHARIA AL ASHRAF

Gawhara
Palace

Muhammad
Ali Fort

Ibn Tulun
Mosque

SHARIA SAYYIDA AISHA

SHARIA SALAH SALEM

al Muqattam
Hills

Zeinhum
Gardens

2

KING KHALED AUTOSTRAD

SHARIA AL IMAM AL SHAFI

SHARIA SIKKET HADID HELWAN

AL KHALIFA

SHARIA AIN AL SIRA

Imam
al Shafii
Mausoleum

1

ASR AL QADIMA

SHARIA AIN AL SIRA

D   **E**   **F**

Picture credits

Abbreviations for terms appearing below: (t) top; (b) bottom; (l) left; (r) right; (c) centre. The Automobile Association wishes to thank the following photographers and libraries for their assistance with the preparation of this book.
Front and back cover: (t) AA Photo Library/Chris Coe; (ct) AA Photo Library/Rick Strange; (cb) AA Photo Library/Chris Coe; (b) AA Photo Library/Chris Coe; Spine, AA Photo Library/Rick Strange.

AKG, LONDON 13cr (Erich Lessing), 25t, 26b, 27cl (Tony Vaccaro); ALAMY 9t (Bob Turner), 11c (Helene Rogers), 71 (Eddie Gerald) 89 (Art Kowalsky), 102t (Robert Harding Picture Library), 143b (Miamnuk Images); THE ART ARCHIVE 23t (Fine Art Museum, Bilbao/Dagli Orti), 26t (Daglit Orti); ART DIRECTIONS AND TRIP PHOTO LIBRARY 28/9, 29b, 191t; AXIOM PHOTOGRAPHIC AGENCY 16/17 (J Morris), 57 (J Morris), 67b (J Morris); BRIDGEMAN ART LIBRARY, LONDON 14c Statue of the Cult of Osiris, (1844-91, Louvre, Paris, France/Giraudon, 25b, Carpet Bazaar. Caorp. 1887 by Charles Robertson, (1844-91) Christie's Images, London, UK; JOHN ELK III 3 (ii), 48b, 63b, 129, 130/1b, 135; MARY EVANS PICTURE LIBRARY 22t, 23b, 24t; EYE UBIQUITOUS 7b, 133t, 140, 152, 158/9t, 178; PATRICK GODEAU 164; ROLAND GRANT ARCHIVE 15t, 15b; ROBERT HARDING PICTURE LIBRARY 8b, 10, 12b, 49t, 63t, 144; TERRY HARRIS/JUST GREECE PHOTO LIBRARY 166; JIM HENDERSON AMPA ARPS 54t, 83b, 96; ROBERT HOLMES PHOTOGRAPHY 111l (Markham Johnson); HULTON GETTY 26/7 (Bettmann), 27t; THE HUTCHISON LIBRARY 12t (Juliet Hight Brimah), 20/21 (Mary Jeliffe); IMAGES COLOUR LIBRARY 14t, 59, 153, 156/7; PICTURES COLOUR LIBRARY 113b, 114, 168; POWERSTOCK/ZEFA 111tr; REX FEATURES LTD 27b, 31; FRANK SPOONER PICTURES 13t (Aynos/Gamma), 13ct, 84t, 92/3, 102b; TRAVEL STOCK 163 (Tim O'Keefe); TRAVEL INK 2 (ii) (Stephen Ballidas), 13b (Abbie Enock), 33 (Stephen Ballidas), 60t (Abbie Enock), 82b (Simon Reddy), 110 (Peter Kingsford); NIK WHEELER 50, 137b; PETER WILSON 52t, 53, 62/3, 139b; WORLD PICTURES LTD 2 (i). 3 (i), 5, 9b, 84b, 87, 107, 117, 179.

Every effort has been made to obtain the rights to use the photograph on page 32.

The remaining photographs are held in the Association's own photo library (AA WORLD TRAVEL LIBRARY) and were taken by the following photographers:
HUGH ALEXANDER 7t, 28l, 30t, 30l, 65, 88, 90; CHRIS COE 3 (iv), 6/7 b/ground, 6/7, 12/13 b/ground, 14/5 b/ground; 14b, 18tl, 18ct, 18tr, 19cr, 19b, 22tl, 28, 29r, 48t, 49b, 51b, 52c, 60b, 61, 67t, 68b, 80, 81, 82t, 93, 99t, 100, 111b, 116b, 118, 123, 131t, 132b, 133b, 134, 136t, 136c, 137t, 143t, 162t, 162b, 165t, 177, 182, 183, 185, 191bl, 191br; STEVE DAY 8/9t, 9t; CLIVE SAWYER 2 (iii), 45, 64/5; RICK STRANGE 2 (iv), 3(iii), 3(v), 6t, 8t, 11b, 19tl, 19tr, 22/3, 24b, 29t, 30b, 46t, 46b, 51t, 51c, 52b, 54b, 58, 66, 68t, 69, 70t, 70b, 79, 83t, 85, 86b, 91, 94/5, 98, 99b, 101, 108, 109r, 115, 116t, 118/9, 1019t, 120, 121, 130, 133c, 138, 141, 142t, 151, 154, 155t, 155b, 161, 165b, 167, 169, 181, 184, 186, 187.

Questionnaire

Dear Traveller

Your comments, opinions and recommendations are very important to us. So please help us to improve our travel guides by taking a few minutes to complete this simple questionnaire.

You do not need a stamp (unless posted outside the UK). If you do not want to remove this page from your guide, then photocopy it or write your answers on a plain sheet of paper.

Send to: The Editor, Spiral Guides, AA World Travel Guides, FREEPOST SCE 4598, Basingstoke RG21 4GY.

Your recommendations...

We always encourage readers' recommendations for restaurants, night-life or shopping – if your recommendation is used in the next edition of the guide, we will send you a FREE AA Spiral Guide of your choice. Please state below the establishment name, location and your reasons for recommending it.

_____

_____

_____

_____

_____

Please send me AA Spiral _____

(see list of titles inside the back cover)

About this guide...

Which title did you buy?

_____ **AA Spiral**

Where did you buy it? _____

When? m m / y y

Why did you choose an AA Spiral Guide? _____

_____

_____

_____

_____

Did this guide meet your expectations?

Exceeded ☐   Met all ☐   Met most ☐   Fell below ☐

Please give your reasons _____

_____

_____

_____

_____

continued on next page...

Were there any aspects of this guide that you particularly liked?

_____

_____

_____

_____

_____

Is there anything we could have done better?

_____

_____

_____

_____

About you...

Name (Mr/Mrs/Ms) _____

Address _____

_____

_____ **Postcode** _____

Daytime tel no _____ **email** _____

Please _only_ give us your email address and mobile phone number if you wish to hear from us about other products and services from the AA and partners by email or text or mms.

Which age group are you in?

Under 25 ☐ 25–34 ☐ 35–44 ☐ 45–54 ☐ 55–64 ☐ 65+ ☐

How many trips do you make a year?

Less than one ☐ One ☐ Two ☐ Three or more ☐

Are you an AA member? Yes ☐ No ☐

About your trip...

When did you book? mm/ y y   **When did you travel?** mm/ y y

How long did you stay? _____

Was it for business or leisure? _____

Did you buy any other travel guides for your trip? ☐ Yes ☐ No

If yes, which ones? _____

_____

Thank you for taking the time to complete this questionnaire. Please send it to us as soon as possible, and remember, you do not need a stamp (unless posted outside the UK).
